LONDON SCHOOL OF ECONOMICS
MONOGRAPHS ON SOCIAL ANTHROPOLOGY
No. 50

CHOICE AND CHANGE

Essays in honour of
LUCY MAIR

edited by

J. DAVIS

UNIVERSITY OF LONDON
THE ATHLONE PRESS
NEW YORK: HUMANITIES PRESS INC.
1974

Published by
THE ATHLONE PRESS
UNIVERSITY OF LONDON
at 4 *Gower Street London* WC1

Distributed by Tiptree Book Services Ltd
Tiptree Essex

USA & Canada
Humanities Press Inc
New York

© *The Contributors* 1974

UK SBN 0 485 19550 X
USA SBN 391 00328 3

Printed in Great Britain by
WESTERN PRINTING SERVICES LTD
BRISTOL

CONTENTS

1. Lucy Mair — 1
   J. DAVIS

2. On some witches and a predicant — 7
   PIERRE ALEXANDRE

3. Conflict and change: establishment and opposition in Malta — 17
   JEREMY BOISSEVAIN

4. How they hid the red flag in Pisticci in 1923, and how it was betrayed — 44
   J. DAVIS

5. The politics of an old state: a view from the Chinese lineage — 68
   MAURICE FREEDMAN

6. The free women of Kinshasa: prostitution in a city in Zaïre — 89
   JEAN S. LA FONTAINE

7. The progress of Greek nationalism in Cyprus, 1878–1970 — 114
   PETER LOIZOS

8. Aspects of underdevelopment and development in northeast Morocco — 134
   DAVID SEDDON

9. Land tenure and 'room for manoeuvre' — 161
   ANNE SHARMAN

10. Cause, knowledge and change: Turkish village revisited 191
    PAUL STIRLING

11. Status and the innovator 230
    SANDRA WALLMAN

    List of works cited 251

I
Lucy Mair

The ten essays which we publish to honour Lucy Mair reflect some of her cross-cutting interests within the discipline of Social Anthropology. When we speak to our students of 'cross-cutting' ties, we generally and unfortunately convey the mental image of a person torn, divided and cut down to small size by multifarious loyalties. Those of us who have been taught by Professor Mair know that the phrase can also indicate a unique integrity, a wholly personal combination of activities and interests bound together by the special skills and intelligence of one excellent person.

After graduating from Cambridge in 1922 Professor Mair spent five years working for the League of Nations Union, in association with Gilbert Murray. In 1927 she joined the staff of the London School of Economics in the department of International Relations: in the early '30s, guided by Malinowski, she went to Uganda and returned to the School as a Lecturer in Colonial Administration in 1932. During the war she worked for the Royal Institute of International Affairs and for the government, moving to Australia in 1945 to advise on the establishment of the Australian administration of New Guinea. She became Reader at L.S.E. in 1947, and in 1955 changed the term Colonial Administration for Applied Anthropology; she was given a personal Chair in 1963 and retired in 1968 after more than forty years at L.S.E., the last two of them as convenor of the department. In that year she went again to New Guinea, and returned to stand in for two years as head of the department at the University of Durham. In 1971 she was appointed Honorary Professor of Social Anthropology at the University of Kent: the post is honorific at least in the sense that it confers honour on the university, where Professor Mair lectures and teaches with apparently increasing vigour.

A glance at the select bibliography in this volume will indicate the intellectual co-ordinates of Professor Mair's position in Social

Anthropology. Three main elements are discernible. There is the broad interest in relations between rich and poor nations, established by *The Protection of Minorities* (1928) maintained in essays which give anthropologically-informed answers to sensible layman's questions (Self-government or Good Government?, 1948), and culminating in *New Nations* (1963) and *The New Africa* (1967). Then, the particular interest in the consequences of western-inspired innovation for 'the societies which at different times have been called primitive, backward, under-developed, developing, and are at the moment officially, it seems, known as less developed' (1969c: 1).[1] This is most manifest in her discussion of administrative innovation, of legal regulation of marriage and land tenure. Her argument has always been that there is no short cut to being an effective administrator of innovation: if there is 'a lesson' to be drawn from the scrupulous study of development, it is that there are no rules of thumb for achieving success; and that an essential prerequisite is to understand the societies in which development is to be induced. And this is the third element, the mastery of the whole field of social anthropology, which begins with *An African People in the Twentieth Century* (1934), is maintained in the articles of the 1950s, and then bears fruit in the major syntheses of the 1960s and '70s: *Primitive Government* (1962), *New Nations* (1963), *An Introduction to Social Anthropology* (1965), *Witchcraft* (1969), and *Marriage* (1971).

It is worth calling special attention to those nine years, 1962–71, which follow Lucy Mair's sixtieth birthday. Her friends and pupils admired her productivity, her colleagues recognised not only her voice but in it, too, the characteristic and authentic L.S.E. usefulness, down-to-earthness, commonsense. When a proper history of the discipline comes to be written I think the five books of this period will be recognised as the *summa anthropologica* they are: it is true that they do not cover all the things anthropologists talk about (notably, economics), but with their immense scholarship and directness they bring order, shape, completeness, into what was formerly esoteric and scattered information. When all the argument is done, what is needed is someone who asks—What do we know now? What can we tell people is true? And Professor

[1] Works by Professor Mair which the contributors refer to are listed in the bibliography immediately following this chapter. Works by other writers are listed at the end of the volume.

Mair has answered these questions in respect of political systems, witchcraft, marriage and the consequences of colonial and post-colonial contact between industrial and non-industrial societies. The answers are not welcomed by all anthropologists, some of whom are disappointed at them; and others have been deceived by their straightforwardness and led to ignore their innovatory contributions. But the reader may care, for example, to search the index of any non-monographic study published before 1961 for entries under *patronage* or *clientage*, and to compare the results with those passages of *Primitive Government* where the spread and growth of political institutions is discussed in lapidary style. *Witchcraft* and *Marriage* perform the same inestimable service: it is not just that undergraduates are given a conspectus which they had not before, but that disputes and controversies are resolved in a comparative context, or are shown to be ill-founded, or that hitherto underemphasised kinds of behaviour are shown to be more important than we had ever thought.

Science operates beyond the boundaries of commonsense. It follows that if science is to progress, what is taken to be commonsense must continually expand. Lucy Mair's contribution to anthropology is thus not only her esoteric and specialist contribution, for she has also, in five major areas of inquiry, brought esoteric knowledge within the grasp of ordinary educated and inquiring people. That is what *summa* are for, and it is how esoteric progress is made.

There are, common to all her works, certain qualities which make them instantly recognisable as those of Lucy Mair. The clarity and wit of her literary style are well-known, but are mere emanations of more fundamental virtues. Clarity is one aspect of an economical approach to intellectual activity, which is also manifest in her ability to produce masterly and original syntheses of a wide range of material while at the same time doing without the spurious general principles sometimes used to create an artificial orderliness. She also abstains from handing down rules for applying anthropological knowledge. Wit is one aspect of a quality which, in addition to her learning and cleverness, has made us think that we should honour her as best we can. That quality is irony—the compassionate confrontation of people's ideals and intentions with what they in fact do and choose to do. It is, perhaps, the necessary condition of excellence in a social scientist:

such irony in Professor Mair's work locates it firmly in the great liberal tradition of the human sciences.

BIBLIOGRAPHY : LUCY MAIR

1928a *The Protection of Minorities: the working and scope of the minorities treaties under the League of Nations*. London: Christophers.
1928b 'The Scheldt Controversy', *Economica*, 8.
1931 'Native land tenure in East Africa', *Africa*, 4.
1933a 'Human Welfare and the League'. London: League of Nations Union.
1933b 'Baganda land tenure', *Africa*, 6.
1933c 'Colonial Administration as a Science', *Journal of the African Society*, 32.
1934a *An African People in the Twentieth Century*. London: Routledge.
1934b 'The Growth of economic individualism in African Society', *Journal of the African Society*, 33. Reprinted in *Studies in Applied Anthropology*, 1957.
1934c 'The Study of culture contact as a practical problem', *Africa*, 7. Reprinted in L. Mair (ed.), *Methods of Study of Culture Contact*, with title 'The Place of History in the Study of Culture Contatact'. London: I.A.I. Memorandum xv, 1938.
1935a 'Linguistics without Sociology', *Bulletin of the School of Oriental Studies*, 7.
1935b 'The anthropologist's approach to native education', *Overseas Education*, 6. Reprinted in *Studies in Applied Anthropology*, 1957.
1935c 'Totemism among the Baganda', *Man*, 35.
1936a *Native Policies in Africa*. London: Routledge.
1936b 'Chieftainship in modern Africa', *Africa*, 9. Reprinted in *Studies in Applied Anthropology*, 1957, and *Anthropology and Social Change*, 1969.
1937 'Colonial policy and peaceful change', in C. A. W. Manning (ed.), *Peaceful change, an international problem*.
1939 'What anthropologists are after', *Uganda Journal*, 7.
1940 *Native Marriage in Buganda*. London: International African Institute Memorandum xix.
1944 *Welfare in the British Colonies*. London: Royal Institute of International Affairs.
1948a *Australia in New Guinea*. London: Christophers.
1948b 'Self-government or good government?', *South Pacific*. Reprinted in *Studies in Applied Anthropology*, 1957.
1948c 'Modern developments in African land tenure', *Africa*, 18. Reprinted in *Studies in Applied Anthropology*, 1957, and *Anthropology and Social Change*, 1969.
1950a 'The role of the anthropologist in non-autonomous territories', in C. M. MacInnes (ed.), *Principles and methods of colonial administration*.
1950b 'Anthropology and the Underdeveloped Territories', *Indonesie*, 4. Reprinted in *Studies in Applied Anthropology*, 1957, and *Anthropology and Social Change*, 1969.
1951a 'Marriage and family in the Dedza District of Nyasaland', *JRAI*, 81.

1951b 'A Yao girl's initiation', *Man*, 51.
1952a *Native Administration in Central Nyasaland*. London: H.M.S.O.
1952b 'Land tenure in the Gold Coast', *Civilisations*, 2.
1952c 'Local government in Nigeria', *West Africa*, Dec. 1952–Jan. 1953.
1953a 'African Marriage and Social Change', in A. W. Phillips (ed.), *Survey of African marriage and family life*, London.
1953b 'Nigeria under the Macpherson Constitution', *World Today*, 9.
1954 'The International Bank Report: Social aspects of economic development in Nigeria', *West Africa*, 25 Dec. 1954.
1955 'Towards a Federal Gold Coast?', *World Today*, 11.
1956 'Applied Anthropology and Development Policies', *BJS*, 7. Reprinted in *Anthropology and Social Change*, 1969.
1957a *Studies in applied anthropology*. London: Athlone Press.
1957b 'Malinowski and the Study of Social Change', in R. W. Firth (ed.), *Man and Culture*.
1957c 'Representative local government as a problem in social change', *Human Problems in British Central Africa*, 21. Reprinted in *Journal of African Administration*, 10.
1958a 'African Chiefs Today', *Africa*, 28. Reprinted in *Anthropology and Social Change*, 1969.
1958b 'The Pursuit of the Millennium in Melanesia', *BJS*, 9.
1958c 'East Africa', *Political Quarterly*, 29.
1958d *Free Consent in African Marriage*. London: Anti-Slavery Society.
1959 'Independent Religious Movements in Three Continents', *Comparative Studies in Society and History*, 1.
1960a 'Mise en valeur de terres pour Africains au Kenya', *Revue de l'Institut Solvay*, 1.
1960b 'Race, Tribalism and Nationalism in Africa', in P. Mason (ed.), *Man, Race and Darwin*. Reprinted in *Anthropology and Social Change*, 1969.
1960c 'Social Change in Africa', *International Affairs*, 36.
1960d 'The social sciences in Africa south of the Sahara: the British contribution', *Human Organization*, 19.
1961 'Clientship in East Africa', *Cahiers d'Etudes Africaines*, 2.
1962a *Primitive Government*. Harmondsworth: Penguin.
1962b 'Old and New Leadership in Africa', *Advancement of Science*, 19. Reprinted in *Anthropology and Social Change*, 1969.
1962c *The Nyasaland Elections of 1961*. London: Athlone Press.
1963a *New Nations*. London: Weidenfeld & Nicolson.
1963b 'Some Current Terms in Social Anthropology', *BJS*, 14.
1964a 'Witchcraft as a problem in the study of religion', *Cahiers d'Etudes Africaines*, 4.
1964b 'L'Afrique Orientale', *Revue Juridique et Politique*.
1965a *An Introduction to Social Anthropology*. Oxford: Clarendon Press.
1965b 'Tradition and Modernity in the New Africa', *Transactions of the New York Academy of Sciences*, n.s. 27. Reprinted in *Anthropology and Social Change*.
1967a *The New Africa*. London: Watts.
1967b 'Busoga local government', *Journal of Commonwealth Political Studies*, 5.

1969a *Witchcraft.* London: Weidenfeld & Nicolson.
1969b *African Marriage and Social Change.* Reprint of 1953a. London: Cass.
1969c *Anthropology and Social Change.* London: Athlone Press.
1970a *Australia in New Guinea*, 2nd edn., largely revised. Melbourne: Melbourne University Press.
1970b 'New Elites in East and West Africa', in V. W. Turner (ed.), *Profiles of Change in African Society and Colonial Rule.*
1971 *Marriage.* Harmondsworth: Penguin.
1972a *An Introduction to Social Anthropology*, 2nd edn. Oxford: Clarendon Press.
1972b 'Witchcraft: a review article', *BJS*, 23.

2
On some witches and a predicant

PIERRE ALEXANDRE

The missionaries expected from the converts a complete breaking away from the past in every field, which was practically impossible: a break from traditional life as expressed in the ancestor cult, the secret societies, etc.

Formerly, important people were buried with several of their slaves, and many heads of cattle were sacrificed during the funeral, the idea being that they were sent to the dead ancestors to curry their favour. This practice is on its way out, replaced by another based upon the same fundamental principle. Following a Christian's death (as well as a pagan's) his friends buy clothes and blankets to be buried with him so that the coffin is crammed up with clothes of every kind and size, the underlying notion being that the dead man will convey them to his friends' deceased relatives. It can be said that he acts as an intermediary between the living and those who dwell in the other world. Is not this an integral copy of the ancient practice now transposed into the church?

The descriptions quoted above have not been extracted from the field report of some anthropologist. They are statements of faith—or should I say statements of fact?—by a presbyterian minister, a pastor of the Cameroun Evangelic Church. Excerpts, to be quite precise, from his dissertation for the degree of Bachelor in Divinity, Paris, 1967 (pp. 59, 72).

In 1965 I was offered the lectureship in religious anthropology at the Faculté Libre de Théologie Protestante in Paris,[1] a post with little prestige and no pay, yet, or so it seemed at the time, with some responsibility, as the Faculté trains many of the ministers not only for various French denominations but also for several Protestant churches in French-speaking Africa.[2]

[1] The Faculté has ceased to be part of the official French university system since the churches were disestablished in 1905. It is interdenominational, as is the Société des Missions Evangéliques (SME).

[2] Students from Cameroun belong chiefly to Eglise Evangélique du Cameroun and Eglise Baptiste Camerounaise, both created by SME, and, to a lesser extent,

8 ON SOME WITCHES AND A PREDICANT

In 1966 I was appointed to supervise the final B.D. dissertation of Rev. D.N., a pastor of the Cameroun Evangelical Church. Rev. D.N., a thirty-year old man, had been trained at the Theological College of the Paris Evangelical mission, at Ndoungué, and had served for several years as a parish minister in his native district (Mungo *département*) before being sent to Paris for complementary training. He had attended my course without any special reaction and I think the supervision of his dissertation was assigned to me chiefly because it bore on an African topic.

I must confess the title—'La puissance de l'Evangile face au paganisme Minieh'—did not look specially appetising. Nor was the preliminary draft any more exciting: it reminded me of the worst type of Sunday school literature, the bowdlerised versions of missionary travels, brimming with dastardly superstitious sorcerers and soapy Uncle Tommish converts. And it rang palpably false.

I gave my opinion, rather bluntly I am afraid, to Rev. D.N., and he broke down, explaining he had not expected his dissertation to be supervised by a layman and, even worse (or better?), by a layman with some African experience. After consulting with some of our common African friends in Paris (and, as I heard later, writing to people who had known me in the Cameroons) he agreed to write down what he really thought—what, in fact, obsessed him—, that is a discussion of missionary attitude vis-à-vis witches and witchcraft. The present paper is essentially a résumé of this dissertation.[3]

'Minieh' is a glossonym—literally 'I say'[4]—designating a group of 'tribes', in fact large patriclans, straddling the border of W. Cameroun (formerly Southern British Cameroons), a hundred miles or so north of Duala. These patriclans—Bakosi,[5] Bakaka, Ninɔŋ, Manmenaŋ, etc.—are also known as Banbengo, 'children of Ngo', after their common ancestor. They are divided into

to Eglise Presbytérienne Camerounaise, created by the American Presbyterian Mission (MPA). EEC and EBC are active in the coastal region and its hinterland and on the Bamileke plateau, EPC in the 'cocoa belt', on the interior plateau between the Sanaga river and the Southern border.

[3] I failed in my attempt to preserve in translation the special flavour of the Camerounian variety of French Chanaanese. Any quaintness in the English is therefore mine and not Rev. D.N.'s.

[4] A common way of designating tribal groups in Southern Cameroons; thus: *mbanae* among the Diwala, Ewodi, Malimba, Batanga; *majónâ* among the Yewondo, Bulu, Fang; *mäkaâ* among the Kozimɛ, Bajw̃e, Mvumbo; etc.

[5] According to Dugast's *Inventair ethnique* the Bakosi belong to another group.

exogamic major patrilineages, and those in turn into minor patrilineages at village level:[6]

> Extended families [i.e. minor lineages] often have some common signs..and in most cases these signs are animals. Our own family has got as its signs the leopard and the snake..The public appearance [of one of them] is a sure sign that a misfortune is about to strike the family..
> One can be possessed [by the 'totemic' animal] when angry or when fighting an enemy..This is very dangerous and can prove fatal for the possessed person..if he is far away from home, for he can be quieted down only by somebody with the same [totemic] animal..
> The family can use this animal to set free one of its members if he be kept prisoner..The animal goes..searching for the prisoner.., opens the door of the gaol and lets [the prisoner] out..But those who used to know how to manage this kind of thing are becoming scarce and young people are no longer interested [in learning]..(p. 5)

Political authority was diffuse, as it usually is in segmentary societies. At village level it was in the hands of a college of elders led by the minor lineage headman. Above that level there were two cult associations with a political role; one (*mwankum*) seems to have been operating within the major lineages, the other (*ngwe*) across lineage affiliations. Membership in both *mwankum* and *ngwe* was restricted to men; women had their own association, of which nothing is known.

Significantly enough Rev. D.N. deals with these associations under the heading 'Means to increase power and to ensure order', 'power' to be understood as individual and 'order' as collective.

Both associations are said to have been invented about six generations ago (end of eighteenth century?); each met at a special enclosure in the forest; initiation in each of them had to be paid for in cattle and goods (it was more expensive in *ngwe*).

'The role [of *ngwe*][7] was to preserve the established social order, to enforce law and justice.. [especially in cases of] adultery, theft or murder' (p. 28). Sanctions were physical—splinters of bamboo

---

[6] All ethnological data are interpreted or derived from Rev. D. N.'s dissertation. There is a dearth of anthropological literature dealing with this area.

[7] According to Rev. D. N. *ngwe* has been invented by the Mwanmenan of Manengumba. Yet associations with name—*ngil, ngïwi*—, insignia and social function quite similar to those of *ngwe* are found among the Basaa-Bakoko and Beti-Fang groups as far south as the Ogowe valley in Gabon. There might be also a possible relationship with the Ekoi *ngbɛ*.

thrust under the scalp—, and financial—heavy fines in cattle—, as well as magical. When a physical, or magical murder had been committed, a chapter of *ngwe* was called in from another place, to conduct the purification rites, arbitrate the blood price, and in general terms to prevent a feud between lineages.

Mwankum seems to have been more restricted in its field of action, more closely linked to local lineage segments and to the family structure. It was apparently in charge of organising the male *rites de passage*. Generally speaking it seems to have been essentially concerned with village affairs, and its control of those to have been more 'medical' (using, of course, magical medicines) than judicial. Thus:

When a member [of *mwankum*] dies too suddenly to have time to share out his estate or to reveal his secrets..you can make him speak even when he has been buried for three days. You have but to mix some herbs and to pour some water on his grave and then ask the dead man your questions and he will answer..with precision either about the origin of this death, or the whereabouts of his goods, or else the people to whom he owes money or who owe money to him..(p. 32)

The power and efficiency of both *ngwe* and *mwankum* were 'based upon the strength of herbs which injured those who rebelled against their decisions, injuring or killing them or making them ill..'

There is nothing in the context to show whether these 'herbs' were (are?) used naturally (i.e. as poisons or antidotes) or supernaturally. In fact it may well be that both explanations are true and that there existed a continuum spreading from pragmatic herbal medicine to magical use of certain plants.

Ngwe was attacked by the colonial administration as well as by the missionaries and eventually destroyed. *Mwankum* activities, on the other hand, seem to have escaped administrative repression and to have only undergone missionary hostility. *Mwankum* disappeared or went underground shortly before World War II, but was resurrected in the late 'fifties during the violent disturbances which preceded and followed independence: 'a spectacular comeback, with *mwankum* initiation, making and bearing amulets as a protection against the enemies..whoever [bore] an amulet no longer fled from the terrorists for he felt protected by it' (p. 41).

Rev. D.N. clearly seems to be of a divided mind concerning the suppression of these associations. In his first draft he duly copied enthusiastic victory bulletins reporting the fall of idols and the confusion of the servants of Baal. In the final version he finds, to say the least, excuses for the old ways: 'Let us acknowledge the fact that olden times were hard and difficult times which prevented individuals from flourishing..', which also certainly made the cult associations a necessary evil, at any rate lesser evils than witchcraft, 'bad medicines' and spirits which he lists (p. 34) as the most frequent causes of death.

A semantic caveat must be entered at this point. Rev. D.N., writing in French, has only one word—sorcier/sorcellerie—at his disposal where an English-speaking person would use several—witch/witchcraft, sorcerer/sorcery, witch-doctor, herbalist, etc.—and most Bantu languages of this area have at least two.[8] In some cases he uses the phrase *'contre-sorcier'* (counter-witch), a term invented by French-speaking Africans precisely to make a clear distinction (impossible in standard French) between the nefarious witch and the beneficent practitioner of the magic art who in fact fights witches. In other cases he uses *'sorcier'* with a meaning similar to that of 'sorcerer', i.e. more or less ambiguous, a man who uses magic in a potentially useful *and* potentially dangerous way. As Rev. D.N. and I had no Bantu language in common I have been, at times, unable to make sure whether his *sorciers* were witches or sorcerers, or both.

Rev. D.N.'s line of reasoning runs as follows: witchcraft, spirits, sorcerers are a reality in African society; the missionaries 'coming from far and strange countries with a peculiar turn of mind' failed to understand this reality and to adapt church institutions to deal with it; thus witches were able to use the very structures of missionary churches to strengthen their position; so it is now up to the independent churches to find appropriate ways to deal with witchcraft.

He starts with a discussion of the causes of death:

—*natural death* 'caused by God' is 'quite exceptional..[and concerns only] white bearded old men, satiated with days' (p. 34);

—*'voluntary' death*: that of twins, and seers who leave life voluntarily to be reincarnated into another body; this kind of death is not plainly commented upon by the author who seems to imply later on that it is unchristian but not morally wrong;

[8] For discussion of that semantic fine point, see: Froelich (1968).

—'*medicines*' are 'herbs, tree bark, and other magical produces, which when mixed together have the property of making people sick or even killing them'. They 'were' (*sic*—note the use of the past tense) chiefly used by cultic associations;
—'*spirits*', more precisely evil spirits, because some nature and ancestor spirits can be benevolent, and can be used for instance to get barren women impregnated:

..The value [of a spirit fertility cult] is measured by its effects and it happened that sterile women did conceive..Was it due to mere chance or to [the rite]? I felt shy (*gêne*) to decide, yet I cannot refrain from considering this miracle as a granting of prayers rendered unto the dead. (p. 14)

But, on the whole, spirits are unpredictable and generally dangerous; not so much the ancestral ghosts:

Some [of which] are innocuous, while others lie in wait..for those who have caused their death in order to avenge themselves. Formerly this way of avenging oneself was quite common, but nowadays it is well on its way to disappearing..(p. 19),

as the nature spirits. Some of these act in an autonomous way; others have human masters or allies:

..in some places there are men who have secretly married female '*mami-wotas*'[9]..[these] alliances are frequent among the coastal population, and they are not imaginary. They are true..In the hinterland tribes they are uncommon but not impossible. They are most common among wealthy planters..(p. 17)
..[Evil] spirits are bought for money, from fetishers and marabouts. But they are often dangerous for their own masters because they are very demanding and any mistake [on their owner's part] can lead to his death. Generally they kill or injure people as ordered by their master.. (p. 19)

—*witchcraft*, finally, is 'a scourge which has depopulated whole regions in the country'.

A witch is a man with four eyes and in his stomach witchcraft, that is a malignant power allowing him to send his double at night to harm his enemies. (p. 90)[10]

[9] *Mami-wota* = mammy water in Diwala *jengú*, a water spirit incarnated in the manatee, or sea-cow.
[10] Rev. D.N. writes later on 'A man bitten by a snake or wounded by a wild

ON SOME WITCHES AND A PREDICANT 13

[People] give [their children] from early childhood a magical power such as witchcraft. This is a kind of blessing in reverse: such children are much feared, but it can be a danger to themselves, because they are tempted to use that power and lacking in experience..can meet with a premature death by letting themselves be caught by witch-doctors [=*contre-sorciers*]. (p. 8)
..Witchcraft is a kind of passion, when one engages in it it becomes very difficult to get oneself rid of it. Although some witches, once caught, swear to renounce witchcraft, they end up by reverting to it. In fact while it may happen that a witch should confess his crime this will occur only when he has fallen ill, his confession aiming at saving his life. (p. 23)

Rev. D.N. then states very definitely the actual existence of these phenomena; as for spirits:

[Their mode of action] is difficult to define: all I know is they get orders from their master and attack only [his] enemies. (p. 20)
All I can say is that most of these [nature] spirits do actually exist, even if a few of them are imaginary. I am convinced that people who speak about them speak through actual experience. Without any doubt some man has had the misfortune of colliding with one..while taking a walk by the forest or bathing at the river in full daylight..it is after such an experience that he is able to speak of these spirits. (p. 15)
[As for people said to have met with ghosts] we cannot state definitely to what a degree their stories are true, yet we cannot deny them because so many things happen in Black Africa which are incredible but nevertheless true. (p. 16)

Concerning witches he is even more articulate and becomes strongly critical of the official attitude of the churches and missions:

These things are real and those who deny it are wrong; this was the fault committed by the first Christians, who in the name of the Gospel denied this reality, manifest as it was; by doing so they let the door open for witches, with the result that paganism has penetrated the Church. (p. 23)
The Evangelic Church of Cameroun has always denied the very existence of witchcraft and taught that fetishers were liars..This is

animal will say that these things have been sent by enemies of his, that they are incarnations of a witch..(This) can be eventually verified as, if one succeeds in wounding the animal, his master (is injured) as well..This happens quite often in rural areas'. This use of an animal double seems quite different from possession by the lineage totem as mentioned above. Here, so to speak, the witch possesses the animal; with the totem it is the other way round.

wrong because you cannot deny what actually exists. Among the Minieh witchcraft does exist..(p. 74)

Witchcraft is a fact, denying it in the name of the Gospel needs some cheek. Today more than ever before those who deny it must needs consider anew their position if they don't want to fall behind the times. (p. 24)

He explains that at first 'for many [converts] baptism was a remedy against witchcraft and bad medicines' (p. 43), that members of the traditional cultic associations 'mistook Christianity for a new kind of secret society with membership widened to include women and slaves' (p. 46). By refusing to admit the reality of witchcraft the missionaries then turned the 'parishes [into] an asylum for witches of all kinds seeking to shelter themselves from persecution. The very notion of natural death has disappeared and nowadays every death is ascribed to a witch' (p. 35), which according to him (and he is probably right) explains why so many people are deserting the mission-founded churches to join nativistic ones.

Rev. D.N. is not alone in feeling and denouncing this malaise. I have had confidences from other young ministers of his generation, some with university degrees in lay subjects, all pointing the same way. Some of them tried to 'do something' about witchcraft, as described below. This attempt does not seem to have been well received by the missionaries and the older generation of ministers —I was given a definitely cold shoulder when I tried to enquire about it. Anyway:

At Ndoungué mission station[11] some missionaries took notice of this phenomenon [i.e. witchcraft] but they thought it was on its way out. They were forgetting..that witchcraft is a science which can be transmitted from father to son; even by becoming a Christian one does not desist from it because witchcraft cannot be peeled off like a garment..Some native pastors took this scourge seriously and founded an association called *male ma makom*, meaning 'alliance of friends', to build up an anti-witch bloc; each member gave up the secret of the herbs needed to fight that scourge, so that they compiled a document full of recipes of all kinds either to cure diseases or to fight witchcraft. Some people after leaving divinity school became true witch-fighters. Others used the same recipes to become terrible witches themselves and

[11] Seat of the Theological College which trained ministers for both the Baptist and Evangelical Churches of Cameroun before the opening of the new Faculté de Théologie Protestante in Yaoundé.

fight one another.[12] This fight often resulted in the sudden death of the vanquished. In this dangerous situation they could no longer battle witchcraft as they had wished. Others were denying the very existence of witchcraft, thus opening the door of the churches to witches who feared persecution by the populace.

During the Regional Consistory of 1962 we tried to discuss the topic of witchcraft. But opinions were divided: according to some pastors well advanced in age, witchcraft did not exist. It was..a mere invention of Man for, they said, nobody but God can dispose of another man's life..This argument is unfounded..The Bible does not teach us to deny the existence of Evil but [only that it] has been vanquished by Jesus Christ. If magic does exist (Acts 13: 1–12) why not witchcraft? As for us younger members of that consistory we were convinced of the existence of this scourge..To say that witchcraft does not exist amounts to giving the witch a possibility to carry on his work of darkness..Some pastors and church members have been responsible for the penetration of witchcraft into the Church:..unwittingly they made themselves ridiculous to the eyes of witches among their parishioners..

I believe we ought to have a change of policy. Instead of protecting the witches we should accuse them and watch the results. Preach against Evil from the pulpit and denounce it as an evil to be fought. The Church has a prophetic role to play. In this way we could do the State a good turn. I regret that after Independence the Cameroon Government has not taken any official step against witchcraft. (pp. 90–1)

What these steps could be is suggested by this nostalgic reminiscence:

In German times witches were sentenced to death and publicly executed as murderers. This living example gave much to think about to those who had become past masters in witchcraft: they knew in advance the risks they incurred by venturing on that path. (p. 34)[13]

Failing Government intervention, Rev. D.N. suggests self-defence:

..Two years ago at Ewodi young men used to meet whenever one of them had fallen a victim of witchcraft. They went to the culprit, armed with sticks, and beat him to death, which compelled him either to cure the sick person or to flee to Duala or elsewhere. (p. 93)

[12] Literal translation. In fact oral elaboration, and even the following few lines, show that these 'terrible witches' were intended to be witches' witches, so to speak.
[13] In fact the people hanged—for 'sorcery' rather than witchcraft—by the German administrators were, in most cases, either dignitaries of *ngwe* or even 'counter-witches' rather than witches proper.

After conceding that this method may be dangerous ('yet deserves to be considered') as 'one can injustly tax a person with witchcraft', he goes on to describe the non-violent method used in his own village:

> The culprit is confronted with the facts and implored to show mercifulness towards the sick person. Beforehand diviners are consulted, several at a time so as to make no mistake. Following this consultation the whole village is convened at the sick man's house. . and divided into two groups, the sick man's family and the outsiders. . The representative of the sick man's brother speaks first, accusing himself and begging the outsiders to remove this ill, as nobody can shave his own head. . [There follows an intervention of the 'village representative', whose speech and gestures are described in some detail]. . Finally the whole family is accused and entrusted with the care of curing the sick man without any delay. . The family. . own to their responsibility and ask the outsiders to depart and let them have a chance to cure their brother. . It may happen that the sick person either gets well or dies, yet this rite ought to command the attention of those who deny the existence of witchcraft, especially the Cameroun Evangelical Church. (pp. 93–4)

I should have thought the Church likely to be more interested in the more orthodox remedies suggested in the dissertation (praying, preaching and prophesying), which were, on the whole, outside my own province. This opinion seemed to be shared by the chairman of the examining panel, a theologian, who concentrated his questions upon these passages. Rev. D.N. finally got his B.D., *cum laude*, if my memory is correct, instead of the usual *summa* or at least *magna cum*. A few weeks later I was dismissed from my post by a curt three-line note without any explanation. Somebody must have told them I am a witch.

3

Conflict and change: establishment and opposition in Malta[1]

JEREMY BOISSEVAIN

INTRODUCTION

One of the problems which anthropologists and sociologists still face is to explain the institutions they study in terms other than their reciprocal influence on each other and on the society of which they form part. In other words anthropologists usually study the *status quo* and seek to explain it in terms of the *status quo*: they rarely seek to explain the genesis or evolution of the institutions they study. The explanation for this, fascinating as it is, need not detain us here: it is largely an overreaction to the evolutionary theories of nineteenth-century social scientists brought about by the shift in power relations within and between the societies of which these scientists form part (Elias 1959: XXVIII–XLI).

This reaction, combined with the difficulties of studying the history of illiterate peoples, enabled anthropologists to rationalise away the need for an historical dimension in favour of purely synchronic studies. These studies described the institutions of exotic peoples in exquisite detail, and sometimes even compared

---

[1] The field work on which most of this study is based was carried out in Malta during 1960–61 under the terms of a grant from the British Colonial Social Science Research Council. Return visits during the Summers of 1967, 1968 and 1969 were made possible by the generosity of respectively the Wenner-Gren Foundation for Anthropological Research, the Netherlands Association for the Advancement of Pure Scientific Research (ZWO) and the University of Michigan Project for the study of Mediterranean Networks administered by Eric Wolf. Fred Bailey, Anton Blok, Bonno Thoden van Velzen, Klaas van der Veen, Jolanthe van Opzeeland, Jojada Verrips, Carla Jonker and a number of students provided valuable criticism of earlier versions. The final draft was written in the congenial isolation of the Pauwhof in Wassenaar.

them to each other. But they rarely tried to explain how and why the institutions studied came into being in the first place. It is almost as though anthropologists believed in a doctrine of immaculate social conception. It is in fact strange to find this in the works of people for whom the evolutionary theories of Darwin are basic beliefs.[2] As a result the understanding of the internal dynamics of societies—the details of the processes of generation, maintenance and change—still leaves much to be desired (cf. Barth 1966, 1967).

A notable exception is Lucy Mair's comparative study of government and politics in East Africa, particularly her chapter on 'The expansion of government' (1962a: 107-22'. Here she examines the process by which certain institutions evolve. It is an attempt to explain the emergence of an institution, the state, in terms of ecology, demography and the manipulation of power seekers. Significantly she begins her analysis with the patron-client or leader-follower coalition and perceptively suggests that the relationship of clientage 'may well be the germ from which state power springs' (p. 166).

In the following analysis I also set out the process by which institutions—in this case ritual corporations that today compete over the celebration of their respective patron saints—evolved from leader-follower coalitions and continue to change. The aim is of course to derive insights into the course of such transformations, in the hope of finding certain regularities in the dynamic process by which the social institutions of which they form part are modified. In the course of this study I examine critically the still widely held notion that conflict within a given political structure takes place between more or less evenly matched groups, according to a set of mutually accepted rules which assure that the competition stays within reasonable limits (Bailey, 1969). Some writers have even maintained that such internal conflict strengthens the structure of the society in question (Gluckman 1959; Coser 1956).

The concept of a structural balance, of a normative order mirrored in and deriving from a set of rules, is I suggest, one of the major obstacles to understanding the internal dynamics of conflict

[2] The teleological elements inherent in structural-functionalism may of course also be viewed as the working of the evolutionary process of the survival of the fittest: only those institutions persist which are best suited for society, though here again there is no explanation of how the institutions are generated.

CONFLICT AND CHANGE IN MALTA 19

groups and thus to the understanding of the changes taking place in all societies. This notion of structural balance derives from the organic or systematic model of society, developed by Durkheim, Radcliffe-Brown and Parsons, on which most of the present generation of English-speaking sociologists and social anthropologists have been raised. Change is consequently viewed as a function of homeostasis: as movement towards a new social equilibrium—which is regarded as the 'normal' condition of a society—in order to 'control and counteract variations which would destroy the system if they exceeded more than a limited range' (Emmet 1958: 62). The impulses which trigger this movement towards a new social equilibrium are seen as coming from outside the social structure. In Bailey's words, 'The seeds of change lie in the environment of a political structure' (1969: 190). The possibility that there may be *internal* forces which bring about change in all societies is ruled out by the organic or systemic model of society.[3]

THE VILLAGE AND PARTITI

The setting

Malta's history has been greatly influenced by its small size and strategic location in the centre of the Mediterranean; for centuries it has been run as an island fortress. All government services are administered from Valletta, the capital, by civil servants; there are no mayors, headmen, or councillors who represent or administer the individual villages. The parliament is composed of elected members representing fairly large districts. In the absence of secular authorities at the village level, parish priests emerged as the traditional spokesmen for the fervently Roman Catholic population in both religious and secular affairs. Malta, long a British colony, became an independent nation in 1964.

Though it is somewhat smaller than most Maltese villages, the central features of Hal-Farrug, the village on which this study focuses, are much the same as those of its larger neighbours.[4]

[3] Emmet also observes that the key terms in the organic analogy 'will therefore not be terms like "growth" and "development", but such terms as "norm" and "equilibrium" ' (1958: 63). The validity of the homeo-static model of social change, clearly formulated by the Wilsons (Wilson 1945) 25 years ago, has recently been restated by Bailey (1969: 12-13, 186-226) and Gluckman (1968).

[4] Further details on Malta, the village on which this study focuses and the

Authority is distributed between the parish priest, the police, and a host of elected and appointed office holders representing the interests of the many formal and informal associations and groups in the community. These persons form a circle around the parish priest. Until parliamentary democracy was introduced, only the parish priest and the police were able to back up their commands with sanctions which compel respect, if not obedience. Today the representatives of the political party in power also form part of the local power élite.

Seven different parish priests have been assigned to the village since the end of the war. Most were transferred after running foul of the village's many conflicting groups. The people of Farrug occasionally remarked that there are too many clubs and societies for the size of the village. There are two brass band clubs, a football club, and committees of the two leading political parties.[5] There are also two sections of Catholic Action, a male branch of an ascetic lay society and three confraternities (devotional brotherhoods), dedicated to the Blessed Sacrament, the Holy Rosary, and St Joseph. Farrug seen as a village has no leader, it owns no property, its inhabitants never meet as a village. But seen as a parish it has a formal leader in the parish priest, and it owns important property: the parish church. The only time most of the village meets as a group is in some religious or political context: for worship, devotional processions and certain feasts or to listen to an election speech. The most important occasion is the annual *festa* of the patron saint. These *festas* provide the chief public entertainment of the countryside, and the good name of a village depends upon its ability to celebrate a lavish feast. Thus most of the issues and decisions which affect the village as a group have to do with religious matters. These are usually decided by the parish priest and the clique surrounding him (which includes the canvassers of the conservative Nationalist Party). They form the local establishment.

The oldest division in Farrug is that between the followers or *partit*, of St Martin, the patron saint of the village, and the *partit* which supports St Joseph. The latter is a secondary saint with

various conflicting groups may be found in several other works (Boissevain 1964, 1965, 1969) to which reference will be made from time to time.

[5] Although the present tense is used I am referring to 1968, the last time I studied the village.

regard to his official position in the parish, but one who has come to assume an importance almost equal to that of the titular saint in the social life of the community. A more recent cleavage is that between the supporters of the Nationalist Party and the Malta Labour Party.

Partiti

Each *partit* in Farrug has its own band club, the officers of which are the leaders of the *partit*. Each band club has elaborate premises, and arranges the organisational aspects of the external feast of its patron saint. They are the nuclei of the *partiti*. The religious confraternities are also aligned with the *partiti*: the older confraternities of the Blessed Sacrament and the Holy Rosary support St Martin, while that of St Joseph celebrates the feast of its namesake. Several of the *partiti* leaders are also officers of their respective confraternities. In addition to the formal members of its band club and confraternities, each *festa partit* has a rank and file of men, women and children who are not members of either, but who still support the *partit* against its rival.

The *festa partiti* compete with each other over almost every aspect of their *festas*, from the decoration of the streets and the adornment of the statue to the number of guest bands and the quantity and quality of fireworks. Even the exact number of communicants, the number and size of candles on the altars and the amount of light bulbs illuminating the façade of the church enter into the competition. During 1960, the year I spent in the village, St Martin's supporters spent over £1,400 on the centenary celebration of their patron while their rivals spent almost £600 on the annual festa of St Joseph. Most of the money was spent on illuminating the streets and the church, on guest bands and on the raw materials for the fireworks which were made in the village by the partisans.

The members of the *partiti* now rarely change sides, although this often occurred in the generation or so following their establishment, nearly a century ago. Today a person is either born into a *partit* or he marries into it. Children normally support the feast of their parents and an outsider marrying into the village generally supports that of his spouse. Children of mixed marriages support the feast of their favourite parent: boys normally follow their father and girls their mother. Marriages between members of rival *partiti* are regarded as undesirable although they occasionally do take place. Thus 72 per cent of the marriages contracted within the village were intra-*partit* marriages. The high incidence of intra-*partit* marriages is probably due more to the class orientation of the *partiti* than their ritual rivalry. In terms of status and power, like tend to marry like.

Though each *partit* claims that it is larger than its opponent, the band clubs each have a membership of about 80 men, and I found that the village was fairly evenly divided between the two. Forty-eight per cent of the men and women supported St Martin, 42 per cent St Joseph, and 10 per cent were uncommitted. Of those uncommitted, 63 per cent were outsiders who had married into the village.

There is strong correlation between occupational class and *partit* affiliation. In general, the supporters of the titular saint have more prestigeful occupations than their rivals.[6] As shown in the table below, 83 per cent of the village's professional and white-collar workers belong to the St Martin *partit*, while only 38 per cent of those engaged in agriculture do so. In contrast 62 per cent of the village's full-time farmers are in the St Joseph *partit*, while only 17 per cent of the professional and white-collar workers are found there.

Partit affiliation and occupational class in Farrug: 1960

	Number	Percentage of Labour Force	St Martin	St Joseph
Professional and clerical	12	4	83%	17%
Service and skilled	115	39	55	45
Semi- and unskilled	124	42	48	52
Agricultural	45	15	38	62
Total	296	100		

We may also note that there is no territorial division between the *partiti*. There is a tendency, however, for more St Martin supporters to live in the better residential area near the church, and for St Joseph supporters to live in the less desirable sections of the village. This is a reflection of their occupational class, and their

[6] I have discussed the relation between status and occupation elsewhere (Boissevain 1965: 49–53; 1969: 44–50).

relative prestige and influence. Social mobility does not involve a change of *partit* though it is often linked to a change of residence.

History of the 'partiti'

The story of the origin and development of the *partiti* in Farrug is in many respects similar to the accounts which I collected about *festa partiti* in other villages. The conflict began almost a hundred years ago. Before 1877 there were no *partiti* in the village; everyone co-operated in the celebration of the feast of St Martin, the patron of the parish. By all accounts this *festa* was a humble one. This period is described as an idyllic time, a sort of mythical period during which the village was happy and united. Much of the organisation of parish affairs, including the celebration of the patron appears to have been in the hands of a clique of influential persons. This often happens if the parish priest is weak. But in 1876 a new parish priest arrived and the scene began to change. Dun Guzepp, the new priest, was young and strong minded. He was determined to wrest control over local affairs from the establishment clique. He began to organise a rival force. As he was from a village where there was a strong secondary *partit* devoted to St Joseph, he first established a confraternity dedicated to his namesake. He thus began to recruit followers and enrolled them in a formal moral association under his direct leadership. This gave him a considerable hold over his followers. The first feast in honour of St Joseph was celebrated in October 1878 to mark the formal establishment of the new confraternity. Although the new secondary feast was at first a simple affair, it and the titular feast grew rapidly during the next few years. In 1880 the new confraternity dedicated an altar in the church to its patron. By 1886 some persons were beginning to grumble about having to pay for another feast. There was a feeling of 'you collect for your feast, and we'll collect for ours'.

In 1888 an incident occurred which changed the course of the rivalry between the supporters of the two saints, which until then appears to have been rather mild as most people celebrated both saints. Dun Guzepp, who was the financial administrator of the parish tried to increase the rent on some of the parish property. There was an outcry. Some persons went to the bishop to complain. Not only had Dun Guzepp been diverting parish funds collected for other purposes to buy new street decorations for the new feast of St Joseph, they protested, but he was now raising rents on church property to continue this work! The complaints resulted in an investigation, following which the administration of the parish church was taken from Dun Guzepp and given to a prominent member of the village who favoured St Martin. This was an important loss of power and, in this poor living, a serious loss of revenue, for the administrator receives a three per cent commission on all fiscal transactions. The parish priest had lost the round to the local establishment, which traditionally organised the celebration of St Martin. This defeat, not surprisingly, infuriated Dun Guzepp. From that day onward, according to the accounts, he threw his full support behind the feast of St Joseph, and in so doing divided the village openly into opposing factions, forcing all persons to choose sides. He eventually built up the feast of St Joseph to a scale that rivalled and eventually surpassed the celebration of St Martin organised by his rivals, the local establishment. He recruited his following from anti-establishment or, as I have called them, the opposition elements in the village: the uninfluential, the poor and, so several informants indicated, the young. Through the new cult they could gain offices and perform functions which hitherto had been monopolised by the circle of the village élite who had surrounded the former parish priest. Today the supporters of St Joseph still occupy the lower rungs of the local prestige ladder.

Some time after this, each *partit* formed its own social club. According to St Martin's supporters, their club grew out of a pre-existing band club, but that of their rivals was not established until after the first world war. They thus consider that they have seniority. St Joseph partisans deny this. They maintain that both clubs came into being when the pre-existing club split around the turn of the century. Consequently they have equal seniority. Both clubs claim that the records crucial to the question of seniority were destroyed by enemy action during the last war. There is thus no documentary evidence which can prove or disprove either claim. This makes for deadlock whenever the issue of seniority is raised.

Dun Guzepp ruled the village for over 56 years. When he finally died in 1932 at the age of 90, he was blind and deaf. Through a variety of means at the disposal of a parish priest he had succeeded in wooing or coercing three-fourths of the village into his *partit*. There are many stories about the old man and the methods he used to recruit supporters. Although many came willingly from the opposition categories, not all did so and genealogies show that the sons of one or two of the élite families joined him. One method he used, according to the accounts, was to make it difficult for people to marry unless they were or became members of the confraternity of St Joseph.

When the old priest died, it was discovered that most of the festal finery of the parish church had been purchased in the name of the confraternity of St Joseph. St Martin supporters were in the humiliating position of having to beg their rivals for the use of the parish valuables in order to decorate the church for the feast of the parish patron. Moreover, while the old priest had firmly controlled the celebration of St Martin within the church, thus limiting it as best he could, he had allowed the lay leaders of the St Joseph *partit* a free hand in planning the religious side of their feast.

The burden of redressing the balance between the *partiti* fell upon the old priest's successors. There were many incidents between these priests and St Joseph supporters, and on several occasions the priests had to send for police protection. In spite of increased pressure from the church after 1935 to limit the extent of the secondary celebrations, the St Joseph *partit* retained its numerical superiority as well as most of the church decorations during the thirties. It was not until 1942 for example that a shrewd parish priest succeeded in bringing the silver altar front out of the St Joseph strong room into that of the parish church, where it has remained ever since. Nonetheless, after the war the number of St Joseph followers began to decline slowly and the St Martin *partit* is now slightly larger than its rival. This is in marked contrast to most other villages divided by this type of rivalry. There the secondary *partiti* are larger than their rivals. This decline can largely be explained by the fact that the leader of the St Joseph's *partit*, although a very capable schoolteacher, has not lived in the village since Dun Guzepp's successor persuaded the school authorities in 1932, 'in the interest of peace in the village', to transfer him to another school. His monthly visits are now too infrequent to keep up the high level of activity which younger members need to remain attached to the club.

Most of the details of the competition for power between Dun

Guzepp and the local establishment that gave rise to the hostile factions of the partisans of St Martin and St Joseph have long since been forgotten. The building materials he introduced to recruit and bind his followers to him (Saint, confraternity and band club) provided a complex of structural features which have transformed the factions. Recruitment is now relatively unambiguous. Each *partit* has frequent meetings, a common ideology and a very definite sense of unity and purpose in its devotion to its patron saint. Moreover, each owns important property in the furnishings of its club, the costly street decorations for the annual festa and the instruments for its brass band. In short, in the 90 years of their existence, the factions have been transformed into permanent ritual corporations.

Why partiti?

The ritualised conflict between established and opposition interests, between those who wield relatively more power and authority, and those over whom they wield it, studied here in one village, is general in Malta. Today there are *festa partiti* or at least competing band clubs in 19 of Malta's 44 villages and towns.[7] Ten are divided by the type of rivalry described above. Another four are divided by rivalry between their constituent parishes. Five more are divided by rival band clubs not related to the cult of saints, though those in one village once were. Finally, weak *festa partiti* once existed in another seven villages. But as these were not yet aligned with formal associations such as band or social clubs, they were not well enough organised to resist the firm pressure the Church began to exert after 1935.

All *festa partiti* came into being during the fifty years or so after 1850. This is because a number of new elements were added to the structural conflict between local establishment and opposition interests which had always existed in the villages, as indeed it exists everywhere power and authority are exercised. The first of these was a growing awareness on the part of persons in what I have called the opposition categories that they shared certain common characteristics. The ideology of a working-class movement, developed in the north of Europe, reached Malta during this period. Industrialisation also began in Malta at this time. The

[7] In Gozo only Rabat, the capital, is also divided. But the little island's eleven villages are divided into two blocs, each of which centres on a *partit* in Rabat.

workers' movement propagated an egalitarian ideology of the brotherhood of all men, an ideology which not only highlighted the unfavourable political and socio-economic position of the mass of the villagers, but also clashed with the ideological basis of the hierarchical structure of the Church, and the acceptance of the *status quo* it preached as a means of attaining a better life in the next world. This ideological opposition to the established doctrine of the Church must have created dissatisfaction with the *status quo* and placed in sharp perspective the authoritarian power of the parish priest.

The Church attempted in 1870 to structure this movement in accordance with its own interests by declaring St Joseph, already the patron of the working classes, the patron of the Universal Church. This introduced, or rather underlined, the availability of St Joseph as a religious symbol for the workers. A working man's organisation could henceforth also be a cult group honouring St Joseph. In Malta there are many signs that the devotion to St Joseph was strong during the latter half of the last century. Four new confraternities were dedicated to him after 1850, and he was chosen as the patron of three new parish churches. Moreover, he is the patron of the secondary *partiti* in four parishes (including Farrug). Besides these, two other parishes had St Joseph secondary *partiti* which succumbed to the increased pressure of the Church after 1935. Finally, blue, the colour of the banner and ceremonial cape worn by members of the St Joseph confraternity, is also the colour of most of the secondary *partiti* irrespective of whether or not St Joseph is their patron. The colour of all establishment (titular) *partiti* is red. During demonstrations partisans display loyalty to their respective saints by waving or wearing red or blue flags, umbrellas, scarves, ties and even hair ribbons.

During this period a conception of social organisation relatively new to Malta also gained currency, namely voluntary associations for laymen, and in particular, social clubs for 'gentlemen'. After the establishment in Valletta of the exclusive British Union Club in 1826, and the equally exclusive Casino Maltese in 1850, clubs of various kinds began to spring up in many villages. In most cases the introduction of such clubs, as in Farrug, gave greater organisation to existing village factions by providing a corporate nucleus.

It is striking that everywhere that *partiti* have arisen, they have done so in pairs; one establishment or titular *partit* against one opposition or secondary *partit*. Several titular *partiti* split into two clubs. But all with one very recent exception have merged again. Whether opposition factions became permanent depended largely on whether they had developed the necessary corporate characteristics by the time the Church decided to eliminate them in 1935. All the case histories I collected of factions which did not develop into permanent corporations indicate the same dichotomy between what I have called establishment and opposition, and have involved no more than two factions (Boissevain, 1965; 64-6, 70-3, 111).

Finally, the striking similarity in the anti-Church orientation of the secondary festa *partiti*, and the relatively low socio-economic status of their members indicate that the factions from which they grew arose out of what I have called the opposition category. By making use of the new ideological and organisational building materials which became available in the second half of the last century the members were able to gain offices and perform ritual and organisational activities (in connection with the celebration of feasts) which had hitherto been monopolised by the cliques of village notables surrounding the parish priests. Older informants from Farrug and other divided villages also noted that many young people were among the founders of the secondary *partiti*. In this we can see the universal resistance of the young to the authority of their elders. By becoming active in the new cults, they were asserting their independence from the control of the older generation. In short, the secondary *partiti* grew out of factions which recruited their members from among people disgruntled with established authority. The cultural materials which the original leaders used to gain power and score points off their rivals have transformed the factions into ritual corporations, thus building firmly into the pattern of village ritual life the political conflict between establishment and opposition.

STRUCTURAL ASYMMETRY

Although they are locked in combat in the same arena, it is an error to regard competing *festa partiti* as being in balanced opposition, or even in agreement over the rules which regulate and channel their enterprise. They differ in almost every conceivable way: they are unlike in respect to resources, internal organisation and strategy.

Resources

As already indicated, there is a difference in socio-economic status between the *partiti*. The members of the titular or establishment *partit* by and large tend to be professionals, white-collar workers and skilled labourers. The members of the secondary *partit* are often semi-skilled and unskilled labourers and farmers. Not surprisingly this difference is reflected in the respective influence they can command in their own communities. In Farrug for example 23 of the 30 key positions in Catholic Action, the Football Club and the village's Malta Labour Party Committee in 1961 were in the hands of St Martin's supporters. Moreover, of the 41 priests born in and resident in the 7 villages divided by *partiti* which I studied closely during the same period, no less than 33 (80 per cent) were sons of families supporting the titular *partiti*, although in all but Farrug the secondary *partiti* were equal to or larger than the titular *partiti*.

Congruent with the higher status of its members, the St Martin *partit* enjoys a position of pre-eminence by organising the celebration of the village's official patron saint. Through this the *partit* enjoys a number of privileges, for its position is protected by the formal laws of the Church and by the sympathy which Church officials at all levels show to the representatives of titular *partiti*. Because St Martin and other titular *partiti* form part of the establishment in Maltese society, they can draw on resources which are denied to their opponents. These give the establishment *partit* an edge on its competitor in the various disputes in which they engage, and influence in no small measure the strategy the contestants must adopt.

The special resources of the titular *partit* are varied. To begin with, its constituent confraternities and band club, because they were usually founded before those of its rival, enjoy seniority and thus occupy a more favoured place in the jealously guarded order of precedence in the various religious and secular processions.

There are also a number of Church regulations, enforced by the police (who must grant licences for all aspects of the external celebration of a *festa*) which favour the titular *partiti*. In 1935 the Church in Malta severely restricted the celebration of secondary saints in an attempt to control the rivalry between *festa partiti* and to reduce the scale of the secondary celebrations which everywhere were surpassing the titular *festas*. Thus in 1960 St Joseph supporters like those of opposition *partiti* everywhere on the island were not allowed to decorate streets remote from the church, and were permitted to hold only two brass band programmes, while their rivals held nine (Boissevain, 1965: 75f.).

Because of their superior status and influential positions in their professions and the various associations they control, the members of the titular *partiti* boast between them a more influential network of strategic contacts than do their rivals. They can gain indirect or direct access via their personal networks to important decision makers—such as police officers, members of government departments and, above all, the various *monsignori* at the Archbishop's Curia—who act to settle disputes between rival *partiti*.

Finally, it is worth noting that the opinion of the influential city élite is generally opposed to the rivalry between the *partiti* which takes place in so many of the villages and parishes. It is fair to say that they tend to blame the secondary *partiti* more than the titular *partiti* for the excesses.

Given their superior resources, it is not surprising that over the years the titular *partiti* have consolidated their position and obtained control over a number of the most important symbols and rights. These form the resources and prizes for which the *partiti* compete. They include the position and participation of the club and the confraternity in church processions and at other functions, the routes over which these processions travel and the possession of certain symbols and property and their use and display in the parish church. Any attempt to extend or to reduce these rights is resisted by the *partit* affected, which takes action to protect its interests by trying to influence the Church authorities who must make the final decisions. Not surprisingly the alignment of the symbols important to the people of Farrug is also congruent with the structural positions of the rival *partiti*. For the sake of brevity I have summarized a number of these below.

St Martin	St Joseph
Titular (establishment) *partit*	Secondary (opposition) *partit*
Statue stands on right hand (Evangel) side of church	Statue stands on left hand side of church

CONFLICT AND CHANGE IN MALTA 31

Main altar dedicated to St Martin	Side altar dedicated to St Joseph
Confraternity: oldest	Confraternity: youngest
Confraternity of Blessed Sacrament walks last in procession (high seniority)	Confraternity of St Joseph walks first (low seniority)
Partit colour: red (banner of confraternity)	Partit colour: blue (banner of confraternity)
Symbol: star	Symbol: eagle

Internal organisation

In their competition for valued prizes, their unfavourable position vis-à-vis the establishment presents opposition *partiti* with particular problems. They are at a disadvantage: the titular *partiti* monopolise important resources. Though deprived of the official support of the Church and police, secondary *partiti* have to some extent been able to match the superior resources of their rivals by strengthening their own internal organisation.

Their position in opposition to Church policy has given most secondary *partiti* a certain *esprit de corps* and unity of purpose that their rivals often lack. This has made St Joseph better able to withstand the divisive effects of the political factions which have recently weakened St Martin. It has also resulted in the emergence of stronger leaders. Secondary *partiti* are often united around a single professional-class leader who can hold the *partit* together in the face of the attacks of its opponents, and argue intricate points of Canon Law even with the Archbishop. As we have observed St Joseph has fewer professional-class members who have the status necessary for leadership of an association (Boissevain 1965: 49-53). Consequently competition for the role of leader does not occur so often, and there is a longer tenure of office. By contrast in the *partit* of the titular saint, with its better-educated members, there are more men with the necessary qualities of leadership, and accordingly there is more competition for office and a high turnover of office holders. The competition both creates and results from internal factions which weaken the group. The president of the St Joseph Band Club has led the St Joseph *partit* more or less continuously since Dun Guzepp died forty years ago. He is also just about the only member of the *partit* with the educational qualifications and social position required of a leader. The key positions of the St Martin Band Club, in contrast, constantly pass between about half a dozen educated persons. This divided leadership has weakened the club; and on one occasion it even split in two. The strong leadership and internal unity of the St Joseph *partit*, plus the fact that it rarely presents claims that are not well founded, has enabled it to score many successes in spite of its apparently unfavourable position.

Strategy

The structural position of each *partit* in relation to important resources determines the kind of pressure that it can bring to bear upon the Church. As noted, the Church seeks to build up the celebrations of the titular *partiti* at the expense of the secondary ones. St Martin thus had access to important resources denied to St Joseph and can negotiate from a strong position: its ultimate sanction is refusal to participate in the feast of the village patron, an event which the Church is anxious to see celebrated with great pomp. Secondary *partiti*, on the other hand, are inherently opposed to the Church in matters of *festa* policy. They try to increase the scale of their feasts by introducing new rules, while the Church tries to reduce them. St Joseph thus does not dare to cancel its feast for fear that the Church would accuse it of making trouble and suppress the *festa*, as it has done to secondary *festas* in several other parishes.

In short, the strategy of the St Joseph *partit* is to attack the vested interests and established position of the St Martin *partit*. The latter, secure in its favoured position, is primarily concerned with defending its rights and privileges against the threats of its rival. The establishment *partit* thus defends the *status quo* while the opposition attacks it.

CONFLICT

As noted, the disputes between the *partiti* concern matters which affect their precedence and ability to display devotion to their saints. The course which such disputes take is highly formalised. They usually begin when the St Joseph *partit* petitions the parish priest for a new privilege. St Martin leaders then try to check their rivals by threatening to cancel their feast. At this point the parish priest passes the dispute up to the Archbishop's Curia for judgement. Both sides then use all the influence they can in order to obtain a decision favourable to them. If the decision is favourable to St Martin the dispute usually ends quickly, for St Joseph's partisans cannot threaten to cancel their feast. But if the decision is favourable to St Joseph and his followers, St Martin's partisans refuse to hold their feast for a year or so or until they can wring some concession from the parish priest or the Archbishop. After that a new dispute arises over some other issue and the process starts over again.

From 1952 to 1954 there was trouble over the right of the St Joseph procession to pass along a street over which St Martin claimed exclusive rights. When the parish priest backed St Joseph, St Martin followers not only refused to celebrate their feast, they also exploded a huge home-made paper bomb under the unfortunate cleric's house. Relations were restored when the Archbishop transferred the priest (at the latter's urgent request) and modified the St Joseph procession route. In 1956 the St Martin band club refused to celebrate its *festa* because the St Joseph confraternity had been given permission to renew two of the bunches of artificial flowers which stand on the secondary saint's altar. The following year the St Joseph band refused to play at the installation ceremony of the new parish priest because the Archbishop had denied the St Joseph confraternity permission to hang a new picture over the altar of its saint. In 1960 the parish priest infuriated St Joseph followers when he did not allow the *partit* to participate in the centenary *festa* for St Martin. The poor man's hands were tied, for St Martin supporters refused to have anything to do with the *festa* if their rivals took part in it. Moreover he knew that they only wished to participate in order to be able to sabotage it. Later in 1960 there was also a sharp dispute over which band was to have precedence at the installation ceremony of the new parish priest (i.e. the right to escort him to his house from the church). They could not agree so neither played. (Boissevain 1965: 88–91.)

In 1968 St Martin partisans boycotted the parish priest's fundraising fair because he refused them permission to build a new niche to house their patron atop an enormous new pedestal. Furthermore, the St Joseph's *partit* has been manoeuvring for several years now to obtain permission to build a beautiful new pedestal for *its* patron.

So far only the more important clashes between the *partiti* have been discussed. During the course of a year numerous fund-raising fairs run by the band clubs are also occasions on which the village divides along *festa partit* lines. While supporters of the *partit* running the fair flock to it their rivals either stage their own fair or usually they hire several buses and leave the village for a picnic or a pilgrimage to some shrine of their saint. Rivalry runs highest of course during the *festas*. Then many policemen are required to keep the jeering and abusive rivals—men, women, and children—from coming to blows.

Although most of the disputes at the village level concern small concessions which the parish priest or the Archbishop have in their power to bestow upon the secondary saint, the secondary *partiti* very often challenge specific rules. Thus in the dispute in 1960 over precedence at the installation ceremony of the new parish priest, St Joseph partisans categorically denied their rivals' claim to precedence based on their alleged seniority as well as their past performances as the only functioning band in the village during the preceding five years.

It is also interesting to note that the secondary *festa partiti* have united in an association (which is opposed by the association of titular *partiti*) to bring pressure on the Archbishop as well as on the Vatican to modify the provisions of the 1935 regulations reducing the scale of secondary celebrations in Malta.

It is a misconception therefore to think that the secondary *festa partiti* agree with these regulations, that they agree with the 'rules of the game' because they see them as legitimate or morally necessary. They do not *agree* with the rules, but they are *obliged* to accept them because they are constrained by the police as well as the Church, which can cancel feasts and interdict leaders. Hence I suggest it would be an error to regard this sort of rivalry as Bailey does, as competition according to an agreed set of rules which express ultimate and publicly accepted values. There is compliance with rules, not because they are regarded as legitimate or are mutually agreed upon, but rather because they are backed by the sanctions of Church and State. These are resources to which the establishment and not the opposition has access. Secondary *partiti*, both individually, and collectively through their association, seek to change the rules so that they can expand the celebration of their feasts. The pressure to do so is constant. Thus I think it is closer to the actual situation to regard the competition between *partiti* as determined not by adherence to a set of mutually agreed rules, but as channelled by a set of restrictions. As we have seen these are regarded as legitimate by the side imposing them, the establishment, but are not accepted as such by the opposition, which seeks to change them.

This point is not as trivial as it may seem. For the rules, and the power to impose restrictions, themselves form the prizes for which the contestants compete. If there were agreement upon the rules the situation would indeed be static. Change would have to come from outside the system. But there is no agreement about the rules, as Bailey would have us believe. The 1935 Church restrictions are regarded as legitimate by one side, and as unfair, immoral limitations by the other. To regard such restrictions as mutually agreed rules is to argue from the position of the establishment, which, of course, can usually present its restrictions as legitimate rules. Thus there is continuous pressure from the side of the opposition to modify the restrictions. This pressure in no small measure provides the internal dynamism in a political contest and explains why, in addition to the effects of the processes taking place in the wider society, there is an inherent tendency to change built into the competition. This internal dynamism can only be understood if one views political competition not as a 'game' in which the competition takes place between more or less 'evenly matched' contestants according to an 'agreed set of rules' which 'regulate their conflict' and ensure an 'orderly competition' (Bailey 1969: 1, 2, 16), but as a struggle between unequal partners whose moves are determined by constraints imposed or manipulated primarily by the stronger contestant. In short, I am arguing that, to use Bailey's terminology, political competition is always a fight and never a game, because there is never complete agreement upon the rules, and thus there are always rival rules.

PROCESS

There is a process of continual competition between the two *festa partiti*. Each strives for power and honour. This drive for power causes changes: each side continually seeks to bend, modify and innovate laws and customs that restrict its behaviour in a way which benefits itself rather than its rival. It has been observed that the establishment *partit* can mobilise greater resources and is supported by a body of laws enforced both by religious and secular authorities. Its primary strategy is defensive: it can appeal to precedent, law and can obtain protection from official bodies such as Church and government. It defends the *status quo* from which it derives its pre-eminent position. Its philosophy is essentially conservative in the sense of conserving its pre-eminence. In contrast, the opposition *partit*, given the handicaps under which it must compete and manoeuvre for changes in the restrictions which limit its activities, is forced to use different strategies. Not only is it more apt to place its organisational house in order, it also is more apt to innovate, that is to develop new techniques, new ideas, new strategies which will help it to modify the *status quo* in its favour. Its outlook will thus often be progressive, in the neutral sense of favouring change or reform.

In every conflict situation there is an asymmetrical relationship between those with more and less power. Those with less power, the opposition, are obliged by the situation to innovate and change things in order to score off their rivals. In every conflict situation consequently there is a built-in dynamism which can lead to change, for the competitors seek more power. The seeds of change are present in any conflict situation. This does not mean of course that the impetus for change is always successful or always comes from the opposition: new restrictive policies may be thought up and imposed by the establishment, which may be able to block for extended periods attempts to reduce its superior power. We have seen how the opposition faction in Hal-Farrug by using the cultural building materials available in the environment built the conflict between it and the establishment faction into the cultural scenery of the village. The same happened in other villages. Thus through the action of local opposition factions throughout the island, institutional and cultural changes took place. But because the conflict continued to escalate, the Church in 1935 took the measures which have been discussed.

I suspect (but at present have no data to prove) that the increase in the scale of the secondary feasts just prior to 1935 was also related to the political conflict at the national level which raged during the 1920s and early 1930s between the Church-supported, pro-Italian Nationalist Party and the anti-clerical, pro-English Constitutional Party. In 1933 the British dismissed the Nationalist government for unconstitutionally trying to re-establish the primacy of Italian in the schools and civil service. Following the closure of the Legislative Assembly, the arena at the national level, more political resources were channelled to the still open parish arenas and the level of opposition to the Church-favoured titular *partiti* increased accordingly. In 1935 as we have seen the Church took steps to clip the wings of its increasingly active parish level opponents by introducing restrictive new rules. The opposition *partiti* were bitter, but they were obliged to obey owing to the resources their rivals controlled. As in most if not all political contests, might is right. (Italians have a saying which summarizes this neatly: *Chi commanda fa la legge.* He who commands makes the law.) The new regulations in turn provided fresh fuel for the conflict between establishment and opposition: secondary *partiti* became increasingly opposed to the restrictive policies of the Church. Their constant opposition to the edicts of the Church regarding these matters accented the anti-clerical tendencies of the secondary *partiti*. The action of the Church to restrict the conflict and thus save the position of the establishment *partiti*, provided an issue for conflict which further served to erode respect for the authority of the Church and, I suggest, kept alive and thus paved the way for the anti-clerical orientation of the Malta Labour Party (Boissevain 1965: 9-14, 108-11).

Throughout the ninety years of their existence the power relations between the *festa partiti* as well as their internal structure have been changing. An important impetus for change is the competition between them. At the same time other processes are taking place in Maltese society which also influence them. The more recent conflict between the Church and the Malta Labour Party has also had repercussions on the level of conflict between *festa partiti*: the Labour Party has made a conscious effort to restrict the scale of festivities. It has encouraged its members to boycott the celebration of feasts, which it regards as a waste of time and money that can better be spent upon the development of the country. This has created within the villages a growing category of persons who take no part in the competition. Moreover, many of the younger members of the clergy have also tried to modify the competition. The increasing welfare of Malta, brought about by a boom in the tourist and building sectors of the economy and the growing number of manufacturing industries, is drawing people away from the village. This particularly affects the young. Young men who formerly played in the band, made fireworks and decorated the streets for the *festa* now have money in their pockets, often a car at their disposal and prefer to spend their free time with the increasingly emancipated girls at the cinema or the beach. They no longer spend their free time celebrating the feasts or loafing in the band clubs. Fewer men are enrolling in the confraternities, which as we saw are of critical importance to the *partiti*. Thus the internal structure of and the relations between the competing groups in Maltese villages are continually changing. This is caused partly by the internal dynamics of such conflict, and partly by the processes taking place in the wider society in which these conflicting groups are embedded.

ESTABLISHMENT AND OPPOSITION IN NATIONAL POLITICS

The pattern of organisation and conflict of the establishment and opposition *partiti* at the village level strongly resembles the difference between the Malta Labour Party and the Nationalist Party at the national level.

The Nationalist Party of Malta may be viewed as the establishment party, and the Malta Labour Party as the opposition party. The Nationalist Party is the older of the two. It has been in power many more times than its rival and for longer periods. It has been traditionally supported by the Church, and traditionally it has been the party of the professional classes—the lawyers, doctors, notaries and higher civil servants—who through their network of occupational relations link their clients to the party. Its leadership is diffuse. Although it has an official leader, it is a party composed of professional-class members each of whom has his own private political machine. Thus one of its organisational problems is the clash between the interest its leading figures have in retaining their patronage-based political machines, and the desirability of creating a tight party structure. As the Nationalist Party has had access to government resources for prolonged periods it has been able to use these for patronage: government jobs, contracts, licences and other concessions have been systematically used to keep the wheels of the many small Nationalist political machines well oiled. Both its internal as well as its foreign policy have been markedly conservative. It has supported the Church, and has been extremely reluctant to effect any major changes or put an end to a number of serious social problems such as the housing shortage and in general has let local developments take their own course. Its foreign policy has been to maintain Malta's traditional alliance with the Western powers in NATO through the mediation of Great Britain. In short, both at home and abroad its policy has been to maintain the *status quo*.

In contrast the Malta Labour Party in its present form came into being in 1949 as a coalition led by Dom Mintoff, then an ex-Minister of Public Works and Reconstruction. Almost at once Mintoff began to reorganise the party and established a tightly structured system of village clubs and regional councils. In short he set about putting the party's organisational house in order and built up the image of the party with himself as its chief symbol. Henceforth allegiance was not to be to individual politicians and their personal machines, but to the party itself and its leader. This was highly beneficial to the party. There were few members of the Labour Party (in contrast to the Nationalist Party) whose occupational status enabled them to recruit voters from their professional clientele. This also meant fewer competing big men. The Labour Party is a workers' party and its ideology and membership reflect this. Most members are recruited among skilled and unskilled workers as well as the young. Moreover, the party has made a conscious effort to recruit women into its formal organisation, and for a number of years there have been two MLP women Members of Parliament. There are no female Nationalist MPs.

Its ideological basis has been reflected in its internal and external policy. The party has been strongly anti-clerical and reformist. The first period of government under Mintoff between 1955 and 1958 was characterised by a flurry of social legislation, increased and liberalised educational facilities, and a damming of patronage. Foreign policy has also been highly reformist. After an initial flirtation with a plan to link Malta with Great Britain along the lines of the union with Northern Ireland, it struck out for neutrality and independence from the NATO bloc. This policy has been set forth by the Labour Party since its victory at the polls in June 1971. Both the domestic and foreign policy of the Malta Labour Party can be characterised as reformist and socialist, as progressive (in the sense of favouring change) and anti-establishment. This may be contrasted to the conservative laissez-faire policy of the Nationalist Party (Boissevain 1965: 7–14, 23–6, 122–33).[8]

CONCLUSION

At one time I thought the resemblance between the structure and activity of establishment and opposition parties at the national and parish levels in Malta a coincidence. I no longer think so, for the resemblance is too marked and the explanations too similar. I now believe that they are manifestations of a general pattern in all conflict groups which, I should like to argue are always asymmetrical rather than balanced.[9]

In all societies there are certain persons who control more resources than others do. This enables them to influence the actions of others, if need be against their wishes. They are obeyed because they wield more power. With this they are able to control or occupy all or most of the offices from which authority can be exercised. These persons form the local 'establishment'. Ranged against them, as it were, are the less powerful persons who do not

[8] The transformation which takes place in a party which has long been in opposition once it succeeds in replacing its rival at the control of government is fascinating, but lies outside the immediate scope of this paper. The essential and logical inconsistency of its position ultimately leads to an electoral defeat or the abandonment of ideological premises. If it remains true to its ideals, it will in a democratic electoral system be defeated from time to time and so be able to renew itself. This has happened to the Labour Parties of Great Britain and Malta, for example. The only way that it can remain in power, I suggest, is by adopting some of the characteristics of the establishment party as sketched above: it must become a machine run on patronage and enter into coalition with powerful—and thus conservative—blocs in society. In other words, its ideological as well as organizational characteristics must change in many respects. Certain political movements which unseated colonial powers, such as the Indian Congress Party, provide examples of this. An alternative method of remaining in power is to abolish the opposition through the establishment of a repressive single party state, as happened in Germany and Italy during the 1920s and 1930s and more recently in many communist countries and a number of newly independent countries in Africa and Asia.

[9] This asymmetry is something to which Lévi-Strauss pointed in his perceptive article 'Les organisations dualistes existent-elles?' (1956). Although Professor Mair drew my attention to the article in 1959 it meant little to me. I was then still caught up in the belief system imposed by British structural-functional anthropology, and the notion of the balanced opposition of conflict groups forms a basic part of this way of thinking. Lévi-Strauss also concludes, by different means than I have used above, that while moieties have always been treated as symmetric—as a consequence of the overheavy reliance upon the notion of social reciprocity derived from Mauss, Radcliffe-Brown and Malinowski, alongside which there is little place for asymmetrical relations—they are in fact all asymmetrical.

exercise or share in the exercise of power. These often include those disgruntled with the way in which the 'establishment' administers the resources it controls, the poor, the failures, the oppressed, the weak, the eccentrics, the drop-outs, the social misfits and, often, the young. These form an anti-establishment or 'opposition' category. These are social categories from which coalitions may be recruited.

Now the more powerful rivals of the establishment recruit support from the social category I have labelled the 'opposition'. Often opposition coalitions unite to exercise concerted opposition against the establishment, which is forced to consolidate its position to protect and advance its interests. The result of this manoeuvring is most often two rather than three or more coalitions or alliances. Either the weaker ones coalesce to be able to compete with the strongest, or the strongest is able to subvert the weakest coalition member to achieve a clear dominance over its chief rival. There are many combinations possible but they usually lead to the formation of two competing and asymmetric coalitions. Thus it is that factions and other conflict groups appear most often in pairs.[10]

The resources of the establishment and the opposition and the way in which they use them differ considerably. The establishment usually defends tradition. It has a vested interest in maintaining the *status quo*. Tradition provides the charter for its existence. It claims to interpret the norms and defend the moral order. Because it controls most of the formal offices, it can often make use of legally sanctioned physical force, public funds, office and ritual to recruit followers and to defend itself against attack. Moreover, because it defines, defends and interprets tradition and the moral order and has more resources at its disposal than its rivals, it is able to monopolise the most important ideological symbols (right hand, white, high, male etc. *versus* left hand, black, low, female). The establishment thus will usually be conservative (although when a coalition which has long been in opposition gains the upper hand, those newly in power will, at least initially, be progressive, and those in opposition conservative).

[10] For a detailed discussion of the logic behind this process the reader is referred to Caplow's elegant treatise on the subject (1968). His discussion provides an important correction to Dahrendorf's somewhat dogmatic assertion that given the dichotomous distribution of authority in every association there will thus be 'two, and only two, conflict groups' (1959: 173).

The opposition must attack and challenge to gain access to the resources mentioned or to modify the use to which the establishment can put its superordinate position. Given its subordinate position (i.e. unfavourable position with reference to the resources the establishment monopolises), an opposition leader's problem is how to unseat the establishment from its superior position. One way he can do this is by recruiting more followers. Since he does not have access to the resources controlled by the establishment leader, and thus cannot recruit as many followers through patronage, he is therefore more likely than his rival to be attracted to new techniques and ideologies, or to develop them himself, to meet the anti-establishment interests of his potential followers. Besides using new ideologies and symbols to bind his followers to him and his cause, he will also try to fashion his coalition or party into a better, more tightly organised instrument.[11] Only in this way can he hope to win from his strategically less favourable position: an attacking party needs a strong leadership and a streamlined organisation. For these reasons the opposition coalition usually becomes the progressive party. This is not only because it seeks to win a surprise victory over its rival through using a new strategy. By merely *being* progressive it challenges the conservatives. For the same reason it adopts ideologies and symbols which are rivals to those adopted by the conservative establishment coalition.[12]

The competing coalitions may become institutionalised through the introduction of various corporate trappings such as formal

[11] Cf. Bailey (1969: 54–5, 80–4) who gives a penetrating analysis of the management problems of leaders in general and how ways of resolving them can lead to the progressive institutionalization of conflict groups. The reader can easily assume from this analysis that the problems of all leaders are similar, an assumption that is of course implicit in the notion of balanced opposition. Here I have argued, however, that while opposition and establishment leaders share some of the same problems, they also have fundamentally different problems to solve, have access to different resources and so employ different strategies.

[12] Thoden van Velzen (1972) describes 'interest' coalitions formed by wealthy peasants and government experts in Tanzanian villages and 'levelling' coalitions of anti-establishment elements which combine periodically to attack the resources of the leading members of the rival coalition. He suggests that competition between coalitions of this type is found in all societies. Although they are organizationally less evolved than the 'establishment' and 'opposition' coalitions described for Malta, they are analogous and corroborate much of the analysis presented above.

The low level of internal organisation of the Tanzanian coalitions, particularly the 'levelling' coalition, compared to the Maltese *festa partiti*, lies partly in the fact that wealthy peasants of the establishment or 'interest' coalition wield power but organisation, property, permanent symbols and so on. The long-term processes taking place and the cultural building materials available explain the specific content and form that the establishment-opposition conflict assumes. Though the rival coalitions may become institutionalised, they are not static or symmetrical, nor is their competition balanced. Their relations remain dynamic. This dynamism derives from the attempt of the weaker to obtain more power and so topple its opponent. The opposition can only obtain power through change. The impulse to change is thus ever present in conflict situations. The notion that competing political groups are evenly matched or that conflict leads to stability and the preservation of the social order is an illusion, a projection of wishful thinking on sociological analysis. It has, I suggest, hampered our understanding of politics as well as of social change.

The impetus to change is always present in the asymmetry between establishment and opposition, between those who command more power and their rivals who seek more power. Since this asymmetry is present in all societies, the conclusion must be, therefore, that change is inherent in all societies and social equilibrium does not, and cannot, exist.[13]

have no authority. In contrast, the Maltese establishment *festa partiti* cemtre on roles (those of the parish priest and the offices he can bestow) from which considerable authority can be exercised. (For a useful discussion on the distinction between power and authority see Dahrendorf, 1959: 165ff.) Such roles have greater continuity in time than the often temporary command over resources (other than authority roles) from which persons derive power. Hence coalitions which form to contest the exercise of such authority, or to compete for the roles themselves, have a certain continuity. This continuity in turn permits a greater degree of internal organisation to develop.

[13] The argument in this paper owes much to Leach's seminal analysis of the Kachin (1954). The structured relationship I have established between, and the inherent nature of, conflict and change is also similar to the model Dahrendorf developed (1959: 157–240). He failed, however, to explore fully the differing ideological and organisational characteristics of conflict groups as well as the strategies of their leaders. These could probably also have been generated by this model. His failure to do so illustrates, I suggest, the disadvantages of a deductive approach. There is in fact no substitute for the raw data of social behaviour as a basis from which and on which to build social theory.

4

How they hid the red flag in Pisticci in 1923, and how it was betrayed

J. DAVIS

In many communities there are people who have attained, with age, reputation not as leaders but as tranquil sources of wisdom. They have played, perhaps, an active part; they have certainly witnessed the great events, and now are famous for their knot-cutting counsel, their ability to bring new developments into relation with old fascinations, their insight into human affairs. Some people may think it cheeky of me to compare Lucy Mair—who has that sort of position in British social anthropology—to Michele D'Alessandro, known as Pischiniull,—who has that sort of position in the south Italian town called Pisticci. If that were all, of course it would be; but I hope that as Michele D'Alessandro's story unfolds those who read it will perceive that it is about things which have been among Lucy Mair's important interests: the nature of political loyalties, the importance of ideology, the structure of values which forces a son—but not his father—into betrayal.

THE NARRATOR

Michele D'Alessandro, son of Leonardo-Rocco, brother of Giovanni, was eighty-three years old when I recorded this story in 1965. He had lived in Pisticci all his life, and has farmed the same land in the district known as Caporotondo since his marriage in about 1910: the land came partly from his wife whose family had contiguous fields. It is good land, easily accessible, with a fine stand of olive trees. Michele D'Alessandro was an active farmer when I knew him.

Part of his reputation in Pisticci rested on his learning: his remark that his father, who attained high office, scarcely knew how to scribble, is a depreciatory comparison with his own skills. He read widely, not only newspapers and Scaramouche romances. His brother, in America, wrote poetry and 'beautiful letters', and it was partly in order to keep up with him that he kept diaries for 20 years and more. In 1958, acting on caprice inspired by his sense of shame at his poor culture, and by the fear that, after his death, his children would laugh at him, he burned the lot. He had, however, got the habit: and began to keep them again, in school exercise books, from 1 January 1959; I was allowed to copy them up to the end of 1961 (since he was still writing in the volume including entries for 1962). They are usually terse records of weather, travel to and from the town, farmwork done, money laid out, income, and important incidents which he felt it necessary to record his part in—a visit to give condolences at a death, aid exchanged with a neighbour, and some less pleasant interludes. They give a first impression of austerity, even severity: his wife, for example, is referred to throughout the 200 sides of closely-written quarto page as *essa*, she. Elucidation of the incidents recorded, however, reveals a vivid sympathy for and against those around him and close to him. And it should not be forgotten that the very act of keeping a diary in Pisticci displays a vigorous and determined spirit, and an awareness of the value of things lived through, which is one reason why he was admired and respected by most of those he knew.

Shortly after I first met him we talked of books and history. I asked him if he had read Silone's *Fontamara*. No, he had not—was it a history book? I explained it was a novel about the arrival of the fascists in a peasant town in Abbruzzo. 'Good, I like that sort of thing', he said, and proceeded to tell me the story of Pisticci's Red Flag. The flag was, I think, not so much a flag (though it was, in the mainstream socialist tradition, called one—*bandiera*) as a banner of the kind known as vexillum, used in ecclesiastical processions and by our own Trades Unions. A few days later I visited him and recorded the story which is transcribed and translated here. The main difference between the two versions, the one heard and the one recorded, is that the former contained a long comparison between Alessandro Bruni, the Pisticci leader, and 'Masaniedd di Roma'. I think the reference must be to Masaniello, the Neapolitan fishmonger who led the revolt against the Spaniards in 1647, whose portrait was struck on medals with the head of Cromwell on the other side, and whose marked physical resemblance to Spinoza led that philosopher to keep his picture always by him (Croce 1965: 37). This identification leads me to make two tentative points: the first is simply that it was not uncommon in Pisticci to hear things said which quite suddenly opened up vistas over the whole of European idealism and revolution, spanning centuries. While Michele D'Alessandro did not make the connection with Cromwell or Spinoza, the sudden vision which the words of an aged man can give are salutory reminders of continuities and connections which the brash sociologist, intent on describing the meretricious, instrumental, undemocratic 'political system' of an isolated peasant backwater, can too easily overlook. The second point is more particular. In Michele D'Alessandro's version, Masaniello 'got proud' (*insuperbì*) when he got power, and was murdered by his followers in a church. When he recorded the tale, the implicit strong criticism of Bruni was considerably toned down: true, he calls him aggressive (*violento*) [2, 3][1]: but there is no hint that those of Bruni's followers who left him had any justification.[2] The reason for this is that Michele D'Alessandro was anxious not to damage the memory of a man who had recently died, and who had been called 'an outstanding Lucanian man of letters' in a newspaper headline [1]. So, the preliminary to the tale was a reminder that it should not be used to denigrate Bruni, 'for, you know, he died not so long ago...'. I do not think that this present paper does denigrate Bruni: he was clearly an outstanding leader, of whom most Pisticcesi are justifiably proud.

THE LANGUAGE

In making the transcription I have tried to act by certain technical principles. The language spoken by Pisticcesi in 1965 was a

[1] Figures in square brackets indicate the paragraphs of the translation and transcript.

[2] That Bruni may have been more than aggressive is suggested by a report dated 9 April 1916 from the Royal Commissioner in Pisticci alleging that 'Bruni's thugs organised an infamous plot to kill me at the door of my house. If I did not fall victim to the dastardly plot (*scellerato disegno*) it was certainly not for any defect of planning on the thugs' part but by pure coincidence to which I doubtless owe my life'. Although Bruni and seven others were arrested they were later released and were not proceeded against. *Arch. Stat. Potenza*, vol. 289, fasc. 190 Gabinetto: cat. 31 prot. 836.

mixture of dialect, 'bad' Italian and 'good' Italian, and I have tried to reproduce it faithfully—aided, I must acknowledge, by Mrs Ripalta Colclough. I have tried to identify and to eliminate characteristics of speech which are solely attributable to the fact that the speaker was a very old man, but otherwise I have been scrupulous not to alter anything. The combination of dialect with Italian in the same text posed some orthographical problems. It was necessary to distinguish the Pisticcese *e*, which in all dialects of the Neapolitan family is pronounced like *e* in unstressed *the*, from the high closed Italian *e*. In other texts I have used an apostrophe; in this text I use ë. So that an apostrophe in this text means only and always that the speaker has omitted a vowel. In Italian this is quite standard; but in Pisticcese it can be a vowel which, if it were present, would soften a preceding consonant. The reader is thus warned that *sacc'* (= *saccio*, I know) is pronounced, roughly, *such*, not *sack*; and that *c'a* (= *ci ha*, who has) is pronounced, roughly, *cha*[r], not *ca* [r].

There are some instances of 'bad' Italian. *La nottate* [2] 'should be' *la nottata*, and so on. There are nouns with the wrong gender, verbs in the wrong tense. I was at no time tempted to correct these, considering it my duty to produce as nearly as possible an exact transcript. It has been known for some dialect speakers to speak posh when talking with people whom they consider more educated than they. But these characteristics of his language do not reflect such a pretension: first, because the common Pisticcese way of speaking posh is simply to add an *o* to all words with no terminal vowel—at no time does he use that form. Secondly, because when he writes in his diary he reproduces the same features of his speech as I do here—though less frequently. I therefore conclude that he is not using a particular form of speech to me.

There are, additionally, some words which are used in unexpected senses. *Civilisti* [1] has the dictionary meaning of civil lawyers, not plaintiffs or respondents. *Assoluto* [2] would normally be translated absolute, rather than absolved; *Stimolare* [3] as stimulate, not beat; *istigare* as arouse—in which sense it is also used [14]—not to put pressure on [10]. In some cases these 'misuses' exhibit serendipitous creativity of the kind which makes popular language a continuing delight. In the sonnets of G. G. Belli the transition of a word from formal educated language into a popular speech creates a dimension of ironic resonance which is there the mainspring of conscious poetic creation.[3] I do not claim that Michele D'Alessandro is a Belli: but the same associative transformation may be perceived in the 'ignorant' confusion of absolute and absolution; while the ironic understatement in *stimolare* and *istigare* is—whether conscious or not—a fairly typical usage. There remains only one suggestion which I am competent to make: that is that the language is sometimes formally traditional. Enemies are proud (*nemico fiero*) [3, 4], when they are not so continually opposed as to be almost side by side (*affiancato*) [4] and supporters of adversity. They express respect for each other, [5] remorse, [4] and are finally magnanimous when, alas alack (*marro me*), they win. [11-12] I think that this language is derived from Dumas and the many sub-Dumas popular novels which, published by small artisan presses in the rural provinces, are a staple literature. Although the novels are still read by old people, so that one exile from town used to while away winter evenings by translating novels *viva-voce* into dialect for his wife's entertainment, their language does not usually carry over into ordinary discourse: perhaps that only happens when an eminent and respected man recounts great deeds for posterity.

I hope it will be clear from the foregoing that the transcript is as accurate and scrupulous as I can make it without acquiring phonetic orthography and a method for registering the important paralinguisitic pauses and non-word noises. The task has brought home to me, what I knew only in a facile way before, that writing is a very selective way of recording speech.

AN OUTLINE OF EVENTS

Michele D'Alessandro's story culminates in the events of 1922:

> Telegram: Prefect's Commissioner to
> Prefect (Potenza). 22 November 1922.
> The ex-mayor of Pisticci, *avvocato* Alessandro Bruni, left yesterday at 11 a.m. for Matera escorted by a Captain of Carabinieri and soldiers.[4]

---

[3] e.g. sonnet 331: '*er padre sputativo poverello*' where St Joseph's ambiguous fatherhood of Jesus is expressed by the conflation of *putativo* = putative and *sputato* = absolutely clear (*verità sputata*, = literally, spat-out truth).

[4] Most of the documents to be quoted in this section are from Pisticci's municipal

But Bruni had been active in Pisticci's politics since 1910, at least, when he was 34. In 1910 the population of Pisticci was 8,272, while the electors were 619 (of whom 381 voted that year). In 1911–12 Giolitti's government extended the suffrage to all males over 30, discarding proposals for a more partial extension on the ground that they would favour radical artisans: what were needed were illiterate conservative peasant voters. In Pisticci the electorate was thus increased to 2,524, of whom 1,241 voted in the council elections of 1914.

Bruni and his Republican Socialist followers made a clean sweep of the council [3]. Of the twenty councillors, none of whom had sat before, he was the only one with a professional qualification. Twelve were artisans (4 cobblers, 2 tailors, 2 smiths, a barber, a carpenter, a furnace-man, a watchmaker); one was a shopkeeper, one a bricklayer, and five were peasants. The electoral forms still had a column in which the clerk noted the property qualification of the candidates and even though that qualification had been abolished, the clerk filled the column in. Eight of the new councillors including Bruni and one peasant had no taxable property at all. The wealthiest men had L. 6,000 and L. 8,000—which compares with the out-going council: one man with wealth of L. 100,000; five with L. 50,000 or more—and so on. There is no doubt that the personnel of the council and the social group from which it was drawn, was radically different after 1914.

But the council was short-lived: it was dissolved for the duration of the war, and its affairs administered by a Commissioner. New elections were not held until 1920, although in the post-war troubles the Commissioner seems to have relied on Bruni to control the populace, as his colourfully egotistical report[5] suggests. There had been riots in Pisticci in April 1920 which he attributed to the disillusion of returning soldiers, to the inequities of the grain ration, and to the refusal of the contractors building a stretch of railway to take on new workers, or to increase the wages of those already employed. When, on 21 April, grain was taken from Pisticci in a convoy of lorries, a riot broke out, three people were

---

archives to which I was kindly given access by the Prefect of Matera. The filing category I draw on chiefly is: Cat. 1ª, Class. 4ª: Podestà-Vice-Podestà-Delegati, 1–7. The terminology is of course post 1922. The contents go back to the 1860s.

[5] *Relazione del Regio Commissario Straordinario Cav. Avv. Egidio Miadonna sull' amministrazione provvisoria del Comune di Pisticci.* 29 April 1920.

killed and others wounded. He expected further riots on 1 May, and on 18 May (festival of Martyrs), and therefore increased the monthly grain ration from 11 kg for peasants and 12 kg for labourers, to 15 kg for both categories. 'And the population was very grateful to me for it.' With guarantees from the Prefecture that augmented rations would be maintained until after the harvest, 'the horrendous spectre of starvation vanished'. With Bruni, a railway engineer and the local civil police chief he brought the rail strike to an end, achieving a rise in wage-rates of 20–25 per cent; and an enlarged labour force. 'My unheard-of efforts were already crowned by the very best success.'

In the election held on 20 September 1920 Bruni's followers acquired sixteen of the twenty seats, the other four going to people who got about 500 votes each, compared with Bruni's 1,250. This minority consisted of one lawyer, one doctor, one surveyor and a mechanic. Bruni's team was composed of eight of his 1914 men and eight others. He thus lost twelve men who had stood with him in 1914; of these twelve only two had stood for election in 1920, getting three votes each. The new administrative committee (*Giunta*) of six contained three 1914 councillors and committee members, and three new members.

Although the council was later accused, as most out-going councils are, of malpractice and corruption,[6] its dissolution must be seen as the direct result of changes in national government. The collapse of the Bruni administration was relatively slow (see below, IV), but its last moments were not undramatic, as can be seen from the following translation of a draft letter by an unknown author to the sub-prefect at Matera. The letter is dated 7 November 1922.

On the 29th October ex-mayor Bruni, accompanied by a [illeg.] of persons convicted in the affair of April 21 1920 and by [illeg.]...with impudent mien and armed with large cudgels went to the Municipal Building to hold a session of Council, which however could not take

[6] When the council was dissolved in 1915 and Bruni's followers menaced the Royal Commissioner (above, n. 1), the police collected evidence that the ex-mayor and town secretary had compulsorily withheld ten per cent from all wages paid to labourers working on the council's public works projects. It was alleged that the money so collected had been used to subsidise Bruni's newspaper *L'Idea Repubblicana*. (*Arch. Stat. Potenza*, vol. 290 Fasc. 212, Ordine Pubblico, copia Prot. 188 Delegato di Pubblica Sicurezza Pisticci to Sotto-Prefetto Matera, 25 November 1915.)

place for lack of numbers. Their impudent attitude, observed with disfavour, aroused a lively indignation, and local fascists (seizing on the ideal political opportunity[7]) decided.. to act. The Secretary [i.e. of the fascists] was supplanted by an Action Committee which proposed to occupy the Municipal Building and to wreck the ex-mayor's house. Although police were deployed the fascists (numbering about 50) managed to penetrate the building, some gaining entrance through the janitor's house at the back, others through the main door which they succeeded in opening. They managed to elude the vigilance of public forces, profiting by the dense fog and by the fact that the Carabinieri on duty were guarding [illeg.] attentively the door of the Infant School which also communicates with the Municipal Offices. In the morning I was told that the occupation had occurred, and did everything in my power to clear the gathering; but a large crowd collected in the square.. shouting hostilely against the administration and particularly against Bruni.

Bruni was 'extricated' and 'escorted to safety' by the Carabinieri, as recorded in the telegram quoted at the beginning of this section. He was later exiled from Pisticci to Tramutolo [4, 5, 6, 9].

POLITICS AND FAMILIES

Such were the events in outline. Before passing to Michele D'Alessandro's story, I wish to give a brief account of the nature of political loyalties in Pisticci at that time, so far as it can be judged. There is a view of Mediterranean or Latin politics which sees them to be largely instrumental, governed by actors' perceptions of their profit. This is made explicit, for example, by those who argue that in these societies politicians assume that everyone acts to achieve his short-term advantage, and that no loyalties or moral values attach people to institutions or persons outside the nuclear family. Similar notions buzz in the heads of those who apply one of the varieties of exchange theory to Italian or Spanish political phenomena: they wish to impose a calculus on behaviour, and in order to do so may either ignore evidence about commitment, or may claim that unprofitable commitment is itself some kind of reward (or maybe cost) which has to be met in order to secure future rewards. Let me parenthetically add that while the imposition of a calculus in such a manner may appear intellectually disreputable to the innocent reader, it is of course not in the least

[7] This clause has a line drawn through it in the draft.

disreputable: it is done from commitment to the highest conception of Science: not, indeed, because the result is true to reality, but because the result is easier to think about.

In a *Festschrift* for Lucy Mair it is permitted to lapse from ideals of that kind, to insist on examining the complexities of cases, and the mixtures of motivations. Let me begin, then, by examining Michele D'Alessandro's contention that his father 'stayed with Bruni right up to the end. .after the others had left' [3]. We have no direct evidence that this is so, but we do have a series of letters of resignation from the town council. These begin in 1921 and continue until October 1922. Three early resignations, formulated by the council as expulsions for non-attendance, were from the minority group, and only one from among Bruni's socialists. His letter of resignation was not accepted: he resigned 'because he was no longer a supporter and from obedience to orders received from the Socialist Party to which he belongs'. The council rejected it, because he was responsible to the people of Pisticci who elected him and not to the Italian socialist party—sections of which were by then fascist. On 27 September 1922 Bruni wrote to Nicola Grieco asking him to be sure that he attended council meeting because important business would be discussed and also because it would end 'strange and unjustified rumours' of a difference between them. Grieco, reciprocating the affectionate term of address '*caro compare*', replied that he was a shoemaker, that the council was to be held on a festival day and he could not therefore absent himself from his work; he ended by reassuring Bruni that he had no complaints—'*non ho nulla da lagnarmi*', Two days later Grieco wrote to the Prefect notifying him of his resignation: 'absolutely not wishing even indirectly, to be associated with the daily improprieties of the present administration'. Two days later the council expelled Carlo Pastore for non-attendance and a letter from him to the Prefect dated the day after (2 October) announced his resignation 'declaring that for almost a year he had no part in the council's work, and absolutely wished to be dissociated. .'.[8]

[8] This letter was sent also to the mayor a few days later. In council (*Delibere* 18 September 1922) Bruni made a typically outspoken comment: '... only the signature is Pastore's while the rest is written by a pretentiously lettered person (a reference, this, to the consistent use of the third person—a common petty bureaucrat's dignity) who is well known to most councillors because it is equally well known that, to extract Pastore's signature, the same lettered person had to return again and again to the wine-shop where Pastore was drinking. I can reveal that if

This defection was serious for Pastore had been one of the 1914 councillors and a member of the Giunta since 1920. The only other member of the council to resign was the fourth minority member. There were, however, a further five members of the majority who absented themselves from the meetings in the summer and early autumn of 1922. On this count it seems that Michele D'Alessandro's statement is justified at least in part: his father was one of the ten who continued to attend the council and the Giunta and he was also, of course, the trustee of the flag; it may be that the symbolic importance of the flag persuaded him that his father's position was unique in other respects as well.

It is clear from the council documents that as Bruni was put under increasing pressure by external events he became more, not less, belligerent; and his use of his legal training to insist that members should not be allowed to resign but should be expelled, smacks of the enthusiast who is prepared to go down with all flags flying—and the police guarding the wrong door. It is precisely such behaviour, in my opinion, which leads men to resign secretly or implicitly, and to write to hierarchical superiors dissociating themselves from defiant actions. The point is made clearer, I think, by comparing these resignations with the resignations made from administrations run by sounder men. I quote only one, dating from 1909:

> The reproof made to me publicly this morning in the presence of the entire office staff has pained me severely in its injustice. Before I spoke to young Burzo, I made it clear to his father that he should come to you to ask you to take his son on as telegraph messenger and to get formal assurance of your consent and contentment; I went to the Santilio brothers to know what they thought and it was the same as you; indeed I made the strongest recommendations that the nomination should be made urgently, and so to ask the formal approval of the Potenza Directorate. Also unjust was the other reproof that I had allowed the waggoner Castellucci to burn charcoal in a different place from that in which it was cut. For these reasons and for others which I have been aware of for some time in your attitude towards me, and especially in

we had granted Pastore the building site which he inexplicably expected from this Administration, together with many other little favours, each more improper than the rest, which he petulantly asked for in the brief period of his effective membership of the Giunta, perhaps Pastore would not have signed—not even when befuddled with wine.'

your way of picking holes in me and in what I do, while you ignore.. what other members do, I am constrained to resign from the Giunta..

Injured pride, a sense of being undermined in the conduct of business, quarrels about patronage—these are the stuff of which resignations are made. Bruni, aggressive, fluent, merciless and with his back to the wall, inflated the political currency: men resigned to save their skins.

But not all his followers did resign, not all absented themselves from the council. Leonardo-Rocco D'Alessandro, Michele's father, was one of these. He joined Bruni because he had quarrelled with his brother, an opponent of the socialists [3, 14]. The theme of family relations recurs throughout Michele's account: the quarrel of brothers; the death of a wife and mother [7]; the house now occupied by his sister [7]; the land got with his wife [7, 11]; the conflict between legitimate sons and a priest's bastards [14]; the secret shared with his brother [8], and then betrayed by him [10]: all these provide the setting for the attachment to a man recognised to be imprudently volatile; and for the attachment to a symbol—a flag with its banal motto. The connection between them is the act of inscription in the list: 'Don Alessà—write me down!' [3] While the followers are sometimes called a party, sometimes partisans, socialists, that incident and the use of the word *elengo* (= elenco, list) convey the concreteness of the symbol: it is not an association, an abstraction, but a list of names and a flag: when you are on the list you have a duty which takes a clear priority over most others, and which binds your family. The climax of the story is the different relation of the protagonists to the memory of a dead woman: her husband can betray her to save the flag, [9] her son cannot—and the flag is lost. Once again, politics and the family come together, and produce a denouement.

To say that such political activities are instrumental, self-interested, profit-seeking, is clearly mistaken: they are a disaster for all concerned: Giovanni, the younger brother, is faced with a choice between one 'sacrilege' [8] and another, and neither can be accepted with equanimity. To say that these political activities are specialised, take place in an isolated political arena, clearly does not meet the case either. What is apparent, however, is that the ideal and symbols of family life are mixed and intertwined with the ideals and symbols of political life. In some cases, doubtless, all works for the best; in this case, certainly, the unfolding events lead to dishonour: perhaps that is why Giovanni left for America.

THE TRANSLATION

1] For, you know, he died not so long ago, a couple of years ago: he died at Rome. Indeed, I read a newspaper article which said, 'An outstanding Lucanian man of letters dies at Rome',— and they meant, Bruni. 'An outstanding Lucanian man of letters.' That means he was a man of understanding, to be sure. He came to Pisticci to be a defender in the court, in the tribunal, and to get accused people off—to get them off, to free them, yes. Because he was mostly a criminal lawyer; a criminal lawyer mostly. For people accused of crimes. He took some civil cases too, but not many at all. Yes. He got his pleasure by helping people accused of crimes. Laws. And he got them off. Yes. He had such skill, such flair—Ah.

[2] One day he allowed himself to quarrel with the judge, the magistrate here in Pisticci. He had the Codex in his hand. Now, he said one thing and the magistrate another. 'It does not say that.' 'Then, what does it say?' The magistrate said, 'This is the law: this is the meaning of the Codex.' Bruni was aggressive; and he talked a lot. So much so, he couldn't contain himself any more. He took the Codex volume, and threw it at the magistrate's head. Ah! 'Guards, guards! Guards, guards! Arrest this man.' Bruni left quickly and vanished. He vanished very suddenly. Oh! Without hesitation he went to hide somewhere in Croci, in a mill, in an oil-mill. Down by Cugghier. Because all his followers loved him. And all the people at Cugghier protected him. Yes. In short: that's where he went. And spent the night there. And during the night his followers took him out to Caporotondo in the country. He spent a few days there until his case was prepared. Because a case was brought against him at Matera: wilful insults to the magistrate. [Wilful] Outrage. Think of it! For the opponents of the Party had exaggerated a lot. Think of it: in order to make a case, they really went to town, so to speak. Now, his adversaries were waiting for when they could take him to Matera in manacles. They wanted to take him: yes, he absolutely had to suffer that indignity. They would have enjoyed taking him in chains. Yes. They did not get their fun. For at night the peasants in the Party, with their beasts, with mules, they gave him a mount and, by

by-ways and highways, they travelled through the night: by by-ways and highways: by valleys and hills, every way they went. And on the morning of the day of the trial he was there ready in Matera. When the gentlemen of the enemy saw him at Matera, in flesh and blood! 'Well! But he's a devil! How did he get here? Who brought him—a helicopter?' They were astounded. His enemies wanted to bring him in in manacles. At the trial (passing on to the trial)—he was absolved. Absolved. Ah! How their noses were put out! So, then, he showed that the case was as he said it was, and not the other way. It was the fault of the magistrate. He was really good at defending.

[3]   So then: Bruni was the son of a man called Nicola Bruni: he had a large farm and lived in Montalbano, but he was born in Pisticci, the father. So the son studied, and became a somebody. But he had a rather aggressive character. And he was magnanimous, big-hearted. Foe to profiteers. Proud foe of the gentleman masters—for we call them gentlemen: they have big houses. So: he was a lover of the working men, of the peasants. He was an educated man of course—a lawyer. But he had no shame in going out to the fields, to this tree, to that one, in going out into the country. He was with the people. So then, after he had got his degree at Rome he returned to Pisticci. He came to Pisticci, but he was poor. He had no means; indeed the friends he had looked after him in their houses, invited him to meals. But he had no means. And so, bit by bit, day by day, people joined with him. And a number of followers was created: he made a list. And then, at that time, which was around 1912, I think, but I don't remember precisely, when he had already gathered a number of socialist partisans..Well. So then—about that time my father too, who had a quarrel with his brother, a priest (it was a family quarrel), and the priest, the brother, was very much against Alessandro Bruni, and they were enemies: proud foes. So, given that they hated one another, my father and his brother, my father went to see Bruni. He said, 'Don Alessà: write me down here'. 'But how can I write you down? You've got a brother', he said—and he meant Don Michele; 'you belong with Don Michele.' 'Don Alessà: will you write me down, or won't you? If you will, I'll sign', he said. 'And if I sign, not even a cannon will move me from beside you. And if you won't, I still have to go along with you.' He wrote him down. And once he had signed, he stayed with him

THE RED FLAG IN PISTICCI 57

right up to the last minute, when the fascist squads came, to defend him. After the others had left. And my father never gave up. [..] When the party was formed, and could feel its strength, then they went to the polls against the gentlemen of the town council. They went to the polls, and the gentlemen were utterly defeated. They had to withdraw. And Bruni took the Municipal administration over. My father was a member of the ruling committee with him. He could scarcely read or write! He knew only how to scribble. Even so, he gave interviews in the Mayor's room, my father did, in that year—but I don't remember well—1912, 13, 14. Then came defeat. For the fascist squads came, in 1920 I think. And they looted and set fire to everything. They treated people badly; they provoked them; they insulted them. They gave them doses of cod-liver oil. They broke people's heads with truncheons. And so on. They were so many scoundrels, layabouts and thieves—spiteful. They were protected by the director. Now the director was Antonio Pelazzi, helped by his kinsman, I forget who—Giuseppe Nicola Pastore. Yes. Both of them have gone out of circulation now. Troubles pass on; yes, they pass.

[4] Now: the time came when Bruni, who suffered much, had to take refuge and go away. We knew that even Antonio Pelazzi had some conscience about having made him go, to escape from the bully-boys. For one day Antonio Pelazzi went to a barbershop at Sant' Antuon as it's called, and my father was there waiting to be shaved. Think of it! He was completely opposed: a proud adversary, no?—who knows how many doses of cod liver oil they gave him? They gave them to a priest, too: even to a priest. Don Domenico Sinisi. Cod-liver oil to a priest. And then they sent to say: 'I've got the squits.' Ah yes. He'd put an article in a newspaper which damaged the fascists then—an article he shouldn't have written. The laxative meant that he should purge himself of his evil principles which he held, and should replace them with theirs. That was why they gave him the squits. Now you see what Mussolini was like.

[5] Well. So then Antonio Pelazzi said, in front of all the people waiting for a shave: 'I admire this man's character: he's a man of faith', he said. 'He'll let himself be killed, torn in pieces, but he won't betray the party and the flag.' Yes.

[6] And in fact, the day came when it was all over. All the power was in fascist hands, Don Antonio ruled the town with Peppe-Col

and his friends. They ruled the town. He wasn't bestial. He treated people kindly. And he was a book-keeper at the bank. But then, when he was a fascist, he became savage; he became brutal; he became cruel. People say that during the war they had in Albania and everywhere, he was made a colonel and so on. Good. And he did atrocities on those poor people, indeed.

[7]   In short, there came the day when—because the socialists were demolished,—[they asked themselves] 'What can we do now?' 'We must hunt out the red flags. All the red flags.' Yes. They went from town to town, from one place to another, looking for red flags. For they were to vanish. It was all black shirts, black shirts. And one day they came to our house, a group of layabouts. 'What do you want? What do you want?' 'We're here to look for the red flag: open everything—drawers, boxes—we want the red flag.' [My father] said, 'We haven't got one. There's none here.' My sisters were present, who were orphaned of their mother: my mother died in 1912, on 24 February. He said: 'You may look where you like', he said, 'because we haven't got a red flag here', he said. And so they went away. Opposite the chapel of San Giovanni, that house just opposite the chapel—that was our house in those days. I lived there. My sister lives there now. That night some of the fascists made a joke on the wall opposite the chapel: they waited, and drew a chalice, and then a bottle, and then they wrote: 'Have a drink!' Quite stupid! But they never laid a finger on my father—not a finger: they threatened to, but they never touched him. Now—about the flag. As I told you, we hid it in the bread-oven, we put it in the furnace, and had it by us a day and a night. Then my father said to me: 'Look Micchè: we must hide it: you must make it disappear. It would be a great pity if it fell into fascist hands'. He said, 'take it into the country; take it into the country and bury it'. And so I did. I took it out to Caporotondo. I made a hole two or three feet deep, put it in a barrel, in a keg, inside a sack, and covered it over. In short, I buried it. There was not a trace of it. Nobody could tell where to find it.

[8]   Sometimes not a day passes, not a day passes without a disaster. We were taking straw from the stack. The finial of the flag was on top, among the straw, so that it couldn't be seen. A finial is—on top of the flag there was a brass thing, like an axe: that's called a finial. We hid it there. It was hidden under the straw: and my brother Giovanni saw it, my brother Giovannin

who was about 15 then. He said: 'What's this thing here?' [I said] 'How did it get there?—I threw it there to hide it.' 'The flag', he said, 'where is it? What have you done with it?' 'Why do you want to know?', I said. 'I've seen it [anyway]', he said, 'I've seen it.' 'You've no need to know', I said. 'Where it is, it's alright.' 'But I want to know.' Well! 'Do me a favour' [I said], 'don't insult me.' 'But I won't tell—I don't want to know. . .' He made a to-do about it. 'So: do you want to know? I'll tell you, once for all. Now I'll tell you. And you know that I'll kill you; if you let out one word, I'll kill you. If you let anything out, you'll be guilty of sacrilege. This flag must stay in our keeping', I said, 'for it's valuable.' 'But I won't tell. .' Well. In short: I showed him. Would I never had! Ah!

[9] That same evening I went home and found Antonio Pelazzi talking with my father, in the evening. So I, as soon as I got there, I said—for he was affable, not a proud man—'Don Antò, how do you do; what's up?' 'Oh, we've come here', he said, 'to talk with uncle Nard-Rocco, about the red flag', he said. 'But he's so pig-headed, he won't tell us where he's put the damn flag.' So I, in order not to give cause for suspicion that it had been in my hands, I said: 'Father: if you've got the flag in your keeping, there's no need', I said, 'give up; give it up. Enough's enough. It's all over', I said. Yes. 'I told Don Antuon, I did, that he [i.e. Bruni] took it with him to Tramutolo. That's all I know', he said. 'But is it really true that he took it to Tramutolo?' 'Of course it's true.' They made my father swear to it. And he swore. He swore it. 'On the ashes of your wife.' He swore. Do you see, he was so loyal, he trampled on the memory of his wife. How attached to the party he was, not to betray it, and the flag. In such moments, you get thoughts in your head, how to get out of it, no? How to find a solution.

[10] He said: 'But in all the time you had it here,' he said, 'we came several times and searched the house', he said, 'and we never found it.' 'Well, now', I said, 'do you think I'm so stupid (excuse me) that I'd let the flag be found in the house', I said. Just like that, I spoke. 'But where did you keep it?' 'It was alright where I kept it, but it's not there now at all.' 'But,' he said, to soften me up, 'where did you have it hidden?' 'I kept it in the old oven in the side of Uagna, by the Madonna delle Grazie.' That's to say, in the ravine. It was the evening, night-time, about nine o'clock, and

raining too. 'Well boys', he said, for he had his fellow members with him, 'let's go there now'. And they went. They went. 'But', he said, 'who'll show us this oven?' Well: since there was my brother Giovannin and, yes, Leonardo Prudente, who also knew: 'Take us', he said, 'come with us.' And he took them. They came back empty handed, of course. But they still weren't satisfied. They took the boys, and took them to the fascist office: both of them. First they interrogated one, then [the other]. 'Now, you know where the red flag is.' [He] and Leonardo Prudente said: 'You can kill me; you can cut me in pieces, but I know nothing about the red flag business'. Yes. 'And you?' 'Not even I', [he] said, 'what if I do know where he put it? And I don't know, no.' 'But you boy', he said [to my brother], 'you're naughty; you know—but you won't tell—well, tell me: go on. We'll give you a nice watch.' 'What's a watch to me', he said, 'if I don't know anything? I don't know. I don't know.' They put great pressure on him. Then they began to try threats: 'Now we'll put you in a cell, and we'll make you suffer.' 'Do what you think, but you'll get nothing from me: I know nothing.' 'Do you really know nothing? 'Really!' 'Well then: swear it [on the ashes of your mother].' My brother refused the oath: 'If my father has sworn, [nevertheless] I will not swear.' 'Well now—you know where it is. You know about the flag. Now let's go there; now you can take us.' Among all those bullies, knaves they were, layabouts; a poor boy as he was—they ought not to have. He took them to Caporotondo. At night, too.

[11]   That night: the new house wasn't there in those days, only the old one. I lived there. Alas! But I wasn't there that night: I was away. An old woman, my mother-in-law was there. My wife's mother, asleep. She didn't even notice the noise they made. I was in town, and that night I was making oil at the mill in Piazza Plebiscito. Making oil. When the next morning came, and we were reaching the end of the oil, a woman came to the mill: 'Eh', she said, 'don't you know anything?' 'What?' She said, 'Don't you know they've found the red flag?', she said. 'They've found—'. Well: it had been in my keeping; I had it for that while: 'Then it's a lie', I said. 'But it's true!' Eh. 'It's so true, they're going to have a procession today.' 'And where did they find it?', I said. She said, 'Where the old woman lives'— she said, but she was mistaken—'where the old woman called Troccoceron lives.'

[12] So that day, that day, those layabouts let everyone believe there would be a procession. They would take my father, mount him on a donkey, and lead him round and about with the red flag; and when they got to the square they would have a bonfire, and they'd make him put the red flag in the fire—so they made everyone believe. But it never happened. It never happened. And I don't know what they did with the red flag.

[13] Now there was writing in gold metal letters on that red flag:

'To those who work, the fruits of their toil
Light, land, life belong to all.'

That's what was written.

[14] The people who were the chief troublemakers against the socialist opponents were the sons of my uncle the priest: he had no less than seven children. Seven children. So. Well these—no! Eight. Eight sons. Four girls, four men. But these four sons were all dissolute, without skills, without a trade, without any profession. And they were dedicated to crime: to thievery, to meddling: and adversaries of the socialist party. In short, they followed their father, my uncle.

THE TRANSCRIPT

[1] Perchè sapete è morto poco fa, un paio di anni addietro, è morto a Roma: tanto ciò ch'io lessi 'n articolo sul giornale dove diceva: 'E' morto a Roma un insigne letterato lucano',—che era appunto il Brun'. Eh. Un insigne letterato lucano. Vuol dire che a scienza a tenevë, no? Eh. E së vissi a Pisticci difendere nell' assisi e nel tribunale e mettere fuori gli accusati. Mettere fuori, liberare— sì. Perchè per lo più era lui penalista; era penalista per lo più. Per gli accusati penali. E per i civilisti purë pigghiava qualche causa— ma non mica tanto. Si.—Ma a piacë suj' er per gli accusati di pena. Delitti. E metteva fuori. Sì. Aveva un' arte tale, una favella. Ah.

[2] Una volta si permettete di combattere col giudice, col pretore, qui a Pisticci. E teneva u codice in man' idd. Mo, lui diceva d'un modo, il giudice diceva d'un altro. 'Non va cosi!' 'Ma come va?' Il giudice 'ce: 'E' così: così è caparlo il codice.' Eh. Quello era violente, era volubile. Eh. Fu tanto che non ci tenne più. Pigghi u libro d'u codice e lu men' in facc' u giudice. Ah!

'Guardie, guardie! Arrestate questu qui!' Se ne filò subito. Sparì. Sparì di botto. Aoh. Al momento si sci a nascondere alla parti delle Croci da, in un trapeto, in un frantoio. Da, a a Cugghier. Perchè tutto i soci l'amavano. E tutti a Cugghier lo prottegevano. Sì. Insomma: se ne sci da. Passò la nottate. Nella nottata i soci stessi lo accompagnarono nella campagna di Caporotondo. E là ando a passare alquanti giorni a fino a tanto che fu maturato il processo. E perchè adda fa a causa a Matera di lui: offesa arbitraria al pretore. Oltraggio. Considera. Poi gli avversari d'u Partit', com' avrà scen' esagerato, poi. E considera: per adda fà a causë avva sci a mont', per dire. Mo: aspettavano il momento, gli avversari, quando dovevano accumpagnà a Matera ammanettato. Avevano accumpagnà. Sì—per forz' a sta trafil' adda passà. Avevano piaceri ammo a portà ammanettat. Sì. Non ebbero quel piacere. A nott' i contadini appartenente al Partito co gli animali, coi muli u facevan' a mett' a cavadd, e scortë pë scortë a notte camminarono: scortë pë scortë faciorno per i valli, per i monti, e per dovunque. Eh. E il mattino del giorno della causa si trovò pronto a Matera. Quando i signori avversari lo vidano a Matera in carn' e ossa: 'Mah! Ma—custë quà, è un demonio! Ma comë truvat': chi ha portato quà—l'elicottero?'. Si rustorno. E i sirusi avevano piacere che l'avevano portat' ammanettat'. Ma nell'udienza: si va all'udienza—rest' assoluto. Assoluto. Ah! E rustorno cu tantë dë nas'! Dunque: quello dimostrò che la causa va così, e non va così. E' mancante della gente che prësiede all'udienza. Eh. Aveva un modo di difendere.
[3] Dunque, questo quà era figlio di uno..uomo che si chiamava Nicola Brun'. Aveva una masseria e resideva a Montalbano, ma era nativo di Pisticci, il padre. Questo figlio è studiat', poi: divenne un qualcheduno. Ma aveva un carattere un po' violento. Poi—liberale, liberale. Nemico dei pescicani. Nemico fiero dei signori galantuomënë—chiamammo nui galantuomënë: c'hanno palazz'. Eh. Dunque—amante della bassa plebbe, dei contadini. Era certo un uomo istruit'—un uomo, un avvocato. E' vero no s'avviliva a truvà a terrë, a truvà a quell'albero, a quell'altro, a girare per le campagne. Era popolare. Dunque, dopo aversi laureato a Roma si riparò a Pisticci. Venne a Pisticci, ma era povero. Non aveva mezzi, tanto che gli amici poi ch'aveva l'ospitarono in casa, lo tenevano a pranzo. Ma era sprovvisto di mezzi. Così poi mano mano, giorno per giorno, s'accustò la

gente. E si formò un numero di soci. Faceva l'elengo. E allora in quel periodo, ch'era verso l'anno del dodici dico, ma non mi ricordo bene, ch' aveva già gglomerato un numero di partigiani, socialisti, sì. In quel periodo anche il mio padre che aveva dissensio col suo fratello prete—c'era un dissensio di famiglia—e il prete, il fratello, era molto avverso Alessandro Brun' ed erano nemici. Fieri. E dato che stevono in odio, mio padre col fratello, allor' andò a trovare a Bruni. 'Ce: 'Don Alessà: ce segnëmë quà, a me'. 'Ma, comë të possa segnà a te? Cca tu tegnë fratt' ', dice—che era Dommichele; 'tienë a Dommichele'. 'Don Alessà, më vuo segnai? Ci më vuo segnà, me sign'. Dice: 'ci më sign manco nu cannonë më sposterà dal fianco tuo. E ce non me sign', purë lo stess' aggio venì appriess'. Lo segnai. E segnata appena al ultimo momento quando sono arrivate le truppe fasciste s'avvist' accuost' a difenderlo. Dopo che gli altri l'avevano abbandonato. E mio padre non restò. Mo: [il direttore del fascio,] dicemmo mo, continuamente, che quando s'ebbe formato il partito che si sentiva, allora si venne a votazione coi signori del potere comunale. Si venne a votazione: li galantuomënë cë l'hanno inter'. Dovettero ritirare. E pigghiò lu municibbië, Bruni. Mio padre faceva l'assessore delegato appriess'. Un mezz'analfabeta era. Cca manca tantë sapeva appena scarabbocchiare. Sì. Eppure riceveva al gabinetto del sindaco all'udienza, mio padre, in quell'anno—beh, non ricordo bene: dodici, tredici, quattordici. Poi ne venne lo sfacelo: chè arrivarono le truppe fasciste, il venti, credo. Le truppe fasciste cca mëttevano tutto a sacc' e fuoco. Maltrattavano e stimolavono, ingiuriavono e davano purghe ad olio d'arìgine. E rompevano capë coi manganelli. Eccetera. Tanti mascalzoni, sfaccendati, ladri poi, sciagurati. Che venivano protetti dal direttore. Il direttore mo era Antonio Pelazzi aiutato da suo parente non so chi—Giuseppe Nicola Pastore. Sì. Tutte e due non esistono alla circolazione. Passarono quei fumi, sì, passarono poi.

[4] Mo, arriva l'ora che Bruni passando guai, poi, dovette rifugiare un po' per parte. Sappimm' cust' che anche Antonio Pelazzi aveva un poco di rimorso per farlo fugire e scappare dei manigoldi. Chè Antonio Pelazzi un giorno diciamo si trovò in una barberia a Sant' Antuon', la chiamam', e c'era il mio padre che si doveva sbarbare. E considera: er' affiancato avversario, fiero avversario, no?—che chissà quante purghe erano date. Anche ad un prete—pure ad un prete: don Domenico Sinisi. E a prete a

purg' a olio d'arìgine. E poi mannarno a dir': Ho fatto u brod'. Ah sì. Aveva mess' un articolo su un giornale che nuoceva allora ai fascisti—un articolo che non doveva metterlo. La purga serviva a chè si doveva purgare tutto quei principi maligni che tenevanë da parolë, e s'adda mettere chiddë lorë. E chedd'era perchè fanno purgà. Ha vista mai comë a pensav' u Mussolin'?

[5] Mah. Allora disse Antonio Pelazz' in presenza de tantë gente che si dovevano sbarbare, disse: 'Ammiro il carattere quest' uomo: è un uomo di fede'.' Ce: 'Si fa ammazzare, si fa fà a pezzi, ma non baldisce il partit', la bandiera'. Sì.

[6] Tanto, arrivò un giorno che tutt'ora era finito: tutt' u potere era 'n a man' u fascisti, e dominava Don Antonio a potere municipale—e Peppë Col' e compagnia bella. Si dominavono al potere municipale. Non era cattivo. Trattav' a gente. Fece pure il ragioniero 'n d'a Banc'. Mappoi a mano a fascismo divenne barbaro, divenne atroce, divenne crudele. Si racconta poi nella guerra che facevano, Albania e qualunque punto, che lui poi era nominato colonello, eccetera. Bene. E faceva stragge, di quella povera gente, sì.

[7] Insomma, poi arriv' un giorno che dato che venne lo sfacelo dei socialisti: 'Mo—ammo fà?'—'Dobbiamo cercare le bandiere rosse. Tutte le bandiere rosse', sì. Andavono paes' pë paes', comune per comune, in cerca delle bandiere rosse. Chè quello non dovevano più comparire. Erano tutte camicie nere, camicie nere. E un dei giorni së presentarno a casa nuostr' na guant' di fanullone. 'E ce vulit'? E ce vulit'?' 'Amma vedè quà cca aprite tutte cose—cassë, cassettoni,—volemm' a bandiera rossa'. 'Nun tenimm' quà. Nun ce n' è'. C'erano mie sorelle poi, orfanatelle poi di madre: mia madre morì l'anno del diciotto il 24 febbraio. 'Ce: 'Vui putit' cerchë quantë vulit',' dice, 'cca quà nun tenimmë bandiera rossa.' 'Ce: 'C'a a tennë ce sapimm' nui'. E poi tornò un altra volta. Di rimpetto a ddo sta a capeddë San Giovann', quella casa proprio di rimpetto alla capella era l'antica casa nostra: da tornav'ii. Mo ci risiede una mia sorella là. Al muro di rimpetto alla capella la notte quei seguaci fascisti scëron a fà un scherzo: spettarono; fecero il calice, e poi la bottiglia, e poi ne scrissero 'Bevete!' Ma è ridicolo. Ma non lo toccorno, a mio padre, non lo toccavono: lo minacciavono, ma non lo toccavono. Mo: sta bandiera. Comë vi dissi, a tenevam' nascosta in da fornaccë; in da fornacc' a pigghiorno, da teneva un giorno una notte in casa. E mio padre disse a me:

'Micchè, vedi: ci amma cunfermà: mi deve fà sparire sta bandiera. Era un bon peccato ci va in mano ai fascisti'. Dice: 'Portalo forë: portalo forë e mettalo sott'a la terrë'. Pë cusì feci. La portai ii, da Caporotondo. Feci una fossa due tre palmi profondë, la misi dentro un barile, un barilotto, indu nu sacco, e la sotterrai. La seppellì, insomma. Non parevan' le traccie per niente. Nessuno poteva dire dove andar a trovarla.

[8] Quando non passo un giorno, non passo un giorno, quando certe volte deve succedere un incidente. Fecemmo a pigghià a pagghia do pagghiaron'. U gagliardetto della bandiera era susë frammischiato nella paglia per non farlo comparire. Gagliardetto era—in cima alla bandiera c'era la cosa d'ottone, come un accetta: quello si chiama gagliardetto. Allora, lì l'avevamo sparì. Sparì sott'a paglia; e la veddè frattëmi Giovann', mio fratello Giovannin', che allora l'han' dato una quindicina d'anni. 'Ce: 'Custë quà, comë se trova?' 'E comë së trova? A agghia menatë do pë fà sparisce'. 'A bandiera', 'ce, 'dov'è? Ce l'a fatta?'. 'Ce ne vuo sapè?', ii. 'Cca ii l'agghia vist', ii l'agghia vist' '. 'Non è necessario,' dicai, 'a sapè. Dov'è sta bonë'. 'Che lo voglio sapè..' Fò una questione. 'Beh. Vuoi sapè? Te lo dic', e tocc': mo te lo dico: e tu lo sai ch'io t'ammazzo; ci muove parolë, ii t'accid'. Se tu palesi qualchecosa, commett' un sacrilegio. Chesta bandiera adda stà in mani nostra', dic', 'quest'è valorosa'. 'Ma io non dico..' Mah. Insomma. La facevo vedè. Non fosse mai stato. Ah!

[9] Quella stessa sera mi ritrav' a casa e trov' Antonio Pelazz' cca duscurrev' pë Tat', a sera. Io mo, appena arrivai,—cuddë poi era attacat', non aveva superbia, no—'Don Antò, comë scemë', dice, 'ce dic' '. 'Eh—simë venutë cca', dice, 'a parlà a zi Nard-Rocc' pë l'affare d'a bandiera,' dice. 'Per tanto duro, che non vuol mi dire, non vuol accuseddë, dove ha messë sta maledetto bandiera'. Ii mo, per non fà da redere, che ha passato per mani me, sospetti, dicivi: 'Tà: se tu a tien' priesso di te la bandiera, non c'è bisogno', dico 'ceder' arma, dàlli: oramai', dico, 'basta cchiù. E' finito'. Sì. 'Ii ce l'agghia ditë a don Antuon ii, cca la portava idd quann' fu sci a Tramutolo'. Eh. 'Non sacc'cchiù,' di. 'Ma era proprio vero che l'ha portat' a Tramutolo?' 'E' vero!' A mio padre gli daron' il giurament'. E giurò. Giurò. 'Sulle cenere di vostra moglie'. Giurò. Guarda: quant'era tenace, che mese sotto i piedi la memoria di sua moglie. Com'era attacato forte al partito, per non tradirlo,

la bandiera. In quel momenti sono pensieri da a cap', comë t'adda rësolvë, no? Com' adda rësolvë.

[10] 'Ce: 'Ma cu lu tiemp' che ha tenuto appriess' a te', dice, 'noi simë venutë diverse voltë a fà a percusizione dientro', dice, 'e non l'ammo truvatë'. 'Come', dic', 'tanto fesso era ii (scusate) cca fà truvà a bandiera ientro', dic.' Così proprio parlai. 'E dov' a teniv'?'. 'E dov'a tenivë stava bonë, ma non è cchiù manca dà'. 'Ma tu,' dice, per fà më persuaso un poco, 'dovë tënetë sconnutë?' 'A tënevë a intr' a fornaccia vecchia a o cuozz' da Uagnà, a parte della Madonna delle Grazie'. Per dire, costiere. Era la sera a notte inoltrata, verso le nove, e cchiuveva pure. 'Beh,' dice, 'uagnon', (che aveva i suoi componenti membri appriess') 'ce: 'mo 'ma sci dà', dice. Scese pure. Ci anda. 'Ma', 'ce, 'ci m'adda imparà questa fornacc'?' Beh. Giusto che c'era Giovannin frattëmë, e c'era Leonardo Prudente, sì. Che già a sapeva. 'Accumpagnà' dice, 'accumpagnateci'. E accumpagnò loro. Ritoron' a mani vuotë, no? Ma non furono ancora sodisfatt'. Si pigghiorno u uaglion e portav' a l'uffic' d'u fasc'. Tutt'e due. Prima domandarono al uaglion, e poi domandavono a [nui]. 'E vui sapete dov' è la bandiera ross'.' [Io] e Leonardo Prudente ce: 'Vui më putit' accidë, më putit' fare a piezzi, ch'io non sacc' nuddë pë l'affare della bandiera'. Sì. 'E tu?' 'Cca manc' ii,' dic, 'ce me sacc' ii, dov' a puost'. E ii non a sacc', no.' 'Ma tu uaglion,' dice 'tu sei malizios'; tu lo sai, e non vuol dire: beh—dicëmëla, va. Të dëmë nu bel orologgë'. 'Ce n'agghia facc' a n'orologio', di, 'se ii non saccio nuddë', dice. 'Non sacc' nuddë—non lo sacc''. E tanto lo istigavono. Poi ascorno a pigghià con le minacce: 'mo të mettim' in camera dë sicurezza e të faccim' a passà lu uai'. 'Ma faccitëmë chedd' cca credit', che pë me non ottenete niente: chè io non lo sacc'.' 'Davvero non lo sai?' 'Davvero!' 'Allora: giura!' Mio fratello non volle giurà. 'Se ha giurato il mio padre, non voglio giurare io'. 'Allora, beh: tu lo sai. Tu sei consapevole della bandiera. Mo 'ma sci do; mo m'adda portà'. Miezz' a quei ladri manigoldi, birbanti che erano, sfaccendati. Un povero ragazzo com' era, non dovevan'. L'accompagnò a Caporotondo. A notte, poi.

[11] Quella notte: allora non c'era quel fabbricato nuovo, c'era solo il vecchio. Era là che abitavo io. Marro me! Ma non c'era quella notte, io: er' assente. C'era una vecchierella mia suocera. A madre di mia moglie che dormiva. Non se ne avverte neanche di

quel rumore che fecero. Io ero in paese, e quella notte faceva l'olio a trapeto in a cchiazz', piazza Plebiscito. Facevo l'olio. Quando fu dimattina, che allora stemm' in finë per l'olio, arriva una donna del trapeto. 'Eh,' dice, 'non sapetënë uddë?' 'Ce cos'?' Dice, 'Non sapete ch'hanno trovato a bandiera ross'' dice. 'Hanno trova—.' Mo. Cca era passato pure a mani me; a tenevë ii quel po': 'Allora è mente', dic'. 'E' davver'!' Eh. 'E' tantë ver' cca anna fà a festa ogg''. 'E dov'hann'a truvat'?' dic. Dice: 'a ddo la vecch'' dice. Sbagliò. Dice: 'a ddo a vecch' si chiamava Troccoceron'.

[12] Mo, il giorno appriess', tutti quei sfaccendati facevano credere, facevano: avevano a fà festa dà. Avevano pigghiato a mio padre e avevano a mettere a cavadd' d'u ciuc'. Avevano a tirà poi, paes' paes', p' a bandiera ross', che poi arrivava in piazza avevano a fà u fuoc: avevano idd' stess' dà fuoc a bandiera rossa: facevano credere. Ma non fu. Non fu. Non so che ne fecero della bandiera rossa.

[13] Su quella bandiera rossa s'era scritto a carattere indorati metallici:

'A quei che lavora dell'opera i frutti.
La luce, la terra, la vit' è di tutti.'

S'era scritt'.

[14] Quelli che più erano gli istigatori contro i socialisti avversari, erano i figli del mio zio prete, che n'aveva ben sette. Sette figli. Beh, di questi..eh—no! Otto. Otto figli. Quattro femmënë, quattro uomënë. Ma ste quattr' uomënë erano tutti scapestrati, senz' arte, senza mestiere, e senza profession'. E si erano dati alla delinquenza: chi ladro, e chi farabutto, e avversari contro il partito socialista. Insomma, a la mano col padre poi, mio zio.

5
The politics of an old state: a view from the Chinese lineage

MAURICE FREEDMAN

The scholar for whom this book has been written is unique among social anthropologists in her capacity to relate the politics of the small-scale to the politics of the large-scale, treating both with high skill, and demonstrating that her brilliance as a social anthropologist springs from her being more than just that. This essay follows a common anthropological style in the study of the politics of complex societies, in that it gives most attention to the smaller-scale features of the Chinese polity, but, in honouring Lucy Mair, it tries at the end to rise above parochialism in order to suggest how anthropology and history may together produce a more convincing political analysis than either is able to offer on its own.

The study of lineage structure and organisation is one of the main ways in which social anthropology has established itself within the general study of Chinese society. Up to quite recent times—in fact, up to five years ago or so—the Western writings on China normally made use of the term 'clan' when referring to patrilineal kinship groups; and it was of course no *anthropological* discovery that throughout China, although in differing degrees of elaborateness in different parts of the country, groups formed on the ground which recruited their members on the basis of descent in the male line from common ancestors. The existence of 'clans' was responsible in part for attracting anthropological attention to China, for the study of unilineal descent systems played a major role in a major phase of the discipline's development. If we ignore Marcel Granet's work, which is concerned with archaic forms of Chinese kinship, and has paradoxically had more influence upon the general study of kinship than upon the study of Chinese kinship (cf. Levi-Strauss 1949, and 1969 chs. 19-21), we shall find the first attempt to be systematic about the Chinese 'clan' in Hu Hsien-chin, *The Common Descent Group in China and its Functions* (1948). That book, written from within American anthropology, brought together a great deal of evidence from all over China on the functions (ritual, judicial, and economic) of the *tsu*, but it showed less interest in matters of morphology and was very reluctant to treat the *tsu* as one example of a form of kinship grouping widely distributed in the ethnographic record.[1]

The Chinese 'clan'/*tsu* became a 'lineage'—as every social anthropologist will at once guess—because of the diffusion of a category used by British students of African society. The term 'lineage' was brought in to avoid the vagueness inherent in 'clan' and to label those forms of unilineal kinship organisation which were both corporate (in Maine's sense) and based upon the notion that the steps of descent back from the living generations to the apical ancestor could be spelled out. The African literature showed how lineages might form the basis of political life, by furnishing a series of articulated groups; it became clear that some analogies were to be found in China.

In a world of transient families[2] and kindreds an individual was, in many parts of China, a member of a corporation—or of a series of wider and wider corporations—based upon agnatic kinship. Lineages might be shallow or deep, small or large in their membership. They might be in one or more villages. What at one point in time might be small and simple might at another grow to be large and complex—and vice versa, for there was waning as well as waxing. Let us imagine a small nucleus of agnates (even perhaps those within one family) establishing itself in new terrain. (And because we are used to thinking of China as a crowded country, we need to remember that up to about the end of the eighteenth century there were opportunities for pioneers to expand at least to the south-east and the south-west of the country.) The nucleus may for some time continue to regard itself as part of the lineage it has left behind. If it is demographically and economically successful, the lapse of a few generations will see it composed of a number of families tracing their descent, so far as their male members are concerned, from a common ancestor.

---

[1] For another American approach to the matter see Fried 1957 and 1970.
[2] See Freedman 1967: 93ff. for a discussion of the Chinese family as a unit constantly dissolving into new units.

They are now a small lineage which either stands by itself or constitutes a segment of the lineage from which it sprang. A portion of land will have been set aside to finance the rites performed at the tomb of the local founding ancestor or the rites performed at a central ancestral shrine (or both). More time passes, and on the same assumption of success, the local lineage is now a large community which is segmented. Lesser agnatic groups have crystallised within it. The process by which the segments have come into being is the same as that by which the local lineage was created: an endowed ancestral grave or shrine is established to mark the segment and enable it to continue.[3] We shall see later on that this model of lineage growth and segmentation will not alone account for all the forms of agnatic grouping we can find in China; but it will do for our present purposes.

The property aspect of the process has an important consequence for the segmentary order. A sizable local lineage was unlikely to be composed of families at one level of prosperity, and differences in riches were reflected in differences in segmentation. New segments did not come into being in accordance with some rule that operated automatically upon the genealogical framework: a new segment was created when one small group of agnates were able to differentiate themselves from other members of their segment by financing their separation out—either by focusing on an ancestor in whose name the new property was to be held (and who would distinguish them from the descendants of other ancestors), or by a man entailing part of his estate to his agnatic descendants collectively to prevent his property being dispersed. The segmentary order, then, was uneven or asymmetrical.[4] Any family might be a member of a rising hierarchy of segments—a Chinese box within a set of Chinese boxes—benefiting from the resources of each, but different families might be members of a different number of such segments. The poorer the branch of the

[3] Let me cite a literary source. In *The Dream of the Red Chamber* Ko Ching appears in a dream to Phoenix and explains that she is concerned for the future of the house of Chia. 'True, the Chia clan had endured..for hundreds of years already, but blossoming is likely to be followed by decay..Two things were on her mind: the consolidation of the family school and insurance of the perpetuity of the quarterly sacrifices to the ancestors.' There was a need to buy family estates, thereby forming a lasting and inalienable family foundation..A future dedicated to such cultural purposes would, even if the worst came to the worst, be safe from seizures by the State..' (*The Dream of the Red Chamber* 93f.).

[4] See Freedman, 1958: 48f.

lineage to which any family belongs, the fewer the number of segments from which it is likely to benefit—and the higher its chance, as a consequence, of remaining poor.

The male agnates of each family (*chia*) were joint holders of an estate which, upon the death of the parental generation and the partition of the family, was divided equally among the sons, except that an extra share might go to the oldest of them in recognition of that primogeniture which in imperial China was a mere shadow of its feudal self. But the head of a family (as we have seen), or a group of brothers acting jointly, might decide to withhold from the division some portion of the property to form an ancestral estate or to be added to one already existing. Ancestral property, unlike family property, became (in theory) immune to division and acted as the anchor to which a segment was attached.[5] The estates of lineages and their segments might be agricultural land, and often were; but they might also take the form of rice-mills or fishponds. They might be exploited in different ways. Small ancestral estates seem typically to have been passed round, year by year, among member families, the family for the time being holding an estate profiting by the difference between what they could extract from it and what they had to pay out to discharge the duties (providing the sacrifices and so on) that went with the privilege. Larger estates seem generally to have been subject to managements which rented them out and distributed the annual income to all members after paying for the appropriate sacrifices and other collective activities (which might include running a school).

Lineage relations in most cases stopped at the local community. That is to say, the commonest form of lineage we can see (in the literature and, as field workers, on the ground) is the local lineage on its own: it may occupy a village or part of one. But a number of such local lineages might—as we should expect from the model set out earlier in the essay—be aggregated in a particular region to form a higher-order lineage which again was centred on an ancestral tomb or shrine. Those of us who have worked in the

[5] There appears to be another way in which ancestral estates sometimes came into being. There is reason to suppose that when new land was created by collective effort, as in the reclamations along the south-eastern coast, it might at once be established as an ancestral estate and kept out of the family mill which over the generations could grind property into smaller and smaller pieces. Cf. Wakeman 1966: 153.

Hong Kong New Territories are familiar with the case of the Teng (Cantonese: Tang) local lineages which in pre-British days clearly formed a powerful higher-order lineage dominating the economic and political life of a large part of the county of Hsin-an. (Cf. Baker 1966.) Now, once we reach this level of organisation we need to be careful about our terms and about the evidence for the existence of such agnatic groups. Local lineages might ally themselves temporarily for some political purpose (as in the pursuit of an interlineage struggle or against the county administration); they might be of the same surname, and therefore, in the Chinese view, of ultimate common descent, but they were not by that fact alone a single higher-order lineage. It is only when an alliance of that sort was made permanent and expressed by the establishment of an estate that we may say that a new higher-order lineage had come into being. Again, Chinese genealogists casting about for the ties which might be assumed historically to have linked lineages now widely separated might draw up accounts that made it seem as though groups of local lineages belonged together in one superordinate unit; but in reality these units were, and might well remain, artefacts of historiography and are not to be confused with organised entities.

Let us turn to the place of lineages within Chinese society. In what sense were lineages treated as political entities and, perhaps, legal persons? We come up against an interesting feature of the Chinese political system: the relations between central power and individual subject were intended by the state to be mediated, up to a point, by his kinship ties. The *chia* (family) was, in the official view, a group of people owning a common estate and standing responsible for one another in some realms of conduct.[6] Beyond *chia* the state looked to the mourning grades (*wu fu*) (cf. Freedman 1958: 41ff., 101ff.) for a definition of the range within which an individual could be said to be involved in relationships such that his obligations to the state were modified. That is, we may say that at the levels of *chia* and *wu fu* double loyalty was institutional-

[6] There is a fascinating example in Bodde & Morris 1967: 193 of the way in which this official view could get worked into judicial reasoning. When two or more men were clearly not members of a single domestic group, but it was desirable to treat them as though they were in order to increase the penalty awardable to somebody who had wronged them, then the term *chia* might be stretched to cover even more or less temporary associations between men provided they could be said to have economic resources in common.

ised. In the eyes of the state, a Confucian state, kinship was eminently respectable and could be held in some ways to cut across obligations to the sovereign. (Of course, the conflict between the two kinds of obligation could be rationalised away by asserting that a man who fulfilled his kinship obligations was by that fact a good and loyal subject.)[7]

So far we can be carried along in the argument by the standard sources. But there is more to it than that. Confucianists did not usually philosophize about lineages (as against *chia* and kinship in general),[8] but when they were officers in the bureaucracy and had, especially in south-eastern China, to deal with lineages, they treated them as respectable entities which embodied, on a larger scale than *chia* and *wu fu*, the Confucian virtue of kinship solidarity. Moreover, the lineage could be looked to to police itself and help in the smooth collection of taxes. Whatever view we may take of the range of duties and functions of the Chinese county (*hsien*) mandarin, it is obvious that the maintenance of public order and tax-collecting were the two basic activities. His legal duties were defined in such a way as to make public peace to a large degree measurable by the absence of court business. Small-scale disorder which was contained within local units (villages or local lineages) and which could be prevented from being evidenced in the *yamen* (the mandarin's court) was no disorder;[9] and the administrator was not tempted to go out looking for trouble. Accordingly, lineages capable of managing their own affairs and blocking off attempts to raise disputes to the level of the *yamen* were certainly a very good thing. In a like manner, while in theory every individual owed a duty to the state to pay his taxes to its representative, a well-organised lineage capable of producing the necessary yield from its members was clearly an administrative convenience.

We shall have to go on from this point to consider the limits to the state's tolerance of lineage organisation, but for the moment we must turn back to the internal order of the lineage to understand how it articulated with the external order. There has been a

[7] See Fung 1949: 18–30 for some interesting observations on the relationship between *hsiao*, 'filial piety' (and, by extension, duties to kin), and *chung*, loyalty to the sovereign. At pp. 29f. he says that conflict might sometimes occur between the two classes of duty, and then 'it was the duty of the son as a son that should receive first consideration'.
[8] But note Chan, 1967; 227ff., and Baller, 1892: 19–25.
[9] Cf. J. Cohen, 1966: 1215ff. on 'extrajudicial mediation'.

tendency (which in part arises from a confusion of lineage with family) to speak of lineages in China as though, when they were more than small groups, they were characteristic of the rich and the powerful and not to be found among the poor and the weak. That view shuts off a more rewarding one: the most interesting feature of Chinese lineages is that they were often heterogeneous in their membership. While it makes good sense to speak of some lineages being richer or stronger than others, the richer and the stronger the lineage the more it was likely to be differentiated into rich and poor, strong and weak. One must be careful to distinguish between statements about the standing of lineages and statements about the standing of families and individuals within lineages. Of course, many individuals and families in rich and strong lineages were poorer than individuals and families in poor and weak lineages. The differences within strong lineages were an aspect of the system of uneven (asymmetrical) segmentation discussed earlier in the essay. Riches and power accumulated unevenly in the lineage. Members of rich segments had better access to education and to the sources of power outside the lineage, and greater opportunity to exercise control over lineage affairs as a whole.

We have now to make a distinction between political leaders and ritual elders. Within a lineage and within each of its formal segments the oldest man in the most senior generation was the ritual elder; that is, he took the chief place in the performance of the periodic rites of ancestor worship, either at the ancestral hall altar (or shrine) or the key tomb. That role was given genealogically. But the roles of political and economic management were held by lineage and segment elites formed by men whose standing rested, not upon genealogical position, but upon their riches and their ties with the greater social world beyond the lineage. In some lineages, the powerful political leaders belonged to what is often nowadays referred to as the 'gentry': the titled scholars, who had competed successfully in the state examinations or who had bought themselves equivalent titles. As soon as we picture to ourselves a lineage in which there were both actual and potential mandarins on the one hand, and uneducated farmers on the other, we realise that we are dealing with something very different from the homogeneous rich lineage that as a false stereotype sometimes infects the literature.

A very few lineages included in their ranks men who had attained the very highest positions in their society; and at once we see another crucial aspect of Chinese society. The study of lineage organisation shows us, as does that of other features of the society, that no hard and fast distinction can be drawn between rural and urban society (cf. Cartier 1970). One does not expect lineage organisation to take the same form in town and country (see Baker, in press, and Fried, 1966), and it is obvious that urban conditions inhibit its development; but to move from countryside to town in traditional Chinese society was not to leave one social world and enter another. We are certainly not studying a society in which all that was rich and sophisticated was in the towns and all that was poor and naive in the villages. True, the richer and more educated a man, the more likely he was to have dealings in the towns, and even perhaps establish a house there. (Cf. Elvin 1970: 105f. on cities as centres of 'landlord power'.) But he was not by those facts alienated from his rural home. On the contrary, home was in the village with which his ancestors were linked, and he was likely to spend a great part of his life there, even if, as an official, his work often took him elsewhere. Both through the hierarchy of administrative centres (from the county seat upwards to the imperial capital) and the hierarchy of market places (cf. Skinner 1964-65, and 1971: 272ff.), the lineage was linked into the wider society by its politically and economically more mobile members. These were the men through whom lineages could maintain their position and assert their rights vis-à-vis the county mandarin and those who stood above him. That county mandarin might have within his jurisdiction one or more lineages that included members who outranked him or, at any rate, who were strong enough to prevent him exercising fully the authority vested in him by the state.

It follows that a poor family in a powerful lineage was inferior and exploitable at home yet in a privileged position against the wider world. The riches, renown, and power that from one point of view were the prerogative of the lineage elite were from another the property of the lineage as a whole, all its members sharing in it. Whom the elite might oppress at home they might protect abroad. They might effectively rob the poor of their rightful share in the lineage estates and rig the rules about ritual privileges so as to monopolise them, but in his transactions with the members of other lineages the poor man in a strong lineage could stand with powerful co-members behind him.

Having to deal with organised lineages, led often by powerful men, the state found itself in a dilemma. Clearly, agnatic organisation was to be approved; it demonstrated its orthodox virtue by the ceremonialised piety of the ancestral sacrifices and the lavish care of graves. At the level of ideas and ritual no exception could be taken. But say a lineage grew to be a great power on the local scene, engaging in acts of organised violence against other lineages and extending the area of its control; and say, even worse, that such a rising lineage began to form, along with other lineages of its surname in the area, a superordinate lineage by manipulating genealogies and setting up higher-order tombs and shrines; why then, the state took fright, and what had up to then been agnation respectable became at once agnation perilous. In other words, the Chinese state was responsible for creating a stick for beating its own back. It legitimated agnatic organisation. It gave power to lineages by *de facto* recognition of their corporate nature; it fed the power of lineages by providing their elites with influence and prestige. And always the state ran the risk of that power being turned against its own interests—whence the screams against fraudulent genealogies and the sporadic attempts to put down interlineage fighting. On that last topic I have written a good deal (Freedman 1958: 105–12; 1966: 8f., 104–15) and I do not want to go over familiar ground, but I might add to the evidence a passage from Alabaster (1899), a source I have not before used.[10] He writes of the 'clan fights' which 'occur especially in Kwangtung and Fukien' that they are

the direct result of the clan system...and cause perpetual turbulence and often great loss of life. Many allusions to these occurrences appear in the Peking Gazette, and the evil seems to be an organised one, not capable of effective repression by the administration. Even where a case attains to judicial process, the employment of false witnesses, and assumption of responsibility by the whole clan, renders it a hard matter to reach a fair issue (p. 451)..In the south of China special provision is made for the repression of the clan fights which flourish there, and care has been taken when dealing with affrays to settle whether they come under

[10] I remember that I have Professor Lawrence Crissman (at the time a graduate student at the London School of Economics) to thank for drawing my attention to the relevance of Alabaster's book to my interest in this theme.

these special clauses or not. That there are a number of people engaged, and that one side belong to one part of the country and the other side to another, does not necessarily constitute a clan fight. The points to determine are whether there was a feud to start with, whether the fight was premeditated, whether men were hired to take part in it (there being regular professional fighters—free lances—open to engagement), and whether the factions went armed to the field. When it appears from these facts that it was a deliberate clan fight and not a chance or ordinary affair, the organiser will be held responsible as well as those actually taking part in the fight—the punishment being regulated by the number of men there were engaged upon the side of the organiser, and also by the number killed upon the other side. Nor are *both* sides to be brought under the clauses, unless the fight was prearranged between them—the attacking side ordinarily coming under the operation of the special statute (pp. 459f.).

I would add only that the most bellicose lineages were the great ones (a fact still to be observed in the Hong Kong New Territories, although of course there the hostilities are more effectively restrained); and the great ones were precisely those most closely bonded to the state. What power the state gave them they could turn against it. In the field of lineage organisation we are able to see in the clearest light the fact that political order in traditional Chinese society was based upon a tension between ties to the state and ties to kin. To make the most of both called for the exercise of great political skill.

I want now to turn to the big question of the uneven distribution of deep and large lineages in China. The first point to be made is that the evidence flies in the face of any theory that makes developed lineage organisation the primeval pattern of Chinese society. (Since most writers on China recognise that the lineage as we now know it did not develop until the beginning of the imperial period and was not generalised within Chinese society for some centuries, it would perhaps be better to say that the evidence contradicts a theory that at some unspecified time in the past all Chinese were grouped in deep lineages, the smaller agnatic units now to be seen being taken as broken remnants.[11]) The fact is that

[11] Ho (1968: 32) furnishes an exact date (1050) for the creation of the 'modern-type patrilineal clan..which became more and more common during the Ming and Ch'ing, especially in the southern provinces'. The historical reference is presumably to the institution of the Fan 'charitable estate' about 1050. See Twitchett 1959. One might imagine a somewhat less abrupt incursion of the lineage into Chinese history.

developed lineage organisation appears precisely where Chinese society is most recently established and appears to be largely absent where it is longest established. It is not for nothing that the provinces of Fukien and Kwangtung, on the south-eastern border of the country and comparative latecomers to Chinese civilisation, are singled out for mention whenever the subject comes up; they are not alone in presenting evidence of developed lineage organisation on a wide scale, but they form the region where that model of organisation has been most persistently followed. The lineages that we are still able to study (see especially Potter 1968, and Baker 1968) because of the academically happy accident that Britain acquired a 99-year lease of a large part of Hsin-an county in 1898 and made of that acquisition the New Territories of Hong Kong, are creations of the last 800 years, many of them tracing their points of origin to times much closer to the present day than that. Through the evidence we have accumulated, we can see them establishing themselves in unoccupied areas, expanding their agricultural lands, fortifying their settlements with formidable walls, watchtowers, and moats, and coming to dominate, politically and economically, the lesser lineages growing up around them. The south-east was a frontier area where new land could be brought into cultivation and where state control was weak. Lineages could build up large holdings, many of them entailed in lineage and segment estates, and at the same time amass huge local power. The area has one further feature that may be relevant to the problem under discussion: its agriculture is based upon wet rice, a highly productive crop that has allowed land to be set aside in inalienable estates—those estates which, as we have seen, lie at the heart of the segmentary system.

That argument I have set out before (Freedman 1966: 159-64). It has been taken up by Potter (1970): drawing upon his field data from the Ping Shan Tang lineage in the New Territories and other sources, he adds commercial development to the budget of factors (wealth created in trade being invested in land) and concludes, in his penultimate paragraph, as follows:

The evidence represented by the Ping Shan data would support a hypothesis that the strongest lineages would tend to be found in the agriculturally most productive two-crop rice regions of China, in frontier regions far from central government control, and especially in areas where industry and commerce were highly developed. The weakest lineages would tend to be located in North China's poorest agricultural areas, in long-settled areas where effective government control was present, and in regions characterized by subsistence agriculture and little commercial development. Moreover, in all areas lineage organization would tend to be weaker under strong dynasties and stronger in interregnal periods or under weak dynasties (p. 138).

But the argument has come in for some comment from another quarter. The general view of the Chinese lineage I formed long before I had ever studied in the New Territories was confirmed (especially in regard to lineage segmentation) by the anthropologists who went to the New Territories with lineage organisation at the centre of their attention. The first was Potter (1968, 1969, 1970), the second Baker (1966, 1968); and other material collected in the New Territories has, along with data picked up here and there in the sources on the mainland of China, tended to reconfirm the general analysis. But there is another important group of anthropologists at work on Chinese society: the largely American group concentrating, so far as field study is concerned, on Taiwan; and from their researches, particularly those by M. Cohen (1969) and Pasternak (1968a, 1968b, 1969), there has emerged a significantly different picture. It is not that what they say controverts what has been said about lineage structure on the mainland of China (including of course the New Territories of Hong Kong); on the contrary, they accept it by and large as part of the historical background of the Chinese groups they have studied in the more recently settled Taiwan. The new element in their work lies in its tracing of a different process of lineage formation. Cohen and Pasternak, both working among Taiwan Hakkas, have pointed out that when lineages have emerged they have done so by the amalgamation of previously distinct agnatic groups. As I understand their argument, in the earlier phase of settlement of the island, and still today very generally, families proliferated and dispersed in such a way that they were unlikely to be included within some wider agnatic grouping. Local communities were composed of heterogeneous kinship elements. But in some cases a collection of groups of the same surname, scattered over an area, might be brought organisationally together within the framework of a lineage endowed with an estate, even though it was not possible to arrange the various agnatic components of the new unit in a coherent genealogical scheme. Whereas, therefore, the process of lineage formation on the mainland is seen as a matter of segmentation—a small agnatic group growing and gradually becoming differentiated internally by the emergence of new segments, and segments within segments, as in the simple model constructed earlier in this essay—in Taiwan, lineages appear to have come about by a process of fusion, independent units being welded together. To put the matter differently: if frontier conditions on the mainland encouraged small agnatic groups to grow into large ones, each such group striving to increase the territory under its control and maintaining its territorial compactness, frontier conditions in Taiwan (in a more recent movement of southern Chinese that took them over the water to new land) led families to disperse and then later to regroup themselves in fabricated lineage groups that tied together small units scattered over a large area. In mainland Fukien and in Kwangtung the association between agnatic grouping and local grouping was tight; emigrants from those same provinces moving to Taiwan built up a system in which agnatic ties and territorial ties cut across each other.

That is an interesting difference (although it is not clear to me yet how far the alternative model applies to non-Hakka in Taiwan). But it cannot escape our attention that the process of lineage formation in Taiwan, as Cohen and Pasternak have described it, corresponds closely to the process on the mainland by which local lineages were grouped into higher-order lineages by genealogical manipulation and the setting up of tombs and shrines. In other words, a process of lineage regrouping can be seen to have taken place both on the mainland and in Taiwan, but it appears to operate on localised lineages in the one case and on small groups of related families in the other. These two models of lineage formation having now been confronted, it will be found (I suggest) that they are both relevant to all parts of China, and that the closer we look at the evidence (the written genealogies and other sources), the more we shall discover that the Taiwan Hakka pattern is to be detected on the mainland, and that what I have described as the mainland pattern is also discernible in Taiwan. A more sophisticated model of the foundation and growth of the Chinese lineage than that set out earlier in this essay might then include, before the phase of elaborate internal differentiation, a phase during which scattered elements are brought together (territorially and genealogically, or at least genealogically) to form the lineage to begin with. If we re-examine the data on the Hong Kong New Territories (see e.g. Aijmer 1967: 53–9 on Hakka, and Baker 1968: 28–30 on the early history of the Sheung Shui lineage) we may be able to benefit from the analyses made by M. Cohen and Pasternak.[12]

The latter's work also bears upon one of my earlier arguments— to knock it down. In *Chinese Lineage and Society* (1966: 159–62) I ventured to suggest that the establishment of irrigation works in pioneer conditions may have promoted large-scale lineage organisation: dense populations were built up in small areas; the joint investment of labour in bringing new land into cultivation led to the setting up of undivided (lineage and segment) estates. In his 1969 paper Pasternak says that when a frontier area is being opened up and the population is heterogeneous (as it was in Taiwan), co-operative irrigation works will be undertaken by non-agnates, and the significant associations that people form will not of course be based upon agnation. Moreover, when government control is weak and the pioneers have to fend for themselves, the alliances created will be among non-agnates, since the population is agnatically heterogeneous to start with. He writes (p. 554):

It seems to me..that in the absence of effective state force, ethnic conflict in frontier situations might well encourage an initial articulation and cooperation of families and individuals along primarily territorial and ethnic lines rather than in terms of kinship..

..where the frontier situation involves an entrenched ethnic group, challenged by an initially less structural [sic] immigrant group, the emergence of multi-surname villages and non-kin associations of various sorts would be more likely than the formation of single-surname villages and large, highly corporate, localized lineages. For purposes of offense and defense, such communities might themselves be integrated into higher-order associations or alliances through the extension of kin (agnatic and affinal) and non-kin (e.g., ethnic, linguistic, or religious) affiliations.

And at the end of this interesting paper Pasternak suggests the possibility that the full realisation of the patrilineal ideology (on which my own analysis has placed so much emphasis) may be part

[12] Now (October 1973) see Pasternak 1972 and 1973, noting in the latter work p. 261: 'Our [i.e., his and M. Cohen's] more recent joint work in the Meinung [Taiwan] area (1971–72) has convinced me that the two processes, aggregative and fissive [i.e., segmentary], are by no means mutually exclusive.'

of the second, not the first, phase of settlement in a frontier area. He may well be right. I am particularly pleased that he has mounted his argument against me on the basis of field experience in Taiwan which, together with the Hong Kong New Territories, is all we have for the intensive field study of traditional Chinese society. It is reassuring to know that the opportunities are at last being used.

The view from Taiwan reinforces the need to keep the study of the lineage within the framework of the study of *all* groups and relationships. Agnatic kinship is but one important axis along which Chinese society organised itself; and to understand its significance it must be taken in its full social context. The study of all modes of grouping and alignment—not only lineage but also village, marketing community, *hsiang*, secret society, cult, and so on—will show us how complex was the political system within which agnatic kinship played a role. But it is at this very point that the anthropologist, basing himself upon his own field study and those conducted by his colleagues in Hong Kong and Taiwan, finds himself checked in his progress by the nature of his evidence: much of the traditional political system is no longer there to be observed, and some of its remnants are tantalizingly obscure— unless the historian comes to the rescue.

I shall take an example from my own experience. In 1963 I carried out a field survey of the New Territories and wrote a report which contained, in the section dealing with political matters, an account of a system which, at the time of the British takeover in 1899, covered a large part of the area with a network of village-groupings under the name of *yüeh* (Cantonese: *yeuk*), 'compacts/ treaties'. I went on to show how one aggregate of such *yüeh* was involved in the foundation of a new market at Tai Po in the early 1890s and how it had persisted into modern life (Freedman 1963: 5–10; and cf. 1966: 82–9, and Groves 1965). *Yüeh* and another term for a local grouping, *tung* ('cave'), puzzled me greatly, but I was then in no position to start an historical enquiry that would show the extent to which the terms in these specialised uses were general in China, or the significance of the groupings in the nineteenth-century political system. But (1963: 9) I linked up *yüeh* with *hsiang-yüeh* (the public lecture system) and sketched the interpenetration of *hsiang-yüeh*, *pao-chia*, and *li-chia* (the last two being governmental systems of grouping for security and taxation). I wrote:

It is on record that in places in Kwangtung the heads of 'hsiang-yüeh' assumed roles of local leadership in such a way as to take command of local affairs. In addition, 'hsiang-yüeh' were used as a setting for organising 'regiment and drill corps' ('t'uan-lien') for local defence, and it is an interesting speculation that just as the 'ke yüeh hsiang-yung', the village braves of the several *yeuk*, rallied to the defence of Canton against the British in 1842 [a slip for 1841], so we might find on closer inspection that some of the armed resistance to the first British in the New Territories was bound up with the Ts'at Yeuk [the seven *Yüeh*, the grouping associated with the founding of the new Tai Po market] and other *yeuk*-complexes.[13]

That was an anthropological guess, and later research, historical and anthropological, has shown it to be right. A few years after my New Territories Report was written, an American historian published a remarkable study of political developments in the Canton region in the middle of the last century (Wakeman 1966), and within another few years an anthropologist who had been at work in the Tai Po area of the New Territories produced a paper (Groves 1969) in which, basing himself on Wakeman's historical study and the recent anthropological work on Chinese lineage organisation and marketing systems, he demonstrated from the British documents on the takeover of the New Territories in 1899 that the armed resistance to the British was merely one example of a nineteenth-century pattern in which lineage and local organisations were meshed to produce a social grouping able to mobilise sizable forces of village men for local defence.

The parallels with the Kwangtung militia of the 1840s and '50s are evident. Scarcely three weeks lapsed between the first meetings...and the final battle on 18 April [1899]. Within this time, over 2,000 armed men were mobilised and put into the field. As was the case half a century earlier, this was accomplished by means of well established and enduring sets of relationships that reflected the close-knit social structure and organisation of rural Kwangtung province (p. 58).

[13] I was relying for historical data mainly on Hsiao 1960; and I had consulted (by letter) Professor D. C. Twitchett, then at the School of Oriental and African Studies, London, and been advised in Hong Kong itself by Mr James Hayes. Cf. the corresponding passage in Freedman 1966: 87 (with note 2) which shows a slightly later attempt to discover something about *hsiang-yüeh*. As for the mystifying *yüeh*, I was later to find brief but interesting information in Wakeman 1966: 144, 148, and Kuhn 1970: 95 (where, by the way, my own data on the subject are fed into the historical analysis), 169. Kuhn refers to *hsiang-yüeh* at pp. 136f.

Wakeman, the historian, drew for his interpretation in part on the anthropological work on Chinese lineage organisation; Groves, as we have just seen, drew upon Wakeman; since then, a further American historical work (Kuhn 1970), matching Wakeman's in its freshness and importance, builds upon both historical and (of course to a much lesser extent) anthropological research to treat the question of the militarisation of Chinese society in the middle of the nineteenth century. The interaction between the history and the anthropology of Chinese society has been set going.[14]

From this new work, full to overflowing in its significance for our understanding of Chinese society, I want to extract one political point for comment. Looking at the British official papers on conditions in the New Territories at the time of the takeover, I was disturbed by Stewart Lockhart's account of local self-government, for it conflicted both with my general view of Chinese government at the local level and with my understanding of the hierarchy of local units in Chinese society. In 1899 Lockhart wrote:

The gentry and elders in the village council determined summarily cases of theft, disputes about land, domestic squabbles, and cases of debt. As a rule the decision of that council is accepted as final. But if either of the parties to a case is dissatisfied, he can appeal to a council of the Tung, or to a general council, made up of representatives of the different Tung..In addition to a council of a Tung there is a general council for the whole of the Tung [= east] Lo or Eastern Section..styled the Tung [= east] Ping Kuk [Mandarin: *tung p'ing ch'ü*]..If the decision of the council of the Tung, or of the General Council is not regarded as satisfactory, an appeal lies to the magistrate of the district (Hayes 1962: 9f.).[15]

I confessed myself 'sceptical about some of Lockhart's data on local organisation and local tribunals, but I have not yet marshalled enough historical material to be able to enter into a debate on these topics' (Freedman 1963: 10; and cf. Freedman 1966: 81f.). Nor would I have made any progress with the problem, try as I might, without the new historical research by Wakeman and Kuhn.[16] In the event, Groves's paper (1969: 40f.) made the

[14] For another example of the influence of anthropology on history see the work of the historian Professor Johanna M. Meskill (Meskill 1970a and 1970b).
[15] Hayes (1962) presents the picture of the political system as Lockhart painted it.
[16] Although a more careful reading of Lo 1965 (especially pp. 89f., 106) might have put me on the right track.

problem vanish: what Lockhart was clearly describing—one can say 'clearly' now that Groves has written his analysis—was the *t'uan-lien*, local militia system, which seems to have marked a sharp turn in the political life of China from the 1840s onwards.

Although its origins go further back in time (Wakeman 1966: 23f.; Kuhn 1970: 41ff., 64) a system of gentry-organised local militia was effectively begun by the Opium War.[17] The government feared this militia and with good reason, but, especially because of its role in the resistance to the British in 1849 at Canton, to the rebels in the Red Turban rising of 1854–55, and to the British and the French in the Arrow War (which began in 1856), *t'uan-lien* seems to have established itself as a feature of, and a mutation within, the political system of China. Up to that point in Chinese history the control exercised by the government over the countryside rested, *inter alia*, upon the partial dissociation of the local gentry from the people among whom they lived. That gentry had a political role vis-à-vis the local representatives of the government (chiefly the county mandarins) by its informal expression of local opinion and its mediation between the governors and the mass of the governed;[18] but it was not until the *t'uan-lien* system grew to be accepted as legitimate that the gentry were permitted to engage actively and officially in the organisation of local political life and to put themselves into offices within structures over which the government in effect had little control. As the historians have pointed out, the breakdown of national unity in the early twentieth century had among its causes the weakening of government control by the rise of the political power of the gentry in the middle of the last century. (See e.g. Ichiko 1968: 299 for a succinct statement.)

But who precisely were the local gentry? Scholars unfamiliar with the historical and sociological writing on China need to be told that this question cannot be answered from a general survey of sinological opinion; the definition of 'gentry' is hotly debated (and an outsider might well wonder why so much fuss is made

[17] There is of course nothing very recent about military organisation as such in rural China. Cohen (1973) for example, refers to a Hakka system in south Taiwan that goes back to 1685; and Skinner (1971: 280) writes: 'The *t'uan-lien* or local militia.. were normally formed in periods of dynastic crisis and disbanded in the wake of successful pacification by the succeeding dynasty.'
[18] Cf. Michael 1964: xxii–xxvi, and Wakeman 1966: 29–31. And for a recent assessment of the role and functions of the local administrator see Watt 1970.

over a label, and not even a Chinese one at that). And, while the anthropologists sometimes intervene (cf. Fei 1953, and Freedman 1956, 1958: 53–60, 1966: 69f.), they cannot regard themselves as authorities. But I think we may safely say that however difficult it may be in particular cases definitively to assign the members of a given population to one or other of the two groups 'commoners and gentry', there was in traditional Chinese society a class of men who, by their close association with the literary values and their command of the literary skills upon which the governmental system was based, formed an elite in every largish area. Some of these *literati* were themselves officers of the government, but now resident at home because they were between postings or on (obligatory) mourning leave. Some were retired or about-to-be-appointed government officials. A much greater number were *sheng-yüan* or *chien-sheng*, that is to say, titled *literati* not yet of a status to qualify for government office. And of course one must take into account the members of *literati* families who for one reason or another had not attained even to the standing of *sheng-yüan* or *chien-sheng*,[19] and the members of non-*literati* families who by their worldly success had in some way assimilated themselves to the gentry.

The privileges and standing of the gentry within the communities where they lived were based historically on their constituting the pool of talent from which the bureaucracy was recruited. Their pursuits were gentlemanly,[20] even if at times commercial, and their general cultural style acted as a barrier which allowed them to live among and associate closely with 'commoners' without losing their distinctiveness. There was social mobility; the style could be acquired; the many who did not have it could observe it at fairly close quarters. And because in this

[19] On the definition, status, and functions of the gentry cf. Ichiko 1968: 297ff., and Fincher 1968: 187f. And note Kuhn 1970: 66f.: leaders at the lowest level of defence organisation in the *t'uan-lien* system, 'were often lower degree holders—*sheng-yuan* or *chien-sheng*—or those degree aspirants, the *t'ung-sheng*. Such leaders might also be holders of purchased brevet rank. But the leadership of simplex *t'uan* was by no means confined to men with formal degree status, and we can find in the record many examples of commoners who, by virtue of their wealth and community influence, were functionally indistinguishable from titled scholars in community defense.'

[20] Moore (1969: 167) points out: 'Though the scholar-landlords lived in the countryside, unlike their English and German counterparts (even *some* of their Russian and French ones), they seemed to have played no part whatever in the actual work of cultivation, not even a supervisory one.'

fashion the gentry were in but not entirely of their local communities they were no serious threat to the regime. But the extensive local militarisation of Chinese society in the middle of the nineteenth century set the gentry up as local organisers;[21] hitherto the rule of 'avoidance' had prevented them from exercising authority where they were at home; the kind of local hierarchy described by Lockhart at the end of the century could now develop.

One other aspect of *t'uan-lien* is worth comment. Skinner's work on marketing systems (1964-65) has made us sensitive to the difference between what might be called the official and social topography of China: administrative maps drew their lines for marking out jurisdictions which might fit only roughly, if they fitted at all, with the conformation of communities and their groupings. The advent of a local militia system, based upon previous groupings of gentry and the local communities (lineages, villages, and aggregations of lineages and villages) to which they belonged, introduced the social map of China into the official map.[22]

The county (*hsien*) and its official sub-divisions, *hsiang*, together with *pao-chia* and *li-chia* were now not the only legitimate political segments of the society. And I repeat what I said on an earlier occasion (only I had then no clear idea of the historical causes involved): when the British took over the island of Hong Kong as a result of the Opium War, they began by imitating the *pao-chia* system; when they assumed the administration of the New Territories fifty-seven years later they looked to the social map (*yüeh* included) which had by then clearly come to be taken as defining officially accepted areas. (Cf. Freedman 1966: 82 n. 2.)

As an anthropologist one starts from the Chinese lineage and one finishes up on the grand theme of the disintegration of the traditional Chinese political order. Lineage is but one form of organisation and needs to be seen in the context of all other forms. One advances up to the limit of one's competence as an anthro-

[21] In Wakeman's view (Wakeman 1966: 115f.) the events of the 1840s in the Canton region led, via the creation of the system of local militia, to a slackening of the bonds holding rich and poor together in the same lineages. 'As this process went on, the peasantry became disaffected. Greater and greater numbers began to join secret societies that transcended the clan.' Kuhn 1970: 79 n. 32, challenges the truth of this analysis. It certainly would be difficult to test.

[22] Note the remarks in Kuhn 1970: 101f. and 104.

pologist and then turns for enlightenment to the historian. It is not of course for me to speak for the historians, but it is clear enough that they, symmetrically, are on the look-out for data, clues, and lessons from the anthropologists. As I write this essay (August 1971) hopes are being expressed for the resumption of anthropological field study in mainland China. If in that next phase of the social anthropology of China the field workers become again, as they were in the thirties, so intoxicated with the present that they forget that China has a past, they will slide back from the advance in sinological anthropology that has been made, doubtless improbably enough, by its being confined to Taiwan and the Hong Kong New Territories.[23]

[23] Cf. Freedman 1970: 10f. I wish to thank Dr Hugh Baker, Professor Myron Cohen, Mr Robert Groves, and Professor Arthur Wolf for the comments they made on drafts of this essay. I have not been able to take all the comments they made into account here, and I hope to profit by them on another occasion.

6

The free women of Kinshasa:[1] prostitution in a city in Zaïre

JEAN S. LA FONTAINE

To contribute to a *Festschrift* is a somewhat daunting task. There is always the possibility that the quality of the offering may make it appear less of a tribute than the writer intended. In this case the problem is the more formidable in that Professor Lucy Mair's own work is so scholarly, intelligent and clear. Several of my articles owe much to her careful reading and since, by the etiquette which surrounds these occasions, she has not read this one, I am only too aware that it may contain some slip-shod phrase or badly formulated argument that she would certainly have eliminated in draft. However such considerations could not outweigh my pleasure in offering here my token of gratitude and affection to a respected colleague and a good friend.

Prostitution is commonly regarded as an index of social pathology; it has been seen as the unfortunate by-product of divorce and desertion, of poverty and the lowering of moral standards. In spite of the work of Henriques whose detailed and scholarly study (1962-68) has demonstrated for a wide range of societies, both modern and historical, that the evidence points rather to prostitution as a normal feature of certain types of societies, it is common to find prostitution regarded as deviant and socially destructive 'problem' behaviour. In Africa the prevalence of the phenomenon in the new towns and cities of the continent has been taken as an 'index' of the destruction of traditional sexual

[1] Earlier versions of this paper were read at seminars in the departments of anthropology of Manchester and Sussex Universities. I was grateful for the invitation to set out some of my urban field material and profited greatly from the stimulating discussions for which I thank the members of both seminars. The ex-Belgian Congo is now the Republic of Zaïre but as the English adjective is clumsy, I have retained 'Congolese' for its inhabitants.

mores, of 'detribalisation' and of the conflicts experienced by individuals faced by radical social change. The values of members of the societies in question often support this view; they lament the passing of the old days when all women were virtuous and marriage the only form of sexual association. Together with this view it is common to find that the prostitute is accorded low status and often serves as a stereotype of undesirable qualities. Yet in those same societies, women who are identified as prostitutes may enjoy considerable prestige and influence. Such a society is the urban society of Kinshasa, in the ex-Belgian Congo (La Fontaine 1970; Little 1971). As Henriques remarks (1963: 306) 'The problem becomes one of finding an explanation to account for both the high and low status enjoyed by the normal [i.e. non-religious] prostitute in different societies.'

Henriques' own solution to the problem is couched in terms of the interplay of several factors: the nature of family life and changes in it, the nature of the sexual ethos in a particular society, and its demographic features. He remarks (1968: 309). 'While we would support the contention that economic factors are not the main ones concerned in the recruitment of women to prostitution, there are exceptional circumstances in which they appear to be so.' He cites post-World War II Germany as an example of these exceptional circumstances. My own argument will differ from that of Henriques which I have sketched in here, for I consider economic factors more important than he appears to do. The argument that poverty drives women to prostitute themselves is based, ultimately, on the unverified value-judgement that it is a desperate act, undertaken not from choice but from necessity. Sociologically this bias obscures rather than illuminates. Poverty is not the only way in which economic factors influence behaviour. I take the view that it is preferable to start from the more objective starting-point, that a 'prostitute provides a sexual service' (Henriques 1963: 305). It thus becomes relevant to consider why the service is provided. In Kinshasa as in many societies prostitutes are neither slaves nor coerced, either by organisations or individual pimps. I shall hope to show that becoming a prostitute is a strategy, not necessarily irreversible nor unaccompanied by other strategies, which women in the urban situation may choose. This approach will, I hope, illuminate the more interesting sociological features of the phenomenon.

THE FREE WOMEN OF KINSHASA 91

Before setting out the ethnographic material it is necessary to establish the general background against which it must be considered. At the time to which this account refers (1962-63) Kinshasa had suffered major political and social changes. The Congo's rapid accession to Independence in 1960 had been followed by political strife which still continued, although the town and its immediate hinterland was under government control. Following the disturbances of 1960-61, much of the country's economy was dislocated so that Kinshasa, from having been a major entrepot and a centre of light industry and processing, had few major sources of employment for the large urban population, a substantial proportion of which had been born there. This population was nearly doubled in the immediate post-Independence period by the large influx of refugees from the disturbed country and migrants seeking work whom Belgian rural/urban policy had hitherto prevented from moving to town. By the end of 1963 the population had passed the million mark. Goods of all sorts vanished from the shops, except for periodic shipments and there were regular shortages of major food-stuffs. Yet in spite of this crisis situation, many features of town life showed a remarkable continuity with the past. Such conditions served to exaggerate certain features of the urban system, rather than introduce new structures.

Throughout the history of Kinshasa's development, there have been fewer women than men in the city. Although the latest census (1958) showed a ratio approaching a normal one, in the older age-groups there is a sexual imbalance (La Fontaine 1970: 33-6). If the population is divided by tribal grouping the imbalance becomes greater in certain tribes, whereas in a few, such as the Luba, women outnumber men. There is a firm preference for marriage within the tribal group although socio-economic status is becoming an important factor. As a result many young men are unmarried through lack of a suitable spouse. Many married men leave wives and families in their village when they move to town, thus swelling the numbers of men likely to provide the clientele of prostitutes. This is explicitly recognised by men and women; prostitution is associated with an urban way of life. The existence of unattached men in the town is seen by Congolese as a major cause of prostitution.

As a corollary to the view of prostitution as an urban

phenomenon, there is a tendency for men in Kinshasa to regard women who were brought up in town or who have lived there for any length of time as 'spoilt', flighty and immoral and devoid of the proper respect that a woman should show towards a husband. There is an expressed preference for marrying a girl brought up in the rural areas and some girls are sent back to their village kin when they reach puberty to protect them from the influences of city life and so enhance their chances of marrying well. Yet Congolese do marry city girls and there is wide-spread agreement that marrying an unsophisticated village girl does not guarantee a lasting marriage. The prevalence of divorce is a much-discussed feature of urban life.

Belgian administration has left its mark on the institution of marriage (La Fontaine 1970). While monogamy is the legal norm, there are various accepted forms of marriage: religious, civil and 'customary'. A wife's position has been strengthened economically although divorce is still relatively easy and desertion frequent. Belgian rulings on marriage, particularly that making polygamy illegal, were enacted to facilitate the administration of social services, such as family allowances, which were introduced at the same period. Moreover, the decree was supported by various indirect sanctions. For example, monogamy is a prerequisite for obtaining a building loan, a *parcelle*,[2] or a house in a housing estate. Family allowances, sickness benefits, and pension or insurance schemes all allow for only one legal wife. In addition, economic conditions make it impossible for all but a few to support more than one woman. Thus Belgian policy was strengthened by elements in the nature of urban social and economic organisation so that monogamy is now a very generally accepted feature of urban culture.

Since the Kongo peoples represent a large percentage of Kinshasa's population, and an even larger proportion of its married couples, the pattern of marriage among them is an influence which must be considered. A Kongo man pays bride-wealth for his wife, but obtains only limited rights over her and few over any children who, according to matrilineal rules, are affiliated to their mother's lineage. A woman retains rights over property belonging to her lineage, and, most important, may hold property in her own right. Her husband has no rights over this prop-

[2] A plot of land on which the lessee may build.

erty; she may dispose of it in any way she wishes without consulting him. However, she is obliged to provide the food for her household by her agricultural labour. Translated into town idiom, this means that a Kongo married woman may earn money independently of her husband and spend it as she wishes but should contribute to supplying the household's food. If husband and wife are on good terms she will buy additional things for the children or for the house, but she is not compelled to do so. A Kongo woman is thus accorded rights over her earnings and a measure of economic autonomy, which women of other tribes, for instance, are very much aware of.

Social conditions in Kinshasa reinforce the independence of most married women. Legally a wife has the right of maintenance for herself and her children and a life-interest in her husband's town property; she can sue to obtain these rights. Her economic dependence on her kin for support in the event of her husband's death or desertion is thus reduced. If she divorces him, the courts will award her the right to support for her and her children although she may find it difficult to implement the court decision. The general economic situation both provides an incentive for women to work, and enables them to do so. The absence of women's traditional agricultural occupations means that women generally have time to spare. (It is a constant complaint of men in Kinshasa that their wives have too little to do and get into mischief from boredom!) The city offers opportunities for earning money in various ways, and the scarcity of cash provides the inducement (see pp. 105-9). The insecurity of the labour market is another incentive of great importance. Most Congolese are skilled or semi-skilled wage labourers and the earnings are low and jobs insecure. The earnings of all members of a household are thus given considerable significance and affect their relations with each other.

Marriage is considered the proper career for all adult women, although trading as an occupation, particularly for married women, carries no stigma. The occupations open to women are few and not lucrative. Women are generally uneducated or have only a few years' schooling and most have no technical training. Such vocational training as existed for women was largely confined to domestic science courses although there were a few teachers of primary classes who were women. In more recent years the government has actively encouraged the employment of women as factory workers, white-collar workers and in wage-labour generally, with the aim of westernising them. However, there are few openings for the woman with little or no education. Such a woman had three viable alternatives: marriage, prostitution or petty trade. One woman interviewed expressed this clearly saying: 'I am a woman and have no learning; what work is there for me except prostitution?'

It is often said in Kinshasa that prostitution is widespread. It was a problem discussed by the Belgian administration and welfare societies prior to Independence. One authority estimated the number of *femmes libres* in the city as 4,321 in 1958.[3] From the few life histories of older women collected it appears that it is no recent phenomenon, although women who supported themselves entirely in this way were perhaps fewer before Independence. The incidence of prostitution is difficult to determine. While Belgian law required unmarried women over eighteen to register in order to obtain papers allowing them to remain in the city the figures of independent women so obtained were no clear guide to the numbers of women supporting themselves by prostitution. Indeed as my information shows, prostitution as a source of livelihood is often supplemented by other activities.

Although it is convenient to use the term 'prostitution' to refer to the means of livelihood of the majority of unattached women in Kinshasa, the meaning of the term as applied to the activities of Congolese women is inexact. Prostitution—in the European sense of the concept—undoubtedly exists, but prostitutes in the sense of women whose relations with their clients are temporary and on a purely commercial basis are in a minority. In general, the relation between a Congolese prostitute and her clients is both more lasting and less directly mercenary than that of her equivalent in European cities. The word *courtesan* is perhaps more appropriate: however, I shall continue to use the term, distinguishing where necessary between courtesan and prostitutes.

In Kinshasa all women who earn their living by liaisons with men are known as *femmes libres*—'free women'.[4] The term has the double connotation of loose-living and unattached. A

[3] Romaniuk 1961: 39. The female population at that time was 75,406 according to the official census.
[4] The Lingala term is *ndumba*.

femme libre has broken away from the control of her guardians, whether husband or kin. She is free from kin and clan obligations, and her life depends on her own intelligence and management. The verb *échapper* ('to escape') is often used in this connection, with the implication that a *femme libre* has taken a positive step to rid herself of the irksome restrictions of a traditional life; this probably represents the truth for many women. Although she is free of her kin (in that they no longer exercise authority over her), a *femme libre* does not always sever relations with them. She may need the security of good kin relations and in return she may be a source of financial help for them if she is successful. A number of such women interviewed for my Kinshasa survey (La Fontaine 1970: 23) support kinsmen and pay school fees for younger siblings. It is alleged that among some tribes young girls are encouraged to become *femmes libres* in order to bring in money for their families. One informant frequently heard his landlord admonishing his two adult unmarried daughters to stop wasting his money and earn something. The implication was that they should go on the streets rather than depend entirely on their father for support.

A number of young women come to the towns with the intention of earning their living as *femmes libres*. Seven out of the forty-nine female heads of households I interviewed gave this as their reason for coming to Kinshasa. But many women enter the profession when their relationship with a husband or permanent lover breaks up. Divorced women or girls who have been abandoned by a lover when they became pregnant often become *femmes libres*. Some educated girls with good jobs do not wish to marry young and become *femmes libres* of a sort, accepting more than one lover, or drifting from one affair to another. Such women are sometimes referred to as *femmes libres sérieuses* since their main source of income is from wage labour.

Despite the wide variety of social situations which lead women to become *femmes libres* and the variation in income and style of life which, as I shall show below, distinguishes the successful *femme libre* from her unsuccessful rival, the stereotype of behaviour associated with the status of *femme libre* is clear. It is often defined in opposition to the behaviour thought proper for a married woman: wife and prostitute are polar opposite statuses.[5] Married

[5] See also A. Cohen (1969a Ch. II) for a similar contrast among urban Hausa and Pons (1969) for Stanleyville (Kisangani).

women are expected to stay at home. They should only rarely visit bars or public gatherings except for necessary visits to the markets and the public celebrations of rites de passage such as marriages and funerals. Wives do not normally accompany their husbands to meetings or other social gatherings except to visit kin. A respectable woman must entertain her husband's guests if he brings them home but is expected to remain quiet in their presence and to concern herself with the provision of the food and beer that hospitality requires. She should conduct herself modestly and not take part in the men's conversation unless spoken to directly. In short, she is expected to conform to a traditional stereotype which does not include intimacy of companionship between spouses.

Yet men are accompanied by women at dances and in bars—not by their wives but by mistresses, concubines or temporary companions. These women are not bound by the rules of wifely modesty that restrain the behaviour of married women. They talk and laugh with the men, know the latest dances, gossip and joke, wear the latest fashions, Congolese or Western, and they patently enjoy being admired and looked at. Since they have more contact with the masculine world they often have a much greater sophistication than 'respectable' women. Many of them learn good French which few Congolese women speak properly and their poise and self-assurance is in striking contrast to the gaucherie of many married women forced into a modern world. Indeed they adopt the behaviour of western women, as they see it.[6] While most are uneducated and few are the chic cosmopolitaines of the ideal, yet in enacting the role of companions, prostitutes are also 'free' of traditional stereotypes of feminine subordination to a man; husband or father. It is thus intelligible why the label *'femme libre'* is applied to any woman who supports herself in a job, in the modern manner, be she ever so virtuous.

There are thus two conflicting ideals of feminine success current in the town: the traditional concept of the faithful wife who is a good housekeeper, contributes to the household income and rears healthy children, is the one which most men say they hold. Yet they also clearly admire the women who, as famed *femmes libres*, represent a new type of feminine success. Men can be, and often

[6] This claim is substantiated also by the fact that most ethnographers must describe the correct behaviour of the 'traditional' wife by negatives, as I have done, showing an implicit opposition to the model of such behaviour in our society.

are, ambivalent, forbidding behaviour in their wives that they approve in their mistresses, but for women there is normally a choice between two contrasting roles.

It is necessary to consider the impact of western culture still further, although I am far from arguing a simple cause and effect relationship between such values as I shall discuss and the existence of prostitution. The values support and underline the transactional character of interpersonal relations between the sexes, and as such are important in the analysis.

Young Congolese hold ideas on relations between men and women that—if one consults most writings on traditional African society—are totally new. They recognise the possibility or even desirability of relations between the sexes based on mutual attraction and qualities of character, which have little to do with the institutionalised bonds of marriage. Such love affairs may lead to marriage but often they do not. In essence, an affair is the voluntary association of two people in a relationship that is based on sentiment and no external constraints. It lasts as long as the persons concerned wish it to and includes the idea of companionship as well as sexual relations. Lovers enjoy themselves together visiting bars and markets. The educated write long letters exchanging news and their view of life, professing their sentiments in flowery language. Usually lovers sleep together and may set up house together and eventually get married. Often, however, love affairs are broken off, and most young men and girls have several affairs before they are married.

The conception of romantic love has been called a European idea, and in Kinshasa certainly songs and films in the European idiom serve to disseminate and encourage it. Advertising also acts as a medium for the education of the public in European values. The basic ideas behind advertisements are clearly perceived by Congolese and accepted. Physical attractiveness (smartness of dress, clearness of skin, vitality, etc.) results in sexual success, earning the envy and admiration of others. Sexual success, in men and women, demonstrates superiority over others. The successful man demonstrates his personal magnetism and wins prestige by having a numerous variety of attractive women as mistresses. Such values are firmly held by the younger generation of Congolese. Many take the claims of advertisements too literally (La Fontaine 1970: 184), and the wealthier young Congolese men and women spend considerable sums on creams, lotions, and charms in order to enhance sexual attractiveness.

These are new values, although personal success is not a new ideal in this society. The competitiveness of economic and political life is mirrored here in personal relations. The successful young man is the man with many mistresses; the successful young woman has many lovers among important men. This type of fame depends entirely on individual qualities rather than on the performance of a role. It is, perhaps, best described as a form of personal power or mana.

These new values support prostitution in that an essential feature of the love relationship as seen by Congolese is the gifts given to a woman by her lover. Affection, whether in friendship between men or between the sexes, is expressed in gifts. It is thus transactional, that is it is maintained entirely by the continued flow of reciprocity. As one young Congolese put it, talking about love affairs: 'Loving is giving.' A girl expects her lover to present her with the most expensive presents he can afford in order to show his appreciation of her. Indeed she may break off the relationship if she thinks he is not being generous enough, not necessarily for purely mercenary motives, but because he is not demonstrating the esteem and love he professes to have for her. These gifts are usually clothes and personal finery, but they may be cash presents; or if the man is rich, he may give such expensive luxuries as a radio, a refrigerator or even, if he is a Minister, a house. If a girl says to her lover that she wishes to buy such-and-such, she expects him to help her financially. A man accepts such demands for he benefits socially as well as personally. He demonstrates both his wealth and his generosity in his gifts to his mistress, as well as showing his feelings to her. It was said to me of one well-known young man: 'He is so generous he is mad. Whatever his girls ask for they get.' The tone was one of admiration. To a woman the value of the gifts she receives serves to proclaim her worth and personal success. To have many important men as lovers so that she becomes rich is a feminine ambition which many girls appear to hold and which receives reinforcement from the mass media. It is significant that the most successful courtesans are known as *vedettes* ('stars'), the term used for famous personalities in the entertainment world: the ideal types of modern success.

From 'amateur prostitution' of this sort to earning a living from the gifts of lovers is a short step, chronologically and logically. Indeed, many *femmes libres* do not stipulate a fixed price for their services, but ask for a 'loan' or let it be known that they value themselves at so much. In order to maintain a regular or more permanent arrangement a *femme libre* will expect frequent expensive presents. In order to become her sole lover with exclusive rights to her, a man will have to support his mistress entirely. *Femmes libres* pride themselves that they are not to be bought by just anyone, but generally conceal from their lovers the existence of other clients. Nevertheless the threat to encourage rivals may be used to exact generosity in giving.

Several types of *femmes libres* are generally recognised.[7] The characteristics by which informants classify them are character and behaviour as well as personal appearance. The most successful are the *vedettes*, or in Lingala, *Basi ya Kilo* (because they can buy meat and other luxuries by the kilo instead of in small quantities).[8] They are the outstandingly beautiful and vivacious women, elegant and elaborate in their dress, whose lovers are the most powerful and wealthy men of Kinshasa. They usually have only a few lovers who are regular clients and they will not entertain propositions from anyone who does not appear rich. According to Massamanga if approached by a man she considers beneath her, a *vedette* rebuffs him with a scornful glance or merely says: 'YOU? No.' She speaks less coarsely than lesser *femmes libres* and she is generally less vulgar in her behaviour.

The *vedette* is well established financially. She usually lives in a modern house with good furniture and a high degree of material comfort. She employs a servant to do her domestic work and to cook, whom, according to rumour, she pays very little. Some *vedettes* live in expensive hotels or apartments in the formerly European part of town. Their clientele may include ministers, members of the diplomatic corps in Kinshasa, officials of the United Nations or European businessmen. One I met owned and drove a small car and was about to go on a long holiday to Europe via Nigeria (at the invitation of a former lover). It is

[7] Much of my material in the section that follows was collected by my research assistant, the late Zephyren Massamanga. I am grateful for the permission he gave me to use it and deeply regret the death of an intelligent young man, who was training to become a sociologist, a profession for which he had already shown considerable aptitude.

[8] The phrase also applies to a woman of substance, who has social weight.

possible that *vedettes* take contraceptive precautions because they are said to prefer to have only a few children, whereas other *femmes libres* often have quite large families.[9] An alternative explanation is that prostitution may attract barren women whose lack of children has been the cause of their failure to achieve success in the role of married women.

Chambres d'hôtel are women who are prostitutes in the European sense of the word. They are said to be ready to accept any man who offers them their price and they have as many lovers as is feasible. Informants describe their appearance as slovenly, say they have little self-respect, and must find their clientele among the poorer men who give them little. They supplement their earnings by selling foodstuffs in the markets. In the evenings they sit in the more squalid bars, 'flamencos', waiting for clients. The earnings of these women fluctuate from day to day and week to week according to the demand for their services which relates to the availability of money. Their clientele is drawn from wage-earners who have little cash available except on pay-days, usually the middle and end of each month. They are said to fix their prices accordingly, charging according to what the market will bear at the time. The commercial nature of these transactions is thus clear and these women are generally scorned because they sell their bodies for money. That this pejorative phrase is not applied to *vedettes* is an indication that they are not considered in the same light.

The *vedettes* and the prostitutes represent the two extremes of success and failure in the career of an independent woman in Kinshasa. The majority of women should be classified, by appearance, behaviour and standard of living, at varying points between the extremes. They aim at becoming *vedettes* and endeavour to maintain a reputation for choosing their clients carefully. The richness (or otherwise) of their dress is an indication of their standing and degree of success. They are regular frequenters of bars but pay for their own drinks there. During the day they are often at the big markets where they can see and be seen, so that all such women are aware of the extremes, both desirable and undesirable.

[9] There is no stigma attached to a *femme libre*'s having children. On the contrary she is pitied or despised if she has none. Some of the *femmes libres* interviewed in my Kinshasa survey (La Fontaine 1970: 136) declared they would like to have children but did not wish to get married.

A woman's success as a *femme libre* partly depends on her ability to compete successfully with other women according to exacting ideals of elegance. Normally *femmes libres* do not dress differently from other women; they wear the *pagne* (wrap-around cloth) which is the Congolese national dress. The younger ones and *vedettes* do dress in Western style, some of them with considerable chic. A *femme libre* must take care of her appearance, both by attention to her figure and face as well as to her dress. She spends considerable sums on cosmetics, particularly on perfume and on hair-straightening, since this is considered elegant. She must also know how to wear her clothes. There are ways of wrapping the *pagne* which proclaim a woman's sophistication, or lack of it, to a Congolese observer, just as surely as the nature of a woman's dress classifies her in Western society. Fashion must be followed and successful women have large wardrobes. It is said that a *vedette* who dresses in Congolese style will take pride in having a new headscarf each week. In addition, a *femme libre* must adopt the comportment necessary to attract men. These details are learned from other women and by observation and the intelligent courtesan is quick to assimilate the knowledge necessary for success.

Since success in their profession is a matter of defeating rivals and having a certain amount of luck in contacts, *femmes libres* are said to rely on magic. Two types are common. First, there are talismans and charms to protect against the evil magic of others and to ensure good luck. The sellers of these charms are either foreigners (the Nigerians are important in this trade) or Kongo sorcerers, and their prices are often high. Nevertheless, a *femme libre* will pay up to 600 francs (about £4[10],) at the official rate of exchange, for a charm. (It appears that one of the dangers that charms are designed to ward off is venereal disease.) Men also buy good luck charms and magic to protect themselves against the evil intentions of their rivals whether in love or trade.

Secondly, *femmes libres* are said to employ magic to bind their lovers to them and make them generous. Again, this is usually prepared and sold by specialists, but a common feature is the inclusion of some of the woman's exuviae. A potion is added to the food a woman prepares for a regular client or lover in order to make him fall deeply in love with her and remain faithful.

[10] The legal minimum wage at that time was between 2,500 and 3,000 francs a month for a married man; there were many who received less than this.

Love-magic of this sort is also a common preoccupation of young men, who use it on a girl with whom they wish to have an affair and who is not interested or whose affections are engaged elsewhere.

Femmes libres form associations for mutual aid, similar to those formed by men (cf. La Fontaine 1970: 156–8). There are many of these associations, particularly in the Old City, which has a high proportion of independent women living there. They are based on locality, although it is alleged there are some which are tribally recruited. All those of which I have knowledge were tribally mixed. Members assist each other in times of need, both financially and with advice. For example, they may pool their resources to help each one in turn raise the capital required for new clothes. (Since an essential factor in a prostitute's success is her dress, the financial aspect of these associations is vital.) Knowledge of charms is spread among an association's members at meetings. Members of an association are also pledged to refrain from competing with one another; they often visit bars together, sometimes dressed alike. Many of these associations have an arrangement with the proprietor of a bar or shop which serves drinks. They get drinks on reduced terms because their presence at the bar attracts more clients so that the proprietor also profits from the association.

Most associations of *femmes libres* are small. Nevertheless, an insistence on formal organisation is the rule: the group chooses a name, such as *Etoiles de Léo* or *Elégantes de Léo*, and there is usually a president, a secretary, and a treasurer chosen for their professional success and strength of personality. (In some associations all members are title-holders.) Some associations choose a man as head; his role is to arbitrate in disputes between members and to act as adviser to the group. Since he must maintain impartiality, he must not take a mistress from the association. The choice often falls on the proprietor of a bar or restaurant, and he may be either a bachelor or a married man. In the latter case his wife's permission must be given. The position as leader of such an association gives a man the local reputation of being a success with women and a man of ability. It rarely affects a man's standing in the wider masculine world to any great degree.

These associations fill an important need in the life of an independent woman in Kinshasa. Usually deprived of permanent masculine financial support and protection, she is also often disowned by her immediate kin. Tribal associations are primarily masculine organisations and a woman cannot usually become a member in her own right. Some women come to Kinshasa with a lover and are then cast adrift there to support themselves when the liaison breaks up. The association has the dual role of providing a source of support in hard times (substituting for kin and clan) and being of professional advantage to its members. The associations serve as means of spreading conventions of dress and behaviour, initiating the newcomers into the sophistication of town life, the means of attracting clients, and of choosing a permanent patron. The associations thus impose group values on the new recruit and act as instruments of socialisation for a particular level of society. They are thus identical both in form and function with men's urban voluntary associations.

Women's associations of this sort are frequently short-lived. It is significant that *vedettes* scorn to join an association, as proof of their ability to support themselves without assistance and obtain masculine advice and help whenever they need it. Neither do the lowest prostitutes form associations. The association flourishes at the middle level of prostitution and members leave when they achieve success that places them above the level of their fellow members. If a woman does not observe the rule forbidding competition between members, she may either find herself expelled from the association, or, if she is a leading personality in it, the group breaks up.

Some associations are linked to organisations which have a degree of permanence and they are usually both larger and longer lived. The two main breweries ran clubs called the Friends of Polar and the Friends of Primus. Men who were members of these clubs were issued with caps or shirts advertising their beer. It is alleged that they supported associations of *femmes libres* who, in return for their presence at the bars controlled by the breweries, were given a certain amount of free beer. This practice appears to have lapsed, advertising being no longer necessary to dispose of the breweries' output, which falls short of the general demand. The other type of group to which women's associations are linked is the jazz band. These associations are fan clubs, but since unaccompanied women who frequent bars where these bands play are *femmes libres* (either established or in the making), the fan clubs are also groups of *femmes libres*. They usually have liaisons with members of the band, who encourage them partly for the publicity value.

These groups of *femmes libres* are the only associations of women which were not sponsored by a European-dominated organisation such as the Belgian administration (social centres) and the Catholic Church (Legion of Mary). Market women sometimes form small groups in order to raise the capital to buy wholesale, but their association ends with each transaction and may not always include the same individuals. They have no formal organisation as the associations of *femmes libres* have, nor do they recognise a diffuse obligation of mutual support. The reason for this is clear: the *femme libre* is more isolated by her profession and is insecure, both financially and socially. In these characteristics the *femme libre* is not unique: her isolation and insecurity does not derive entirely from the nature of her occupation. The associations parallel exactly the associations formed by men for social security and to raise capital in a situation in which economic competition is acute (La Fontaine 1970: 156). The associations of traders are very similar whether their members are men or women. We are thus led by these similarities to consider prostitution as a strategy for earning one's living in the city.

PROSTITUTION AS AN OCCUPATION

The traditional stereotype of the proper occupation for a woman varies little from society to society, in this part of Africa. An adult woman marries; in exchange for the services she offers she obtains rights to support and an accepted status in the community. It is with the transactional aspect of her roles as wife and mother that we are concerned here. A large anthropological literature has pointed out that rights over a wife must be considered as composed of a variety of different elements, not all of which are transferred to her husband at marriage: the most usually mentioned are rights to a woman's sexual services, to her domestic and field labour and rights to her reproductive powers. As has frequently been pointed out, these last rights are not transferred to the husband in matrilineal societies, although he may acquire rights to domestic authority over his children. A man may acquire the domestic and sexual services of a concubine but no rights to her children. If we look at marriage from a slightly different angle, we can see that a wife gains economic support in return for her sexual services, her labour and her reproductive capacities. In modern terms, in the city she acquires a house to live in, food and clothing and similar support for her children. The city also offers certain other ways of attaining these objectives outside marriage which we must now consider.

Women like men require money to satisfy the basic needs of housing, food and clothing, if these are not provided by a spouse.[11] This they can acquire either by commercial activities or by selling their labour. Petty trading is the occupation of many women, not only the unmarried, for married women supplement their husbands' income in this way. There are two distinctive features of this occupation: capital is required to start in trade and there is competition from men. It is common therefore to find women specialising in those branches of trade which demand little capital and can be defended as the preserve of women. They sell in very small amounts, they sell articles which are connected with the household economy such as food or they specialise in processing the food and sell snacks of various sorts. The latter occupation makes use of one of the traditional skills of women: cooking. Generally speaking, the profits in these trades are small and they are usually found as supplements to other forms of income rather than as a main source of support. Of 49 earning wives of householders studied in my household survey, all but 3 were engaged in commerce, either occasionally or regularly. Competition with men engaged in retail trade means that women are at a disadvantage in most areas of petty trading, for they lack the wider contacts and social skills of men which can be utilised in business.

In Europe domestic labour has long been a province in which women could earn their living. Domestic work allows a woman to offer a feminine skill for a wage. In the Congo, however, opportunities for this were relatively few and were largely in European households. Housework was performed by men, who were eager for the opportunity of such posts and who, unlike Congolese women, more often possessed the knowledge of French or a *lingua franca* which made employment by Belgians and other Europeans possible. Some Congolese women were housekeeper/mistresses to Europeans who left their wives in Europe (cf.

[11] At the time of my study the wives of unemployed men faced problems similar to those of independent women.

Little 1971: 22), but they again were relatively few. Child-minding engaged some Congolese women but the extensive employment of African 'nannies' was not as much a feature of the colonial regime in the Congo as it was and is in ex-British Africa. Moreover, there were never many of these opportunities available and familiarity with the language and domestic routine of European households was an essential qualification. None of the independent women studied in my household survey were domestic servants or nannies.

What is important to point out about domestic posts of all sorts is that they consist of skills which can be considered related to the traditional skills which are appropriate for the adult woman's role of wife and housekeeper. Although in some cases these skills are adapted to the needs of another culture or class, making a differentiation between the housewife and the domestic servant, which allows men to undertake domestic work without loss of status, they are specialisations within the feminine sphere, requiring neither capital nor other than common skills. However, the relationship between employer and employed is one which consists of an exchange of delimited services for a wage: it is thus a single-stranded relationship rather than the multiplex kinship one in which such services were traditionally offered. In Kinshasa, given the lack of wage-opportunities for men there was no criterion which prevented men competing with women for these jobs and, as I have already stated, the field of domestic work was largely monopolised by men.

Concubinage, however, consists of an exchange of sexual and domestic services, not for a wage, but for housing, food and clothing for the duration of the liaison. The concubine essentially offers more elements of the wife's role in exchange for more general, less clearly defined support. The element of sexual services protects this form of occupation from the competition of men but the concubine is restricted in her earnings by the need to depend on the generosity of one lover and by the insecurity of her position. She will usually be sent away if she entertains other lovers. Although she must be tactful not to offend her lovers, the *femme libre* offers no exclusive rights to the man with whom she does not live. She can thus, if she is successful, earn more by specialising in the exchange of sexual services only, unaccompanied by her domestic labour. She is more specialised than the concubine in this respect and her earnings depend on herself rather than the generosity of her partner in the transaction. It is again a single-stranded relationship, from which she obtains benefits and her success lies in manipulating several of these relationships to her own advantage. Such women are often aware of the disadvantages of a more permanent relationship such as concubinage and even if they enter into a more permanent exclusive relationship with one man, may retain their freedom of action by continuing to pay the rent of their own house or room and allowing their lovers to move into it. Two such women were interviewed in my survey of households in Kinshasa (La Fontaine 1970: 137).

A *femme libre* has no security for the future, for age will inevitably rob her of her ability to make money in this way. Many *femmes libres* endeavour to save enough money to buy a plot of land (and build houses for letting), a bar, or a shop as an insurance for old age. Others regard their kin as ultimate security and try to reinstate themselves with their kin group by supporting and otherwise helping them in town. The woman who houses, clothes, and educates her brother's son is building up a claim on him and his father for the future as well as fulfilling her duties as a father's sister. A smaller group of women regard marriage or a permanent liaison as their ultimate aim.

It is difficult to assess the amounts earned by *femmes libres*. Apart from a general reluctance to reveal this to an investigator, many women do not know what their receipts are. They do not appear to budget, but live a hand-to-mouth existence, calling on their clients for money when they need it. A few with regular lovers would say how much they were given a month, but may well have kept silent about their earnings from other clients. A guide to earnings is the subject's assessment of monthly expenditure on food and the foodstuffs mentioned as eaten regularly. Judging by these criteria, my data indicate that many *femmes libres* are better off than single men and considerably wealthier, in terms of what they could afford to eat, than married men with families (see also La Fontaine 1970: 61–2).

Table 1 shows the source of economic support of 56 independent women in a sample of 217 households in two communes of the city. It shows certain features which support the general contention of this paper that prostitution is a profitable strategy for the unmarried woman. Of those 30 women relying on a single

TABLE 1. Independent Women and their means of financial support

Main Support		
Renting Rooms	14	
Rent only		8
Rent and commerce		1
Rent and prostitution		4
Rent and regular lover		1
Prostitution	37	
Prostitution only		19
Prostitution and regular lover		13
Prostitution and commerce		4
Prostitution and help from kin		1
Kin	1	
Regular lover	1	
Trader only	3	
Total	56	

occupation, 19 depended on prostitution, while only 3 claimed to make their entire living from commerce. Eight women derived their sole income from rents; all of these were older women who had inherited rights in a dead husband's land and buildings or who had invested savings in land and built rooms to let. Fourteen more depended on the provision of sexual services with one permanent lover providing the bulk of their earnings. Thus, only 10 out of 43, about a quarter, needed to supplement their earnings, whereas 6 out of 14 or nearly half those engaged in renting rooms needed to undertake other economic activities. Seven women were engaged in commerce; only 3 of them claimed it as their sole support. If we now compare Table 2 it will be seen that of the 235 married women in the sample, 46 were engaged in trade and only 3 others earned money in other ways. It seems probable that a number of married women who received gifts from lovers concealed this fact but it also seems correct to argue that for the unmarried woman at least the exchange of sexual services for economic advantage was the most favoured strategy at the time of my enquiry.[12] The numbers of married women engaging in trade would offer considerable competition for most of them supplemented their

[12] Since then, President Mobutu has been pursuing a policy of creating economic opportunities for women and many more opportunities are said to be open to them (see S. Gilpin, 'Female Wage-earners in Kinshasa' B. Litt. thesis, University of Oxford, 1970). As an initial step Mobutu created an elite corps of female parachutists.

TABLE 2. Earnings of Married Women in Kinshasa (in francs per month) by source of earnings

Source	Irregular small amounts	Earnings				
		Under 500	500–1,000	1001–2,000	Over 2,000	
Occasional Petty Commerce	16	1	2	3	3	25
Regular Commerce	5	1	7	6	2	21
White-collar occupations	0	0	0	0	2	2
Herbalist	0	0	0	0	1	1
TOTAL	21	2	9	9	8	49

Total wives in sample: 235

household's income rather than providing entirely for the support of the family, and thus could also rely on capital not available normally to the *femme libre*.

At this point the question of moral evaluations must be considered. While prepared to admit that prostitution is a means of earning a living and admiring material success, Congolese, not surprisingly, do not take the morally neutral stand of the observer on these matters. Individual *vedettes* may be admired by men and envied by women but in principle, the life of *femmes libres* is considered morally wrong. At the lower end of the social scale, the prostitute who accepts money for sexual services is thought of as degraded and the status is one which is despised. Clearly, as Henriques has rightly pointed out (1968: 337) an element in a society's evaluation of the prostitute is derived from the society's general beliefs about sexual morality. Although it is difficult to claim that members of a complex heterogeneous society such as Kinshasa adhere to a single set of such beliefs, there is much evidence to suggest certain widely accepted attitudes. Of these, the most important seems to be that a sexual association is morally approved when it is an element in a continuing, multiplex relationship. Hence marriage is morally 'better' than a love-affair or concubinage, and a love-affair 'better' than a brief sexual encounter. It is as though the existence of reciprocity in transactions other than the sexual legitimises the physical intimacy. The use of the words 'buying' and 'selling' in this connection as pejorative is significant: a sale is the stereotype of the completed transaction which entails no relationship between the parties to it (see Sahlins 1965: 147-8). The emphasis placed on mutual activities, loyalty and mutual help by lovers underlines the flow of generalised reciprocity. Thus the phrase: 'loving is giving', to which I referred earlier can also be used to distinguish a love affair from the single commercial transaction between a 'chambre d'hotel' and her clients. A further element here is the implication that a love relationship depends on the voluntary commitment of the two individuals. Like friendship, it depends on no external pressures (Foster 1961: 1174); it is a relationship of mutual benefit and pleasure. My data are not sufficient to warrant any far-reaching conclusions and my remarks here are tentative but it seems worth pointing out that there is fear as well as scorn in the attitude to the 'true' prostitute. Such women are said to be without moral scruples, to be thieves and a danger both to their clients and the community. The use of magic which *femmes libres* employ as protection against the uncertainties of their existence, is also commonly thought of as akin to sorcery: a means by which men may be forced to ruin themselves by spending all their resources on the entertainment of the woman concerned. Such supernatural powers are, like sorcery, both anti-social (evil) and dangerous.

Against these imprecise evaluations, which only further research can define more sharply, it is important to recognise other elements in the negative evaluation of *femmes libres*. Married women perceive their vulnerability, in face of the competition for scarce resources that these women who are rivals for their husbands' concern present. This is made explicit by the remarks of many women, who as wives are dependent on the earnings of husbands (cf. Little 1971: 24 n. 1) in an economic situation of uncertainty. The scale of prestige which material possessions mark is widely accepted; housing, dress and food are not only important in themselves but as indices of the success of members of the family. The expenditure of men in relationships with *femmes libres* directly affects the standing of some households; in the majority of instances it may involve material deprivation for the wife and her children. Men often deplore the emphasis on material success which they say induces their wives to resort to casual affairs in order to compete with the standards displayed by *femmes libres*.

Thus both men and women recognise that women compete, through their association with men, for material success.

Finally, we must consider the statements of informants that the *femme libre* disgraces her family. It is usually expressed as a failure of respect for senior relatives and particularly for men. This failure of respect consists of negating the control thought proper to the role of seniors, whether senior by sex or age, by acting independently. *Femmes libres* dispose of themselves and their resources in their own interests, create and manage their own relationships and do not submit to control of these by men, either as kinsmen or husbands. Relationships created through woman in most African societies are relationships of exchange maintained by a flow of gifts and mutual aid; yet, these affinal exchanges are exchanges between men—a large anthropological literature attests to the economic and political advantages that men have derived from manipulating rights over women. It is sometimes stated, but more often assumed, that the interests of women are either ignored or assimilated to the interests of their male guardians. Yet in many such societies elopement is a recognised means of forcing the hand of senior kinsmen, used by women as well as men. (La Fontaine 1962: 102.) The *femme libre* can be said to have carried elopement a stage further and has deprived both her kin and her potential husband of the social profits which might be obtained from an affinal relationship. In doing this, she attacks the basic structure of the kinship system by denying the authority of men over women, of seniors over juniors. In refusing to be the vehicle for the creation of affinal ties, she deprives any children she may have of full kinship status, as they will have no paternal kinsmen. It is thus intelligible that such behaviour is disapproved by both men and women for it denies basic social values. The sympathetic refer to the *femme libre* as having 'escaped' the burden of kinship ties.

In this article I have considered the ethnography of prostitution in Kinshasa in order to show that, at least in this particular case, it offers a strategy for the economic support of women, which is an alternative to marriage and, given the lack of educational background and the general competition for employment it is a more profitable strategy than trade or wage-labour. While noting that the necessity to earn her own living may be forced on a woman by the death or desertion of her husband and the absence of kin, I have not discussed the degree to which this strategy can be attributed to urban conditions as Congolese often say it is. To this question I now turn.

The existence of urban society such as Kinshasa, is in itself both the result and manifestation of rapid social change, which has affected not only the inhabitants of the new centres of population but the rural areas as well. It is in the former that social changes can most clearly be observed: the change to a monetary economy and the specialisation of economic activities deriving from the general trend, long ago remarked by Durkheim, towards simplex rather than multiplex relationships. The scope for individual choice increases and so does the emphasis on contractual relationships and the possibilities for achieving high status. All this is true for women as well as men, although as we have seen the opportunities for women are still relatively limited. Demographic factors can be said to have created a demand for the services that women can supply. This was graphically explained by one woman who declared, in answer to the question 'Why did you come to Kinshasa?', that as a *femme libre* she could not earn her living in the village, where men (i.e., as clients) were scarce but that in town clients were so plentiful that she could support herself with ease. This answer would seem to imply that the role of *femme libre* was not unknown, at least in the rural area these women came from. We have some confirmation that a role similar to that of *femme libre* existed in the traditional societies of Ruanda (Macquet 1961: 78) and Bunyoro (Beattie 1971: 144). Both authors describe the presence of unmarried women at the courts of the ruler or of great chiefs. They are described as 'courtesans' by Macquet, who says 'They received costly presents and were often well-off' (p. 78) and by Beattie as 'maidservants', but he remarks that Emin Pasha 'not unreasonably describes them as prostitutes'. Clearly, while modern urban conditions facilitate the playing of such roles, the role itself cannot be said to be the product of modern industrialised society.

The significant feature can be seen if we consider the comparison I have already drawn between the roles of married women and of *femme libre*. The married woman plays a multiplex role, providing a number of services for one man, her husband; the *femme libre* is a specialist, offering more restricted services to a number of men. These services seem to be elements of the role of wife (sexual services and domestic labour) which become the basis for distinct roles, and thus allow women economic independence. The process then is one of role specialisation, and is associated with a complex division of labour. This can occur independently of urbanisation as the examples of Ruanda and Bunyoro show. Stratification into politico-economic classes and a relatively complex division of labour at the political centres were characteristic of both societies in pre-European times (cf. Macquet 1961; Beattie 1971). It is also true, however, that societies such as Ruanda and Bunyoro were uncommon and contributed little if any cultural influence to the culture of Kinshasa. Hence one can say that the *femme libre* in Kinshasa is the product of social change though not necessarily, as I have argued throughout, the victim of social disorganisation.

I have also argued that the comportment of *femmes libres* which may be unremarkable in European society but shocking in contrast to the correct traditional behaviour for adult women, for whom the role of wife provided the model, is modern rather than amoral. Their models are the images of modern womanhood projected by the mass media, by the *vedettes*, and observed on the public occasions where Congolese and members of 'Western' societies mix. Educated Congolese women, of whom there were few in 1962, and those with experience of living abroad, also model themselves on their European counterparts and their manner is sufficiently similar to that of the Kinshasa *femmes libres* for Congolese to identify them and for some to claim that modern education makes whores out of honest girls. For many Congolese women, independence of men is a new urban possibility; for the sociological observer it is a special instance of the processes of social change.

7

The progress of Greek nationalism in Cyprus, 1878–1970

PETER LOIZOS

In recent years a number of anthropologists have been trying to strike sparks of theory from the 'problem' of their subject's relation with political science. They argued that as the modern state encourages the growth of its agencies in the hinterlands, and tribal societies are swiftly and sharply affected by social change in all its forms, then two disciplines which had often seemingly kept their distance out of mutual disrespect, like it or not were being brought into closer relations. Would one absorb the other? Would both find themselves deeply altered by contact? Would they come together to produce some new, more powerful discipline? Naturally, opinions reflected a wide range of possibilities. Some, like Professor Gluckman (1964), were for sticking to the last. Others, like Abner Cohen (1969b), were so uneasy at the intrusion of political scientists into the reserves of anthropologists that they suggested joining those who could so obviously not be licked. Balandier (1970) proclaimed that anthropology had destroyed the domination of the state in the study of politics. Ronald Cohen (1969) and Weingrod (1967) set out with obvious caution the possible costs and gains of discreet bridge-building between disciplines.

This sober concern for the proper relations between subjects seems to have overlooked the contribution of Lucy Mair to such a debate. She handled the 'problem' with a characteristic directness in a number of works, not by lengthy discussion of the difficulties implicit in an analysis involving two disciplines, but simply and more profitably *by carrying out the analysis*. To mention only one example: Her essay, published in 1960 on 'Race, Tribalism and Nationalism in Africa' is quite specific about possible and probable causes of instability in newly independent states. Had the points she was then making been given more weight, we might have been spared many a work on 'nation building' destined to be found in serious error before its ink was decently dry. My respect for Lucy Mair's approach will, I hope, be expressed in this paper, which starts out with the assumption that there is nothing 'problematic' about an anthropologist discussing the progress of nationalism in a society where he has also carried out intensive fieldwork.[1]

It has become a jaded piety to say that a village cannot be understood without analysis of the wider society; this essay is one consequence of trying to understand the increasing involvement of a village in national politics. The essay will not be 'about' the village—but it would never have been written without it.

The chief aim of this paper is to explain the persistence of a particular political platform in the affairs of Cyprus since her independence in 1960. The platform is the demand by sections of the Greek Cypriot community for *Enosis*—political union with mainland Greece. The demand is problematic for several reasons. First, it has been ruled out of the island's constitution by the Treaty of Guarantee between Cyprus, Britain, Greece and Turkey; secondly, it seems clear that the Greek Cypriot population are more interested in peace than in *Enosis*, if the price of *Enosis* is continued violence. Thirdly, even though few of them seem to want it, Greek political leaders seem incapable of renouncing *Enosis*; and yet, had they done so, a settlement with the Turkish dissidents might have become possible. Fourthly, since from the criterion of simple power relations the Greek majority have clearly won the lion's share in the struggle with the Turkish minority, why should *Enosis* still be a rallying symbol? When the British

[1] I wish to thank the Social Science Research Council and the Nuffield Foundation for supporting fieldwork which led to this paper. Fieldwork was mainly in one village, February 1968–April 1969, but much observation and interviewing took place in the surrounding district and the capital. Shorter visits took place in 1969, and 1970.

Many people have contributed to this paper. For particular insights into relations between religion and nationalism I am indebted to Clive Kessler, and Kyriacos Markides; for many discussions of politics to Edward Hammonds; for many helpful comments to Caroline Ifeka and Michael Attalides. The inadequacies are of course my own.

left the island *Enosis* as a slogan for anti-colonial insurrection had served its apparent purpose and could have been expected to wither quietly away.

To explain the persistence of an apparently redundant nationalism in an independent republic some skeletal review of recent history is inevitable. The island of Cyprus, 3,572 square miles in area, has endured a number of foreign rulers. The Ottoman Empire dominated the island from 1573–1878, when it allowed the British to occupy the island. The British acquired a somewhat run-down, chiefly rural domain, with a population roughly 75 per cent Greek-speaking Christians, and 25 per cent Turkish-speaking Muslims. The Muslims had enjoyed certain privileges under Ottoman rule which ended with the British arrival; the two religious groups were then placed by the British on equal footing before the law, although the Christians, as co-religionists, were somewhat favoured in fact if not in theory.

Certain sections of the Greek community greeted the British arrival with polite requests for *Enosis*. The British noted this but ignored it. The Turkish community equally quietly expressed opposition to the idea. Since the start of the Greek War of Independence in 1821 the influence of Greek nationalism had stirred the surface of Cypriot life, but had, in the main, been firmly repressed by the Ottoman rulers. The British were more lenient, and allowed Greek Cypriot volunteers to leave the island in 1880 and 1897 to fight for Greece against Turkey.

During the first fifty years of British rule there were three main categories of Greek Cypriots who had an interest in *Enosis*. The Church supplied some of the most passionate supporters, partly, it has been suggested,[2] because the British threatened the Church's traditional monopoly of religious and political authority enhanced under the Ottoman *millet* system. First, the British refused to support certain Church prerogatives in taxation; secondly, they created the secular Legislative Assembly, with popularly elected members. Finally, in 1924 they permitted the emergence of a new secular force—the Cypriot Communist Party. The slogan of *Enosis* was the ideal vehicle for Church antagonism to the fruits of British rule, and also served to assert a continuing right to lead and speak for all the island's Orthodox Christians, against the secular challenge of the left.

[2] Kyriacos Markides, personal communication.

GREEK NATIONALISM IN CYPRUS, 1878-1970   117

Some members of the literate urban elite also supported *Enosis*, for to do this was to claim membership in a larger political unit, a *nation* which had only recently and gloriously fought its way (with European help) to freedom from the very same Ottoman rule which had dominated Cyprus. Thus the Greek Cypriot elite at one and the same time reminded the British and the Turks that they had 'glorious' and 'civilised' connections, and antecedents. For Greek Cypriots to have stood alone would have been to stand politically and culturally defenceless; but to assert identity with the Greek nation was to invoke a compelling and attractive defence.

But this section of the population also had a more down-to-earth reason for supporting *Enosis*. As Orr (1918: 160-71) so acutely perceived, the British reserved senior administration posts for themselves, and did not mix freely with the Cypriot elite. By treating Cypriots in this way as second-class citizens, they effectively encouraged protests of all kinds. *Enosis* was one form of protest to hand, and communism was another; the former preached the superiority of Hellenism over other cultures, the latter the superiority—in the long-term—of an international working-class.

The third main category of supporters for *Enosis* were schoolteachers. Under the British education received a major impetus. Between 1881 and 1911 the number of schools in the island more than trebled, and the number of pupils rose from 6,776 in 1881, to 30,557 in 1911. In the same period the population rose from 186,173 (1881) to 274,108 (1911). By 1911 44 per cent of males over 5 years old could read and write to some extent. During this period the numbers of schoolteachers rose to meet the demand for new schools. In these schools much time was devoted to the teaching of Greek history and language, to the celebration of Greek heroism in 1821, and so inevitably, to the creation of a national identity for Greek Cypriot children. They were socialised by the schools to see themselves as members of the nation of the Greek mainland. Every word of 'proper' Greek they learned to read or write taught them that their own dialect was inferior to educated Greek, and made the new identity more definite. This task also identified the teachers with Greek culture; it was after all their bread-and-butter. They were gatekeepers at a point which the rural masses were reaching in ever-increasing numbers. At the gate were a number of signs pointing to 'modernity', 'literacy', 'new jobs' and 'higher status'; 'national identity' was one more such sign acquired through education. As we shall see, some of these signs concealed certain contradictions.

From most accounts, the illiterate and debt-ridden rural population, for whom British rule brought both efficient administration and improved economic opportunities, were not aware to any large extent of the agitation for *Enosis* which Church, elite and teachers were supporting. Only as their children became literate and as new roads brought the politicians to the villages, did their awareness quicken into interest. This interest was probably still slender by 1931, when as if to usher in the decade of economic depression which was to hit Cyprus as badly as the rest of the world, there was an unplanned outburst of pro-*Enosis* violence known as The Uprising, in which the Governor's mansion was burned, martial law imposed, and after which government proceeded by decree for ten years.

During the period 1932-55 two important new factors affected the growth of Greek Cypriot nationalism. One was the development of increasingly organised and articulate political groupings of the left, and of the right, in sharp opposition to each other. Trade unions for example which were officially recognised from 1932, had only 15,480 members in 1945, but nearly 40,000 ten years later.[3] The other was that the second world war showed the Cypriots, as it did so many other colonised peoples, that European power was conditional and unpredictable. and that Europeans were not all one single dominant class of supermen. Many Cypriots received an informal political education in the ranks of H.M. Armed Forces.

Much work needs to be done before the complex relation between changing social structure and political alignment in Cyprus can be clearly understood; here I shall only make hints about possibly fruitful lines of research.[4] First, the small scale of the island, and relatively good communications have allowed skilled and educated men to remain resident in their natal villages, while

---

[3] By 1970, the left unions had 36,000 members, and the right unions 21,000; the left has strikingly lost ground since 1955, and this is partly due to EOKA's role, and partly due to successful anti-leftist policies from sections of the government since independence.

[4] For a useful discussion of structural, organisational and ideological factors in political alignment, see Sartori, in Lipset (ed.), 1969.

working in towns. Secondly, the fact that there are both right and left wing trade and farmer's unions has complicated the relation between social structure and political alignment; in addition, many individuals are aligned by ties of clientage to powerful individuals, making vertical ties often more important than class situation in explaining political support. Finally, structural position is complicated by the degree to which a person knows English: many areas of elite activity involve competence in English, and persons otherwise secure in their elite status, may feel disadvantaged if their English is poor, or they have been educated only in Greece.

One example of this complex relation between social structure and support for nationalism can be suggested. I pointed out that the teachers had a strong interest in creating enthusiasm for Hellenic culture when between 1880 and 1910 most of the population were still illiterate. But later, as more and more villagers became literate, the high social status of primary schoolteachers was eroded—literacy had lost its magic. *Higher* education then became the symbol of high status. Yet the primary schoolteachers I knew in 1970 still seemed strongly nationalist. Only now, their nationalism is the result of social frustrations with their *diminished* status. Their nationalist alignment has remained stable, but the structural conditions for it have changed markedly.[5]

Other notable changes in social structure which occurred during British rule, included continual population growth, which was matched by a rapid growth of the island's six main towns. The increasingly diversified economy was accompanied by an increasingly literate and mobile labour force for whose allegiance the right-wing nationalists and the left competed vigorously. The civil war between right and left in mainland Greece was paralleled by unrest between the island's equivalent political groupings. Constitutional reforms proposed by the British in 1947 were finally rejected by both groupings and in January 1950 the Church organised a plebiscite in favour of *Enosis* which received 96 per cent support from those Greek Cypriots eligible to vote. There the

[5] Boissevain (1965:43) describes how the authority of Maltese village priests was weakened by the spread of literacy. Greek-Cypriot schoolteachers do not normally have ritual sanctions to support them, although they identify strongly with the Church, and hold jobs in an educational system which defers strongly to Orthodoxy.

matter rested until 1 April 1955 when seventy-five years of elite-inspired agitation gave way to an armed insurrection organised and led by a village-born Cypriot called George Grivas who, with the approval of Church leaders, had secretly organised EOKA, a guerilla group with units throughout the island. It drew heavily on villagers, and village-born young men for its militants.[6] It did not recruit known supporters of the communist party, AKEL, and AKEL did not support EOKA's insurrection as such, preferring its own tactics. These involved generally peaceful agitation for independence from British rule, rather than for union with Greece. Grivas believed the left would betray his group and since he had built up a reputation as a fanatic anti-communist in the Greek civil war, there were good historical reasons for non-cooperation between the two sides.

During the years 1955–59 three important things happened. EOKA's rebellion, together with the climate of world opinion and internal policy developments, convinced the British that it was cheaper to give Cyprus independence, than to hold on to it. Secondly, Greeks and Turks in Cyprus tasted the bitter fruits of inter-communal violence; and thirdly the Greek Cypriot population was given harsh lessons in national identity.

One lesson came from the British who, in the frustration of trying to catch hit-and-run guerilas, or cope with stone-throwing schoolchildren, adopted the standard counter-insurgency tactics: curfews, house and body searches, general surveillance, rewards for information, detention, torture of suspects and execution.[7] Since the security forces did not know whom to suspect, they tended to treat the Greek population with impartiality—as all equally suspect. This must have done much over the four years of the Emergency, to create consciousness of common identity among people who might originally have been unsure about who they were. If EOKA's pamphlets did not convince them that they were Greeks and 'suffering' under imperialist rule, then H.M. Security Forces could be relied on to do EOKA's job.

[6] Some information on the social background of EOKA militants who died in action, under torture or by execution is available in Papachrysostomou (1969). Kyriacos Markides has analysed other material, and stresses that although many militants were village-born, they tended to be upwardly mobile (personal communication).

[7] The British did not however resort to the massive general reprisals against the civilian population which the French carried out in Algeria and Madagascar. Cyprus was comparatively fortunate to have been a British colony.

The other lesson came from EOKA, which acted violently against those it suspected of betraying its members, or collaborating with the British. There were numbers of Greeks killed by Greeks, and this extended to a general harassment of leftists. The end result was that whatever people felt about relations with Britain, or the future status of the island, very few were inclined publicly to deviate from EOKA's line of *Enosis* and only *Enosis*. The costs of dissent were seen to be too high. The consequences of this prudent consensus on national goals was to carry over into independence.

It must be stressed that between 1955 and 1970 when in all possibility large numbers of Greek Cypriots were not in support of the militant pursuit of *Enosis* if this implied wide-spread loss of life, almost no-one publicly spoke against either *Enosis* or militancy. In my view this was because most people feared the violent intimidation which might result. It is widely known that militants were ready to administer severe beatings, or even to kill those whom they believed had betrayed them. Public opposition was likely to be interpreted by some fanatics as 'betrayal'. Widespread fear of violent intimidation is an essential component for understanding the *public* expression of political attitudes in Cyprus.

There was an underlying contradiction in EOKA's position and this concerned the extent to which the struggle was a mass one. Clearly, when the struggle started, the island's Greeks were not unified unless the 1950 plebiscite is taken to show *underlying* as opposed to superficial unity. Some were sympathetic to Britain and through commerce or the civil service doing well out of British rule; others were working through leftist trade unions to improve their situations; and others again were too busy earning a living to participate in insurrection. In spite of these differences, EOKA's propaganda appeal was to all Greeks, or all 'true' Greeks. During and after the struggle it was asserted time and again that the entire Greek population (with the exception of a handful of traitors) were 100 per cent behind the EOKA struggle, and that everyone according to their abilities participated in support for it.

Yet this mass struggle was clearly carried forward by a handful of militants, who afterwards were able to say very precisely that some people had contributed much more than others to national liberation. Many people, they insisted, had done nothing; and herein lay the contradiction: the legitimate national struggle, carried on with mass popular participation, had been won by the heroism of only a few people.

EOKA militants were naturally prominent in the first years of independence. Several such young men were included in Makarios' first cabinet, and many others exercised influence from further off, often in organised forms, through the ex-fighters' associations which were formed. For a few brief years former militants seem to have acted as an informal duplicate government, able to intervene in areas of decision which would normally have been left to civil servants. Appointments to civil service posts, granting of educational scholarships, building permits and import franchises were all subject to such intervention. That is, in a situation of competition for scarce resources, a key criterion was the individual claimant's history of militancy, or in default of this, his personal links with militants.

It is at this point that the contradiction between a mass struggle, and a minority of militants becomes critical, for it creates both a justification for almost unlimited claims to rewards, and an inevitable tension over the legitimacy of claims. At the end of the struggle, EOKA's leader, George Grivas, issued a limited number of certificates of service to the national struggle; but he soon stopped doing this. He did not make his reasons public, but it is not hard to imagine what they might have been: too many claimants.

How could it have been otherwise? First, a guerilla struggle is clandestine by nature, and hardly in the public domain, so that unless trusted leaders are prepared to vouch for the veracity of a person's claim to have served, popular scepticism is likely. The island is small, and kinship, friendship, or common village origins serve to link people easily. These factors would inevitably increase the number of persons closely linked to militants, who might have used these links to seek access to available benefits. In the village I studied it proved impossible to draw up a list of acknowledged militants agreeable to a handful of key militant informants, so tangled were the skeins of claim and counter-claim. Furthermore in village culture—and probably more generally—men are unwilling to grant pre-eminence in one sphere to those whom in other spheres they see as their equals.

However, the very nature of the EOKA struggle also served to multiply the numbers of claimants. Many people for example acted occasionally as couriers; sheltered, hid or fed wanted men; took leaflets and scattered them; or daubed slogans on walls; took part in demonstrations or riots; had their homes searched, or their business harmed by curfews or boycotts. These various forms of direct or indirect participation, when leavened by the ideological insistence on mass struggle, led many people to believe that their claims to the rewards of militancy were at least as good as the next man's. A wealthy industrial nation, dealing with the conventional conscript soldier returning home, can pass a law granting special benefits to a known and numbered category of claimants. This is what the USA did through the 'G.I. Bill of Rights' and the Veterans Administration. Cyprus, a poorer country, could not afford to do this, and was not dealing with the clear-cut problem of a well-administered conventional army being demobilised. Instead Cypriot leaders had to make non-bureaucratic decisions about who was and was not eligible to be rewarded for militancy; such decisions inevitably create dissatisfactions.

One sign of the dissatisfaction was to be found in complaints by members of the educated urban elite. Some of them argued that technical qualifications rather than a moustache and a pistol were needed for running a modern state. There were complaints about 'illiterates' being given important government jobs, and people being given scholarships 'for chucking a few leaflets'. Behind such protests was the problem faced by families which had invested heavily in their children's education, only to see the worth of a paper qualification being devalued by the militants' interventions. Nor were the militants tongue-tied. They replied that rewards should go to those who had risked their lives or given their blood for the cause of *Enosis* and Hellenism; and that those who had been pursuing their selfish interests by being educated abroad—often in the bosom of the English enemy—should not benefit simply because they had brought back a piece of paper. Why should those whose very sacrifices had precluded them from getting an education stand by, while lesser men, men who were not patriots at all, were given jobs?

The issues were simple, but not easily resolved. The people who stressed qualifications, bureaucratic processes, professional competence, and the finality of examination results, were often members of the elite, already committed to legalistic, technocratic administration. The other side, usually not members of the educated urban elite were emphasising *moral* qualifications. The two sorts of arguments are in different idioms, and usually come from individuals who have different structural positions, or social experiences. If Cyprus had not had an ethnic minority—the Turks—to draw off the structural tensions in the Greek community, then this issue between Greek militants and the Greek elite might well have become the dominant cleavage of the society. But events were to take—in the short run at least—a different turn.

Before independence there had been ugly rioting between Greeks and Turks; differences were patched up to permit the Zurich–London agreements to be signed. In essence these agreements ruled out *Enosis*, and established Cyprus as an independent republic, guaranteed by Britain, Greece and Turkey. A complex constitution established separate communal representation, a Greek President, and Turkish Vice-President with key veto powers, and a host of provisions aimed at protecting the Turkish minority from political domination by the Greeks. Perhaps the most frustrating provision in Greek eyes was the one which gave the Turks, who were 18 per cent of the population, some 30 per cent of the civil service jobs, with fixed quotas of Greeks and Turks at all levels. The average Greek probably felt that the Turks should only have been given jobs in proportion to their ratio of the population.

There was another major issue, but among the Greeks. The supporters of President Makarios were prepared to accept the island's independent status; but Grivas, the EOKA leader, and his supporters, believed that Makarios had been too weak in his handling of the final negotiations, and that *Enosis*, the goal of the EOKA struggle, should still be pursued. In effect they did not accept the island's status as a republic, and were inclined to think that Turkish opposition to *Enosis* should be ignored. The antagonism between the two leaders and their respective supporters became public knowledge in the first years of independence, but was patched up.

Following a prolonged constitutional crisis serious fighting erupted between Greeks and Turks in December 1963. The Turks retreated into armed enclaves, and the UN arrived to prevent further hostilities. Since then, until the time of writing (September 1972), there have been several short outbreaks of fighting, threatened invasions by Turkey, and more recently protracted negotiations between Greek and Turkish Cypriot leaders, to define a new form of relationship. The Turkish enclaves remain, however, in a state of *de facto* secession.

During the twelve years of independence, the Greek community has been the arena of endless appeals for 'national unity'. No Greek leader has ever renounced the hope of *Enosis–at–some-point–in–the–unspecified–future*, and on the nationalist right most politicians try to outbid each other in claiming to be the true and only sincere advocates of *Enosis–as–soon–as–possible*. In fact all groupings except for AKEL describe themselves as nationalist, while AKEL replies that the right wing have no hereditary monopoly of patriotism. All groups with the exception of Grivas' supporters have continued to express support for the policies of Makarios, which boil down to an attempt to reach a peaceful settlement with the Turks, and acceptance of the island's status as a republic.

In 1969 the nationalist campaign for *Enosis* took a new and dramatic turn with the formation of an underground organisation reminiscent of EOKA, calling itself the *Ethnikon Metopon*, National Front. It claimed credit for a number of attacks on senior government officials, seizures of arms and explosives, and bombings of government buildings, and explained its position in a series of leaflets. Its line was that *Enosis* was still the immediate goal of Greek Cypriots, that the Makarios government contained a number of secret communists, as well as corrupt opportunists who were lining their pockets while betraying the sacred cause.

Makarios declared the EM illegal, but was unable to counteract the climate of fear and suspicion which it produced. There were numbers of minor local incidents around the island, the most spectacular of which involved a dissident EM offshoot, the *Ieros Lochos* (Holy Brigade) which early in 1970 with a force of some 70 men raided the central police station of the island's second town, Limassol, held it for several hours, and made off with a large haul of arms. Many of these men were soon captured, and some twenty brought to trial, where it appeared that most were young artisans who believed that their raid was to have been repeated all over the island, and *Enosis* to have resulted. At their trial they presented themselves as 'true nationalists', while other branches of the EM declared themselves disbanded and loyal to Makarios. There were even claims by some of the accused that they believed Makarios to have given tacit support to the formation of the organisation. The Limassol raid marked the end of this phase of instability in the Greek community and in May-June 1970 the first elections to the Legislative Assembly were held for ten years, in relative tranquillity.[8]

The election campaign of the more extreme nationalist parties was sufficiently similar in tone and content to the EM leaflets to suggest that the elections were the continuation of the EM's rebellion by other means. This is not to suggest that the same individuals were involved, but rather that certain structural contradictions in Greek Cypriot society are intense enough to provide the best political platform for an attack on the elite. The campaign of the *Proodeftiki Parataxis* (PF), a major nationalist party which emerged from the elections with seven out of the thirty-five seats in the house, blended populist with nationalist themes, as a means to attack the *Eniæon Komma* (EK), a party identified with the *status quo*, the urban elite, and the main levers of power in Cypriot society. The party leaders could have chosen, in traditional right wing nationalist style, to make the key target of attack the communist party, AKEL, but this they significantly failed to do; nor did they put much energy into attacking the socialist party EDEK. Instead, they attempted to discredit the claim of the EK to be a pro-*Enosis* pro-Hellenist party, to brand its leaders as 'false nationalists' while representing the PF itself as the inheritor of the patriotic EOKA legacy. That is, the same sort of claims which characterised the struggle between EOKA militants, and urban elite in the early years of independence, over jobs and other resources, was repeated in the 1970 election, in the attempts to monopolise the platform of 'true nationalism'.

To understand the reasons for the use of claims to 'true

[8] Before the 1970 elections two other sensational events occurred. One was an assassination attempt on President Makarios. The other followed shortly afterwards, and this was the shooting of Yorgadjis, who until his resignation a year previously had enjoyed great personal power as Makarios' Minister of the Interior. Yorgadjis was widely believed to have been involved in the attack on Makarios. In any comprehensive analysis of Greek Cypriot politics since independence, the role of the mainland Greek governments, NATO, Turkey, Britain, the USA and the USSR would all need to be fully taken into account. This paper has been limited to the *internal* factors involved in Greek Cypriot nationalism.

nationalism' as an ideological vehicle in the struggle for resources, it is necessary to look at the parties and their appeals in more detail.

The EK broadly supported a constitutional, negotiated settlement with the Turkish community through intercommunal talks, private property, business interests, anti-communism, and Greek nationalism. It is also thought by many people to be 'the NATO group'. It tried to be all things to all men, promising free education, rural development, and stability, while denying the right of any one social class to speak for society at large. Its leader was Glafkos Clerides, a man generally popular with the urban bourgeoisie, an English-trained barrister, President of the Legislative Assembly, and Makarios' sole negotiator with the Turkish community. Its other leader, until his murder in 1969, was Yorgadjis who had been the former Minister of the Interior. It was widely believed that the patronage machine operated by Yorgadjis in the police force and parts of the civil service was still working during the campaign for Clerides and the EK, although perhaps not as efficiently as it would have done had Yorgadjis been alive to supervise it. That is to say, a large number of people who directly (or at one patronage remove) owed their jobs to Yorgadjis, worked and voted for the EK during the campaign.

The Progressive Front (PF) was led by Nikos Sampson, a famous EOKA militant who had acted for a number of years as a focus for those militants who were discontented with the *status quo* but who drew the line at outright support for Grivas. The PF is a party for people who are willing to come in out of the cold if Makarios allows the sun of his pleasure to play upon them. The party leaders did not in 1970 attack Makarios, but they certainly criticised his former ministers, particularly those who were now with the newly-formed EK.

In the district I observed the PF spent its entire electoral energies attacking the EK. It is the idiom of this attack which is particularly revealing. In speeches by the party's leader, Nikos Sampson, the following themes appeared time and again: the EK was the party of opportunists, of false nationalists, of the men who 'for the last ten years' had lined their pockets at the expense of the masses, and of true patriots. During this period, EOKA militants had been gunned down in the streets for political reasons, for wanting *Enosis* too passionately, and their killers had not been brought to justice. Men who had fought first the British and then the Turks, had asked for a job or a pension, a scholarship for their children, and had been refused, while those who had done nothing but line their pockets had been provided for. Sampson told his audiences he understood their struggles to educate their children in Greece, as Greeks. He knew how after five years self-sacrifice these children returned from the best universities in mother Greece to be told their qualifications were not good enough, and yet people who had been to tenth-rate universities in England and America, who had thus proven their contempt for Greek education and things Greek came back to Cyprus and instantly got the same jobs.

Sampson even alluded to the fact that Clerides is married to a non-Greek woman, and hinted that perhaps his daughter had not been baptised. True Greekness, Sampson explained, did not mean worshipping Buddha and having unbaptised daughters.

The substance of Sampson's charges needs a little background detail: the urban bourgeoisie to which Clerides appeals, has strong commercial and cultural links to Britain. There is keen competition in this category to educate children at the island's exclusive English School, a school to which very few non-elite children manage to gain admission. Mastery of English is considered the mark of sophistication in the elite, and often there is open hostility to the culture of the Greek mainland, especially since the 1967 Greek coup. The Greek Cypriot elite are internationalist in taste and values, however much they publicly speak in support of Hellenism. This is a factor which adds fuel to the PF's attacks. Crudely stated, the less English one knows, the more ideologically important Hellenism becomes; the more one is committed to Hellenism the more important it becomes to denounce the 'dilution' or 'contamination' of Greek culture by English or American influence, whether in education, in dress, personal style, sexual mores, political values, or anything else that comes to hand. Speaking out for things Greek, and speaking out against the elite become almost the same thing.[9]

CONCLUSION

Symbols are usually defined as unstable, and harbour several meanings; in politics this is one of the major advantages of symbols

[9] Inglehart and Woodward (1967) have a useful survey of the relation between national languages, blocked mobility and political conflict.

GREEK NATIONALISM IN CYPRUS, 1878-1970 129

over more literal, or directly representational abstractions. *Enosis*, a slogan which at face value aims to bring about the union of Cyprus with Greece, has been a dominant political symbol in the island's life for over a hundred years, in which time it has excluded other possible nationalisms, for example, a *Cypriot* nationalism which would have sought to unite the island's Greek and Turkish populations. In this paper a number of different meanings, or uses, for this symbol have been discussed in four main phases.

Phase one 1878-1931: *Enosis* served church leaders as a claim to speak for all Greek-Orthodox Christians, to represent a Hellenistic culture; the church in effect asserted a sacred link between religious, cultural and political leadership, which it sought to pre-empt in the face of challenges from a modernising, somewhat secular and democratic colonial regime. *Enosis* appealed to the urban elite because it helped them say to both the British and the Turks that they were not an isolated, uncultured and defenceless island people, but part of a distinguished and powerful culture. and it served to express their frustration with the British monopoly of top jobs. Such symbolism also appealed to the increasing numbers of teachers and other *clercs* but with the added interest that it was for them a bread-and-butter issue as well, for through supporting it they held the role of cultural gatekeepers; controlling access to the mysteries of Hellenic identity, which also meant to meal-tickets and mobility.

Phase two 1932-54: during a period of gradual political development, with the growth of differentiated right and left wing parties, to be pro-*Enosis* became a key attribute of right wing identity. The right tried to define good Greeks as pro-church, pro-Greek monarchy, and anti-communist. This was because they wished to define the left as 'bad Greeks', a view inevitably aggravated by the bitter civil war in Greece.

Phase three 1955-59: during these years the militant nationalist organisation EOKA attempted to rally mass popular support by using *Enosis* as the key slogan of the insurrection against British rule. The argument was that the British must go because the rightful place for Cyprus was within the Greek state, but for many people the wish to get the British out may have been sufficient motive.

Phase four 1960–70: there have been two quite different meanings to calls for *Enosis*. For most people most of the time (and this includes the majority of political leaders) support for *Enosis–Eventually* is a statement of Greek cultural identity in a plural society. It serves to rally 'Greeks' in opposition to 'Turks'. It is hard for any Greek leader to openly abandon it because after a hundred years of nationalist education it has become impossible to separate the notion of Greek culture from that of wanting *union* with Greece. It has become intellectually difficult (as well as physically dangerous) for people to say that one can obviously share in Greek culture, the social identity of Greekness, *without* becoming politically incorporated into the Greek state. Ironically this is the direction that most moderate leaders would like to take. But they have been under attack from the extremists.

Hence the other meaning of *Enosis* since independence, which can be paraphrased as the wish for *Enosis–Now*. This has been a vehicle for protesting radical dissatisfaction with the *status quo*, and is an alternative to the docile but practical critiques of the left. The supporters of *Enosis–Now* often have a strong sense of grievance. They believe the wrong men are in power, that Hellenism is being diluted and adulterated by a cultural attraction to things British, as the English language becomes more and more vital for success in the business or governmental elite. There is a millennarian note in their protests, of the kind which Kedourie (1970: 1–147) has noted. The most ardent see the island as deeply corrupted, and find enemies everywhere. Their arithmetic counts a single 'true Greek' as worth a dozen Turks in battle; their view of redemption is spectacular and cataclysmic. For such true believers, *Enosis* can never be achieved by gradualism, still less by constitutional bargaining. For it is not like a percentage split in a wage settlement, but an identity and a vision.

In discussing the differing appeals of a political symbol there has also, however obliquely, been a discussion of causes; I shall comment briefly on how the Greek Cypriot material bears on two recent attempts to explain the emergence of nationalism.

Elie Kedourie's approach (1960, 1970) has been to stress the role of European intellectual traditions in the growth and diffusion of nationalist ideas. To its philosophical origins he adds an assumed need for a new social identity in the face of an intrusive market economy, industrialisation, social change, and the levelling power of the modern state. His position is developed with impressive scholarship and elegance, but Kedourie does not seek to explain why nationalism should continue to draw support when social conditions have become generally more controlled.

In spite of the fact that social change has been continual and profound in Cyprus over the last century, one looks in vain for the 'atomized society' or 'disoriented and disorganised multitudes' (Kedourie 1960: 112) which he calls forward, to explain the power of nationalist leaders to attract followings. Kedourie's obvious dislike for the excesses of nationalism makes it hard for him to explain its impetus, without the masses having first been put into a state of suggestibility by disruptive, pathological social change.

Another problem for his approach is that in stressing the manmade nature of nations, the potential for organisation that language or other cultural uniformities offer becomes problematic. A homogenous culture ends up in his hands as a white rabbit conjured out of the nationalists' hat. The role of culture, and the emergence of roughly uniform cultures under conditions of social change are better explained by the approach of Gellner (1964 and no date), Gulliver (1969), Argyle (1969) and Abner Cohen (1969a). Taking Gellner's theory (the earliest and most explicit) to represent all four writers, there is a concern to explain why culture can be so explosive. Apart from the expression of artists' aesthetic abilities, what is culture—and particularly literate culture *for*? Why in most societies in which new jobs arise through development and increasing literacy is conflict so readily generated over the issue of an official language, or a national culture? Gellner suggests close links between an increasingly complex division of labour, mass education, citizenship and the economic importance of language in competition for scarce resources between groups of different cultures. This kind of view avoids an assumption of massive social disorganisation (to account for 'hypnotised masses') and instead assumes merely a widespread but concrete and more plausible competition, particularly for jobs.

Perhaps Gellner—like Kedourie but for very different reasons—places too much stress on the *erosion* of traditional memberships under social change. Since he sees industrialisation and modernisation as a massive transition, a giant step away from 'traditional society', he tends to be less concerned with intermediate states, mixed types, and the extent to which traditional social relations are carried over into modernity. Yet anthropologists have been concerned to show that the widely reported particularisms which seem to threaten notions of unmediated citizenship rights persist (whether on tribal, regional, caste or other bases) precisely because people do not believe that they have or will ever have unmediated citizenship. But in these same countries, both nationalism and popular education have often been present for a long time; they simply do not require citizenship, and nor does the theory.

Gellner's theory looks most convincing when tackling the nationalism of modern industrial societies. Yet clearly he wishes to explain the intermediate position of many pre-industrial states as well. Perhaps the best defence of the theory is to break down the stages of modernisation, to separate the developing from the industrial stages, and to bridge the gap by arguing that in developing countries political leaders in fact see the implications of literate culture for the allocation of resources long before their societies show any signs of using universalistic criteria, or their subjects feel that they are citizens. For reasons which are not clear Gellner wishes to see nationalism as an *abstract* loyalty. Yet his theory explains very well why this often need not be the case. Nationalism, as explained by Gellner, is as concrete and down-to-earth a loyalty as one could wish for.

Many factors have contributed to the emergence and persistence of nationalism among Cypriot Greeks: a historical legacy of conflict between Ottoman Muslims and Byzantine Christians; the role of the Ottoman Turks in conquering and dominating the Cypriot Greeks; alien rule by the British which in reforming the administration of the island permitted new forms of political expression and social mobility; the challenge of modern, secular government to the power and leadership role of the Orthodox Church, which encouraged Church leaders to use nationalism to re-affirm their right to lead the Greek-speaking Christians of the island; the refusal of the British to admit Cypriots as equals, in the administration or in social life; the special role of schoolteachers as the gatekeepers of Hellenic culture, and therefore upward mobility; the emergent competition between left and right wings in the island, one of which seized on nationalism as a key symbol of political loyalty; the need of EOKA for an insurrectionary slogan which would rally wide support from the island's Greeks; the need for Greek leaders, faced with a Turkish challenge at independence, to maintain solidarity among their followers; lastly, and most lately, as a vehicle to attack an English-oriented elite.[10]

From this list it will be clear I have little sympathy with writers who suppose nationalism to have a quiddity, or to be a coherent 'ism' which can be quickly and simply explained by the manipulation of a few variables. For I have argued that Greek nationalism in Cyprus, as symbolised by the *Enosis* platform has meant very different things, at different times, to different categories of people, and there is simply no intellectual short-cut to explaining this. As an anthropologist committed to contextual explanations of small-scale events, it comes as no surprise to me to find that for events in a larger-scale unit, the delineation of shifting contexts, interests and meanings is as important as it is at village level. Different, but just as necessary.

At the start of this essay I described how some anthropologists see serious difficulties in any close relation with other disciplines, in this case with political science. It does not greatly matter if one calls this attitude 'tribalism' or 'nationalism'; the main point is that the attitude assumes some loss of identity or *virtu* will result from the contact. In her writing Lucy Mair has consistently adopted a much broader view of social anthropology's scope, and by doing so has encouraged those she influenced to do the same.

[10] The main sources I consulted for historical material for this paper are: Adams (1971), Alastos (1955), Christodoulou (1959), Foley (1964), Grivas (1964a, 1964b), Hill (1952), Jenness (1962), Kyriakides (1968), Orr (1918), and Stephens (1966).

8
Aspects of underdevelopment and development in northeast Morocco

DAVID SEDDON

If one accepts the traditional distinction between 'pure' and 'applied science as applicable to the social sciences then Professor Lucy Mair has always demonstrated, in addition to her many interests within the sphere of 'academic' or 'pure' social anthropology, a much broader concern for the 'practical' problems of those countries in which the majority of social anthropologists have carried out their field research, namely 'those countries that are sometimes called "under-developed" and sometimes, more hopefully, "developing"...(Mair 1963a: 11). Furthermore, she has always maintained that 'the anthropologist's field of study is society' and has never been afraid to include within that field the study of nations as well as of tribes and other small-scale societies; indeed, one of her major concerns in *New Nations* was to analyse the way in which local communities (small-scale societies) have become integrated into wider social and economic systems and the effects of this process on the structure of social relations within these local communities.

In fact the distinction between 'pure' and 'applied' is almost always misleading, in the case of the social sciences at least, and few have done more than has Lucy Mair in her work to show that theoretical problems and practical problems are closely related. The application of social science to problems in the real world inevitably involves the construction of adequate theoretical and analytical frameworks within which such problems may be considered. To take action on the basis of an inadequate or mistaken analysis is to set out on a perilous and unpredictable journey.

In this paper I attempt to outline some of the practical problems

UNDERDEVELOPMENT IN N.E. MOROCCO 135

facing Morocco today and to examine the way in which efforts to solve those problems have been conceived within a particular theoretical framework and also within a particular socio-political context. I refer particularly to a major irrigation project in the northeast of the country and the effects that this has had on social relations, both actual and perceived, at the local level. In order to understand changes that have taken place as a result of 'development planning' I argue that it is essential to understand the changes that preceded state intervention, both at the national level to explain the form of intervention and at the local level to explain the responses to intervention. This essay is merely an outline, introducing more problems than it solves, but I hope that it demonstrates the necessity of considering 'practical' problems and 'theoretical' problems as interrelated and also the need to consider local changes as an integral part of changes at the national and even international level.

UNDERDEVELOPMENT AND DEVELOPMENT

Continuing and persistent underdevelopment in the politically independent countries of the so-called Third World has been explained in a number of different ways by social scientists, but these explanations may be seen as falling into two broad categories. In the first are those based on a view of underdevelopment which considers the striking economic inequalities, as well as the social and political differentiation characteristic of the underdeveloped country, to be reflections of an essentially 'dual' society and economy, of which only one sector has been importantly affected by the outside world. This sector, it is argued, has become 'modernised' and relatively developed precisely because of its contact with the developed, metropolitan countries of western Europe and the United States, while the other sector, deprived of this advantage, remains archaic, traditional, subsistence-based, non-market oriented, or merely isolated, and therefore backward. Underdevelopment exists, in this view, because an insufficient proportion of the national economy has been integrated into the world economy (dominated by western capitalism), and because the backward sector, being archaic and traditional, acts as a drag on the economy as a whole, and thus prevents or impedes proper development (Boeke 1953; Fei & Ranis 1964; Jorgenson 1961, 1967; Lewis 1954, 1958).

According to explanations of the second type underdevelopment is a direct result of the ever-increasing involvement of the countries of the Third World in the international capitalist economy and of their increasing dependence on the developed, metropolitan powers of Europe and the U.S.A., in such a way that a period of colonialism has been followed by a period of what has been termed 'neo-colonialism' or 'imperialism'. The underdeveloped countries were exploited and in certain respects impoverished by colonialism but, despite political independence, are today even more dependent economically than before. Social scientists holding these views suggest that, within the capitalist system, development is achieved only at the expense of others; thus the development of one sector of the world economy, or national economy, is actually generated by the exploitation of another and by the realisation of the surplus thus extracted elsewhere than in the sector or country where it was produced. The relatively developed sector (or country) may, in turn, be exploited (and underdeveloped) by a third, the third by a fourth, and so on, to forge a chain of economic relations between exploited and exploiter (or underdeveloped and developed) which will extend from the poorest manual or agricultural labourer up to the wealthiest member of the ruling class, and from the richest and most developed sector of the underdeveloped country to one, or more, metropolitan developed countries. The greater the degree of involvement with a more developed sector or country within the capitalist system, the greater the degree of exploitation and the greater the difficulty of generating autonomous development. Given such a view of the relationship between development and underdevelopment, in which both are merely aspects of the same phenomenon and process and constitute an integrated system, it is argued that 'development planning' based on the conception of a 'dual' economy and society, whether directed at the national, regional or local economy, is likely to clarify and exacerbate social and economic differentiation and exploitation and also to intensify and perpetuate the very conditions of underdevelopment and dependence it is supposedly designed to remedy (Frank 1969a, 1969b; Griffin 1971; Laclau 1971).

UNDERDEVELOPMENT AND DEVELOPMENT IN MOROCCO

Morocco in 1971, nearly fifteen years after political independence demonstrates nearly all the characteristic indicators of underdevelopment, including a high rate of population growth, economic stagnation, massive unemployment and underemployment, food deficiencies in the mass of the population, illiteracy and increasing social and economic inequality throughout the country (Amin, 1966; Green & Seidman 1968: 34; Lacoste 1968: 21; Waterbury 1970a: 87; Waterbury 1970b: 304–315). A general decline in GNP followed the departure of the Europeans in 1956, for the period of vigorous economic development experienced in the French Protectorate after the second world war up until 1953–54, was in fact a typically unbalanced product of colonial rule, from which only a small—and predominantly European—section of the population benefited at the time, and which left the country's economy ill-prepared for broad-based autonomous development and economic growth (Amin 1970: 25–9).

Only a tiny minority of the Moroccan population enjoyed the educational and cultural effort of the colonial administration; a small group underwent military service with the French and occupied the few administrative posts available to indigènes. The first group was largely urban and the second rural, with little overlap. The two taken together inherited administrative and military power after 1956, and constitute, together with the small group of important businessmen who managed to develop under the Protectorate, Morocco's ruling class. The bulk of this power elite is recruited from a broader social elite, the prestige and rank of whose members are defined by economic and political power, locally or nationally, or else by religious or cultural criteria, or, often, by a combination of both. Members of the power elite frequently have as clients and supporters local notables and dignitaries in the various provinces.

The outstanding member of the power elite is the King, who intervenes directly and continuously in the political process. In 1970, before the attempted coup d'etat of 10 July 1971, one experienced observer wrote:

the monarchy has achieved for the moment remarkable control of elite politics, and the two aspects of its domination have been, on the one hand, a policy of elite division through the manipulation of punishments and rewards, and, on the other, the direct subordination of the armed forces and police to the throne. The essential dilemma of such a monarch is to promote economic development without upsetting the delicate political stalemate that he has helped maintain. (Waterbury, 1970a: 318)

The re-organisation of the economy needed to produce effective social and economic development, whereby the overall level of production and the standard of living of even the poorest might be drastically raised, and the dependence of the country on more powerful economies reduced, would inevitably also produce some degree of social and political instability. This would run directly against the interests of the Palace and of the power elite. But it is crucial to realise that the alternatives may well also produce serious problems, possibly even more fundamental ones.

Since political independence in 1956, and the large-scale withdrawal of foreign capital by departing Europeans, economic growth has in fact been negligible, while the substitution of a new set of interests for the old colonial 'ruling class' has resulted in the development of even greater social and economic inequality. As one observer wrote, in 1965:

The direct consequence of independence and the subsequent European exodus has been the establishment of new and relatively privileged classes; for the broad mass of the population neither the level of employment nor real income per head has improved; indeed, quite the reverse. (Amin 1970: 223)

It is some indication of the nature of economic inequality in Morocco that, out of a total population of well over 13 million, a small minority of about 800,000 have an income per head of over $1,400, while the vast majority average only $80 a head. It is also significant that the calculated average income of the rural inhabitants in the predominantly 'backward' areas (who constitute about 75 per cent of the Moroccan people) is between $45 and $55 (Amin 1970: 219–46; Morocco 1; Oualalou 1970: 13).

The increasing centralisation of political control behind a façade of democracy, the massive growth of the State bureaucracy and the emergence of new privileged classes are phenomena found at all levels and in all regions throughout Morocco and which have stimulated the growth of a system of patronage which threatens to strangle or to obscure all other modes of socio-political articulation. The absence of significant economic development and the failure of the Moroccan government to bring about the necessary restructuring of the economy are directly associated with these trends in social and political organisation. For economic policy is always, and must always be, also socially and politically determined and in Morocco those in power are unwilling so risk their own position by introducing radical reforms. What change there has been has resulted predominantly in the growth of social and economic differentiation throughout the country and within each region.

NATIONAL AND REGIONAL DEVELOPMENT PLANNING IN MOROCCO

If radical restructuring of the economy is precluded for political reasons it is nevertheless clear that something has to be done. In the absence of significant economic growth and any expansion of employment opportunities the rate at which the population is growing constitutes a major problem for central planners. In 1965 the population of Morocco was well over 13 million. The rate of demographic increase has risen from 2.7 per cent per annum (in the period 1956-60) to a current rate of c. 3.2 per cent, while mortality rates dropped from 25 per 1,000 in 1956 to 15 per 1,000 in 1966. If nothing is done to control the rate of growth the population will double between 1965 and 1985 (Seddon 1970). The family planning programme, started in 1966, is unlikely to have any real effect for a considerable time. The alternative to reducing the rate of population growth is increasing the rate of economic growth to promote broad-based economic and social development.

Both the alarming rate of population increase and the feeble rate of economic growth in Morocco since independence, as well as the prevailing inequalities within the economy, the society and the country have been explained by some as effects of colonial occupation and exploitation between 1912 and 1956 by the French and the Spanish (Belal 1968; Bencheikh 1968). This is certainly true to some considerable extent, but these explanations do not account very convincingly for the inability of independent Morocco, fifteen years after decolonisation, to reverse those disabilities inherited from the colonial period and to reduce the degree of underdevelopment.

Moroccan national development policy has been, for almost a

decade, conceived of largely as a struggle to eliminate the traditional sector of a 'dual' economy based on the belief, as expressed recently by the Minister of Agriculture and Agrarian Reform, that 'the Moroccan economy remains dual: a modern sector and an archaic, traditional sector that is more or less at subsistence level'.[1] So far, as has been suggested, the success of planned economic development in Morocco since independence has been severely limited, while development on other fronts has proved even less spectacular for, despite their constant invocation of 'major social and political reforms', it is clear that the Moroccan government 'has achieved little in the way of fundamental change at the local level to hasten the development process and that what changes have occurred involved only small segments of an already urbanised, relatively advanced minority of Moroccans' (Ashford 1967: 23). Hopes of a genuine radical reform of the national economy raised by the Five Year Plan for 1960–64 (conceived in the transitional period of 1957–59 when 'left-wing' voices had some impact) have faded as all aspects of political organisation have become increasingly centralised and controlled, and the chances of 'popular participation' in the construction of a democratic, developing nation have grown ever more remote (Amin 1970: 180–93; Bencheikh 1968: 41-4). The maintenance of the status quo and the attempt to encourage foreign investors and international aid have, together, induced a hyper-cautious approach to the question of reform of any kind on the part of the Moroccan government and of the ruling class from whom the government is drawn. It may well prove, however, that widespread minor reforms (although almost certainly nothing more radical) will be necessary in the future both to maintain the overall status quo and to keep the favour of those considering investment and aid for Morocco.

Present government policy for the rural areas is founded on the belief that technological change can produce economic development without radically altering social and political structures while radical measures of a broader socio-economic nature—like a genuine land reform—are likely to produce social and political ferment without necessarily improving production (Bencheikh 1968; Goussault n.d.; Goussault 1962). There are already indications that both these assumptions are generally incorrect, but for

[1] An interview reported in *Le Maroc Agricole*, no. 8–9, 1969, pp. 5–8

UNDERDEVELOPMENT IN N.E. MOROCCO 141

these and other subsidiary reasons the top priority for the countryside is the 'modernisation' and mechanisation of the backward, traditional, subsistence sectors and the development of cash-crops, predominantly by irrigated farming. A number of major projects are now being implemented along these lines, and with the cooperation and assistance of foreign experts, as part of the Five Year Plan for 1968-73 (Houston 1954). One of the more important of these is the completion of the Lower Muluia Irrigation Project, which straddles the provinces of Ujda and Nador, in the northeast of Morocco.

The province of Nador lies on the left bank of the Muluia river, and the completion of the Project involves the irrigation of three plains on the left bank before about 1975. The province of Nador is generally regarded as one of the poorest and most 'backward' in Morocco (Morocco 1 vol. III: 271-87; Troin 1967: 28-32) and, despite the existence of some mining in the north (Mennesson 1961), the region is clearly both poor and underdeveloped. Within the province itself some areas are significantly less well off than others; one source gives Nador an average income of $72 a head, with a range of between $100, in the wealthier districts around the urban centres of the north, and $30 in the predominantly rural south, while another puts the average per capita income in the rural areas as low as between $18 and $20 (Morocco 2, 4; Morocco 3 vol. I: 37).

The total population growth in Nador between 1960 and 1973 is calculated on the basis of a probable rate of c. 3.5 per cent per annum. Despite a significant rural exodus throughout the province and relatively high mortality rates, figures suggest a high rate of population growth in the countryside, rural population density per cultivable square kilometre showing an increase from 231 in 1960 to 291 in 1968 (Morocco 1 vol. III: 272). Unemployment and underemployment within the province are rife, and this, together with the constant rise in the cost of living, has caused considerable hardship over the last decade. Illiteracy is widespread and the present rate of school-going gives little hope for improvement in the near future.[2] Medical facilities are poor, and diseases associated with poverty and low standards of hygiene are common.[3]

[2] 47.6 per cent of boys of school-going age and 7.5 per cent of girls, compared with a national average of 49.3 per cent and 22 per cent, Morocco 1 vol. III: 278.
[3] An average of 21,000 inhabitants per doctor compared with a national average of 12,000 to 1.

Farming is increasingly regarded as a hazardous and uncertain occupation, all too dependent on the vagaries of the climate and the fluctuations of the market. The major crops are wheat and barley, grown in predominantly un-irrigated fields (although some cotton is produced for export in pump-irrigated plots in the north of the province), and the yields are generally low. The province is frequently obliged to import grain and other agricultural produce as well as manufactured goods. Industry is almost non-existent and the major alternative sources of revenue for the reluctant farmer include trading and commerce (usually on a very small scale), smuggling, service in the administration, the army or the police, local unskilled or semi-skilled labour on various private or public enterprises, and, since the early 1960s, labour migration to western Europe. The growing importance of wage labour, together with the stagnation of the farming economy and the generally low price for grain on the market, have brought about a number of important changes in local social and economic organisation. Many of these changes have their roots in the profound alterations induced by the Spanish colonial occupation,[4] but certain developments in the region over the last decade have accelerated the rate of change.

The possibility of irrigating the lower-lying areas on the left and rights banks of the Muluia river had been foreseen as early as 1917, but no real progress was made until 1947–8, when work began on the right bank, in the French zone. It was only in 1954 that preliminary work on the left bank began, and it was not until 1956 that water started flowing from the dam at Meshra Homadi to the Triffa plain on the right bank of the Muluia (Morocco 3 vol. 1: ii, 2–5). The re-unification of Morocco facilitated the continuation of the project, and in June 1960 a retention dam at Meshra Qlila was inaugurated by the King and construction work began. In 1964 an important study was made of the whole area within which irrigation was to take place (ibid. vols. I–VII) and by 1965–6 the development project in the 'Basse Moulouya' was well under way.

Even before water started flowing on the left bank in 1970 the project had made a substantial impact on certain aspects of social and economic life in the region. Changes that have occurred so far

[4] The Act of Algeciras, signed in 1906, placed Morocco under the protection of several of the European powers, but with France and Spain as effective holders of mandates over the southern and northern parts of Morocco respectively. See Seddon 1973.

make certain general forecasts possible. Over the last few years the landscape has been radically and irrevocably changed and the ecology of the whole region substantially altered. Private landholdings within the actual irrigation perimeters have been completely re-organised and re-located, but, apart from this, and the allocation (by the State) of a small number of new plots to new owners, there has been no major land reform (Ben Barka 1966: 55). The price of land within the irrigated perimeters has inevitably soared and several illegal transactions in land have taken place;[5] further, there has developed a whole new area of conflict among the local inhabitants, and especially between kinsmen, over rights to the potentially more valuable and productive land within the perimeters. New laws relating to forms of ownership, inheritance and actual exploitation of land have been promulgated with the express intent of controlling the development of cash-crop farming within the irrigated zones. The degree of dependence on credit, equipment, advice, seed and fertilizer provided by the State has increased dramatically, especially in the case of the smaller farmers, and the control both of production and of marketing is passing increasingly out of the hands of the farmers themselves.

Besides aggravating existing tensions and producing new material for conflict between different sections of the local rural population, preliminary work on the Project has been responsible for a growing dissatisfaction throughout the countryside with the actions of the various representatives and agents of the *makhzen*,[6] who are seen as 'outsiders' responsible for the imposition of a totally new pattern of agricultural activity upon a local population that has had little or no say in the planning or implementation of the project at any but the lowest and least significant level, and whose personal and immediate (let alone long-term), benefit is by no means clear. These two areas of hostility and cleavage would appear to be complementary, in so far as the local population is most clearly divided into those who are likely to benefit from the 'development' of the region and those who are not, those who are likely to benefit the most (the larger farmers, traders and entrepreneurs), being identified increasingly as friends or clients of the *makhzen*.

[5] Land transactions within irrigated perimetres was forbidden by law in 1951.
[6] A term widely used throughout Morocco to refer to the 'government', the 'administration' or local authorities, and the 'State'.

The two areas directly affected by the Lower Muluia project up to 1971 were the Sebra plain, in the southeast of the province, in the rural commune of Zaio, and the Bu Arg, slightly to the north, where the territories of four rural communes (Qaria-t-Arkeman, Nador, Selwan and Zaio), meet. The irrigation of the Sebra and the Bu Arg, and possibly, by 1974, of a third plain, the Gareb, is seen by national and regional planners as the most effective way of developing some of the backward areas of an isolated and backward province. It is hoped that the production of cash-crops for foreign export and national consumption will lead, not only to an improvement in the national balance of payments situation,[7] but also to the establishment of processing factories and other light industry in the area, within the decade, and that this will improve production both in agriculture and in industry, increase opportunities for local enterprise and local employment, raise the overall standard of living in the province and introduce a significant input of wealth into the region as a whole.

In the field of agriculture there is little doubt that superior equipment, information and techniques, together with State financial assistance and State control of farming procedures, will result in far greater farming efficiency, but, in the absence of any major changes in the local economic or political structure, the changes are likely to benefit only the wealthier minority, to create new difficulties for the less well-off and to increase inequality and social differentiation.

Looking ahead, and keeping our focus primarily on the local situation, we would suggest that those who are likely to benefit most from 'development' within the area will be those who already own, or are in a position to buy, (or acquire an interest in), large tracts of irrigated land and those able to participate on a large scale in the process of marketing produce into and out of the region. Such individuals are relatively rare and where marketing is not controlled by State enterprises it is probable that big entrepreneurs will be attracted from outside the region. Most of the larger land-owners are likely to prosper, as are the wealthier co-owners of jointly-owned inherited land within the irrigated perimeters who are able to buy out their poorer kinsmen. The re-location of presently scattered homesteads into nucleated settle-

[7] It is debatable whether a concentration on export crops could in fact achieve this. (Green & Seidman 1968: 37–51; Amin 1970: 232–46.)

ments will attract entrepreneurs of various kinds from outside the area, and the bigger local traders will increase their custom, as new commercial opportunities develop in the rapidly growing village and urban centres. Small land-holders with fields in the plains may improve their positions somewhat, if they can ignore the demands of their less fortunate kinsmen outside the irrigated perimeters or without land at all, and not sell their newly valuable property to would-be buyers with more capital to invest.

Those who have been allocated land within the perimeter from the 'public domain' may have a new source of revenue, but their farming will be so strictly controlled by the State to produce according to 'national needs' that they will be, in effect, agricultural labourers on their 'own' land for a State capitalist enterprise. Those who have land only in the dry zones will be increasingly at a disadvantage unless substantial efforts are made to improve conditions in these relatively deprived and underdeveloped zones.[8] Finally, those without either sufficient land to maintain a livelihood or the capital to establish themselves effectively as entrepreneurs in the more 'stable' areas of the tertiary sector are likely to suffer, as unskilled or semi-skilled workers and as part of the floating population in the 'unstable' areas of the local economy, from the overall rise in the cost of living and from ever-increasing competition from the landless labourers of the even poorer mountain areas of the central Rif.[9]

Whether the 'development' of the region will in fact benefit Morocco as much as is hoped is not a concern of ours here, but there are some indications that whatever 'development' takes place in this region it will be an 'underdeveloped development', a development stunted from the start by its dependence on and exploitation by more developed sectors of the national economy and by foreign interests (Oualalou 1969: 175-205). What does seem clear is the probable direction of change for the mass of the local population of Nador province as a result of the 'development' of certain areas within the region.

[8] The development of the hillier, non-irrigated zones has been relatively little considered and investment to date in these areas has been absurdly small.
[9] For a discussion of the relationship between the 'stable' and 'unstable' sectors of the economy, see Frank 1969b: pp. 276-97.

UNDIRECTED CHANGE IN NORTHEAST MOROCCO

It is necessary, at this point, to reiterate the fact that changes brought about by 'development planning' are very recent in this area, and that, in most cases, such planning has merely accentuated certain types of conflict and accelerated existing trends. We would be in a better position to make forecasts about the likely direction of changes in local economic and political organisation over the next few years if we considered not only developments since independence but also the changes that have taken place in this region over the last century or so as a result both of 'planning' and of unplanned, but systematic change in the national and international economic and political 'environment'.

Although Nador today is undoubtedly both poor and underdeveloped, it is impossible to agree with the suggestions of the planners and of certain other observers, that the region's so-called 'backwardness' is the result of its longstanding physical, economic and political isolation (Troin 1967: 29). There can be little doubt, when the evidence is reviewed, that 'the area has long since passed the stage of a pure subsistence economy and its inhabitants are well aware of the significance of the market system in which they actively participate..' (Morocco 3 vol. 1: 88), and, in fact, the region's involvement in the international capitalist economy, (both colonial and post-colonial), dates back to, at least, the first half of the nineteenth century, when labour migration from the eastern Rif to French-occupied Algeria began. Even before 1830 and the beginning of colonial military penetration in north Africa, the inhabitants of the northeast were by no means isolated, either economically or politically.

As early as the seventeenth century the tribes of the eastern Rif were involved in an extensive trading and smuggling network which linked the Moroccan hinterland with Europe and made possible the exchange of local materials for arms and ammunition (Brignon *et al.* 1967: 239). That such commercial contacts continued throughout the eighteenth and into the nineteenth century is adequately documented, and, indeed, illegal commerce between the tribesmen of the northeast and European traders became so substantial that in 1813 the Sultan sent a punitive force to the area in order to bring local commerce, and also local mining concerns, under the control of the central government (or *makhzen*) once more (ibid.: 253, 266; Miège 1963 II: 29-30; Houdas 1969: 194-5). In the first half of the nineteenth century much of the traditional commerce between Morocco and the regions to the east continued, and even expanded, while new sources of trade and income developed with the installation of the French. The absence of all customs control between the territories held by the French and those still in Algerian hands made it possible for British goods, imported illegally through Tetuan in the west, to reach western Algeria via the eastern Rif. Abd-el-Qader, the leader of tribal resistance against the French in western Algeria, received supplies of all kinds, including arms and ammunition, from England via Gibraltar and northeast Morocco; he also had his own contacts and supporters in the Rif. Two governors of the Spanish praesidium (and town) of Melilla were recalled after their association with local agents of Abd-el-Qader was discovered (Miège 1963, II: 202), and when, in 1847, the Moroccan *makhzen* sent three columns to the northeast to prevent further assistance to the Algerian leader, they found him with his loyal supporters in the small fortress at Selwan (ibid.: 205-6).

The nearest towns to the essentially tribal northeast were Melilla, Taza, Ujda and Fes (the capital and heart of the *makhzen*). Commerce with Melilla, although limited, increased during the latter part of the nineteenth century, especially between 1880 and 1909, and included the unofficial sale of arms by the Spanish garrison to the surrounding tribesmen (Payne 1967: 63). Some tribesmen went as far afield as Fes to buy foreign imported goods and to sell their local produce, both vegetable and animal (although an important market for livestock lay closer at hand near Taza),[10] and much of the iron ore extracted by simple mining techniques was exported from the mines around Melilla to the capital.

The region came, in theory, under the jurisdiction of the Pasha of Ujda, the highest representative of the *makhzen* in the whole of the northeast, and political contact was frequent between the agents of the *makhzen* and the local tribal leaders. The *makhzen* had never maintained more than a relative monopoly of coercive means within the country and the spread of fast-loading rifles throughout the tribal areas during the latter part of the nineteenth century tended to reduce still further the effectiveness of the

[10] Taza had been an important centre and market for animal products since the fourteenth century. Brignon 1967: 154.

makhzen's control and to strengthen the position of local leaders. Nevertheless, taxes were still frequently exacted from the tribes of the northeast, and both political and economic pressures could be exerted (e.g. Houdas 1969: 142, 183, 190, 193–5).

Even before the military penetration of the Spanish into the area, in 1909, therefore, the northeast was by no means cut off or isolated from either the national or the international economic and political system. For well over a century, every household and family has been an integral part of the regional, national and international economy, by virtue of its participation in the market system, its consumption of imported food-stuffs and manufactured goods, whether Moroccan or foreign, its payment of taxes to the government and its role as a source of labour on the national and international labour market. Iron ore, livestock and animal products and labour have, for a very long time, been exported from this region, although the mass of the people have benefited but little. Neither the poverty and underdevelopment of the northeast, nor the increasing inequality and social stratification found there, can be explained as a result of backwardness and isolation; they should rather be seen as deriving from a combination of factors, of which perhaps the most important has been the region's growing involvement in a wider capitalist economy. The integration of the northeast into this global economic political system predates the Spanish occupation. Nevertheless, the Spanish military expansion into northeast Morocco, in 1909, from a bridgehead in Melilla, and their subsequent occupation, pacification and colonisation of the whole of northern Morocco until 1956, brought about radical changes throughout the area and also accelerated and accentuated many of the changes already taking place (Waterbury 1970a: 35; Seddon 1973).

THE PRE-COLONIAL PERIOD IN THE NORTHEAST

In Nador province, at the present time, there are clear and significant differences between the north and the south, both in terms of average income per head and in terms of degree of 'modernisation' and urbanisation; social inequality is also probably more marked in the generally better-off north. There are also certain differences in population density, patterns of landownership and, indeed, in the basic farming economy between the largely agricultural north and the still heavily pastoral south

(Seddon, in preparation). These latter differences reflect, among other things, differences in local economic organisation that date back to pre-colonial times. The major geographical contrast between the hilly north of the region and the relatively open south was reflected, during the nineteenth century, in both the economic and, to some extent, the political organisation of tribes, although they showed certain fundamental similarities throughout the northeast (Seddon 1973).

Economic and political organisation throughout the region, in the latter half of the nineteenth century (or at least up until the 1890s), appears to have been based essentially upon the complex interaction of individuals and groups forming, breaking and re-forming alliances, coalitions, contracts and associations of various kinds, in a continual attempt to gain advantages or to minimise disadvantages. These associations gave the individual a framework for social, economic and political activity, while his individual perception of the range and flexibility of existing and possible alternative alignments provided him both with a conceptual model, or set of ideas, regarding the way in which his 'society' was constituted, and with suggestions as to how the usual forms might best be used and manipulated (Seddon 1973).

It has been suggested that a basic trait of Moroccan political behaviour is the remarkable flexibility of political actors and groups (Waterbury 1970: 7, 66), and it is certainly true that, in the northeast, the kinship idiom, the concept of 'friendship' and that of political coalition (called *leff*, pl. *elfuf*), provided tribesmen with principles of considerable flexibility by which associations could be formed and maintained for a variety of purposes. Kinship comprised several, more specific, principles of association and cooperation, of which the dominant (i.e. the most valued and most frequently invoked), was that of patrilineal descent. In practice, here as elsewhere, although political organisation was frequently described in terms of the segmentary lineage model (Middleton & Tait 1958), and agnatic descent claimed to be the crucial principle of association—whether for economic, political or other social reasons—the existence and utilisation of other principles of association meant that the segmentary lineage model did no more than set out and express one set of values, which frequently contradicted, and were contradicted by, one or more other sets of values (Favret 1968; Peters 1967).

TABLE I

Circle	Rural Commune	Annex/Tribe	Language	Total Pop.	Pop. density
L'Uta	Zaio	Ulad Stut	Arabic	10,500	24
	Ras el Ma	Kebdana	Berber	30,700	50
	Qaria-t-Arkeman	,,			
	Hassi Berkan	Beni bu Yahi	Berber		
		Beni Ukil	Arabic	18,800	15
	Tistutin	Beni bu Yahi			
		Beni Ukul			
	Driush	Metalsa	Berber	28,100	17
	Ain Zohra	,,			
Gelaia	Nador	—	—	18,500	—
	Ferkhana	Mazuja	Berber	28,000	126
	Had Beni Shicar	Beni Shicar	Berber	21,500	127
	Iazanen	Beni bu Gafar	Berber	8,300	131
	Tleta Jbel	Beni Sidel	Berber	22,900	73
	Tleta L'uta	,,			
	Selwan	Beni bu Ifrur	Berber	25,200	123
	Beni bu Ifrur	,,			
Rif	Dar Kebdani	Beni Said	Berber	31,700	78
	Tazarhin	,,			
	Ben Tiyeb	Beni Ulishek	Berber	22,100	100
	Mehayast	,,			
	Kemis Temsaman	Temsaman	Berber	36,800	87
	Budinar	,,			
	Trugut	,,			
	Ijormauas	Beni Tuzin	Berber	39,000	64
	Midar	,,			
	Tleta d'Azlef	,,			
	Tafersit	Tafersit	Berber	8,200	130

Population figures refer to 1957 and were taken from Mennesson, 'Importance social des exploitations minières dans la région de Nador', *Mines et Geologie*, no. 14, 1961.

According to this dominant model of social organisation each tribe was divided into a number of segments, which in turn were subdivided into their constituent sub-segments; these sub-segments were again internally segmented. The model set out an ideal pattern of relations between segments (defined as 'descent groups' by the principle of patrilineal descent), and within segments at all levels, in which members of a given segment (or descent group) co-operated together and united in opposition to another segment (or descent group) of the same order, while at the same time being internally segmented along lines given by the rule of descent. Even during this early period, however, the abstract principle of 'kinship solidarity' was only one of a set of principles guiding the actions of individuals, and by no means controlled completely the nature and direction of economic and political activity on the ground. Vertical cleavage, produced by the principle of kinship solidarity and the manipulation of the segmentary lineage model, both within and between descent groups (and tribes), was frequently nullified by alternative possibilities promoting horizontal cleavage extending throughout the region.[11]

On the other hand, agnates did often co-operate in economic and political matters, despite differences in wealth and status. Also, if economic security and political success were to be obtained by membership, or still better by control, of an effective coalition or political association (*leff*), as well as by the possession of a personal network of alliances and contacts throughout the region, agnates provided the basis of such a coalition in the majority of cases. In fact, a virtual prerequisite for the acquisition of an effective following was the ability to control, and even manipulate, one's closest kinsmen, for they provided the surest and most satisfactory base for the recruitment of a wide-ranging support group.[12]

Typically, an ambitious man seeking economic and political pre-eminence would himself seek to marry or to marry his children outside the descent group, and frequently outside the tribe, despite the value given to marriage within the descent group as a way of maintaining the 'solidarity of the descent group', in order to extend his range of potential allies. At the same time, it was in his interest to persuade co-members of his descent group, (by the invocation of 'descent' and 'marriage within the descent group'), to marry within a circumscribed social field so that their affines were still his agnates, and therefore susceptible to his influence and authority.

The construction of flexible alliances between equals and the need to attract a sizeable following founded on support from one's agnates and close kin (or else to belong to such a support group),

---

[11] Inequality was an integral part of pre-colonial economic and political life, but the development of a class structure was limited.

[12] For discussion of a strikingly similar situation see Barth 1959a, 1967; Montagne 1972.

were related to the insecurity and unpredictability of the natural and social environment (Waterbury 1970a; 68) and produced considerable instability in the distribution of wealth and power. The extreme difficulty of accumulating wealth that could be regarded as more or less permanent (especially among the pastoral groups), and the problems involved in maintaining a position of political superiority, explain, to a large extent, the degree of interdependence that existed between kinsmen, between the more and the less powerful, between the richest and the poorest individuals both within the descent group and between descent groups, and, indeed, throughout the region.

There are indications that this situation was changing throughout the last two decades of the nineteenth century (Seddon 1973); that the social distance between the more and the less powerful, the richer and the poorer tribesmen was growing as rapid integration into the wider economic and political system had an ever greater effect on local social structure and social organisation. This process was tremendously accelerated by Spanish intervention and subsequent military expansion in the northeast between 1900 and 1912 (Seddon 1973).

THE COLONIAL PERIOD IN NORTHEAST MOROCCO

From 1912 until 1927 the Spanish were primarily occupied in pacifying their 'zone' and in bringing the whole of northern Morocco under effective colonial rule, but, even during this short period, they transformed the very foundations of social organisation in what they termed the Rif Oriental (and which today is the province of Nador), by integrating it completely into the Spanish colonial economy and the Spanish colonial political and administrative system. From 1927 onwards until the mid-1950s, the Spanish so controlled the economic and political life of the entire northern 'zone' that, in effect, as one observer has remarked: '..the Blad l-Makhzen, for the first time in history, included all of northern Morocco..' (Woolman 1969: 197–214).

The construction of villages, first as military camps and strongholds and later as commercial centres and market places; the opening up of the mines by private Spanish companies; the appropriation of land for colonisation and farming; the establishment of a regional administrative capital 14 kilometres south of Melilla (Villa Nador); and the employment of the local inhabitants on a large scale as wage labourers, 'native police', minor bureaucrats and functionaries, and soldiers, all drastically affected the population geography of the region, as well as political and economic organisation. These factors in turn increased individual geographical mobility and stimulated the drift off the land into less stable employment, thereby altering the nature of economic relations between kinsmen, the average size of households and the economic position of the nuclear family.

The suppression of inter- and intra-tribal violence,[13] by the colonial *makhzen*, together with the establishment of an official 'presence' throughout the countryside, radically changed the nature of political organisation. Despite the maintenance of tribal divisions and subdivisions (for administrative purposes), interdependence and co-operation between members of the same 'descent group' weakened rapidly as men strove, not to find support in the construction of a following, but to develop and maintain good relations with the *makhzen* and to make the most of the new mobility to establish a wide-spread network of 'friends' and patrons throughout the region, and elsewhere.

With the emergence of a stable and all-controlling *makhzen*, and the development of new investment possibilities, accumulation of both wealth and power became possible for the small minority looked upon with favour by the Spanish, and for these individuals the need to cultivate their poorer relatives and fellow-tribesmen as a form of social investment and insurance became increasingly irrelevant. At the same time, the attempts of the less-favoured to invoke 'kinship solidarity' and kinship obligation as valid reasons for providing them with assistance and support became increasingly ineffectual, for the most part.

In the southern parts of the region the settlement of the previously transhumant, tent-dwelling tribes, that took place gradually during the 1930s and 1940s, was related largely to their absorption into the colonial economy, which required wage labour more than it needed animal products and provided incentives to leave the herds for employment elsewhere. The substantial growth of population, as a result both of immigration into the area from adjoining areas and of natural increase, together with a drastic reduction in the average size of herds and a rapid

[13] Violence in the form of feuding and raiding was an integral part of precolonial political organisation among the tribes of the northeast.

increase in the proportion of land devoted to agriculture, produced firstly an extension of cultivated land, and then, very soon afterwards, an ever-increasing pressure on the land. The dominant form of land-ownership shifted, within a few years, from communal descent group ownership to private ownership by individuals as heads of households,[14] the wealthier and more powerful members of the descent group being able generally to secure sizeable tracts for themselves and their immediate families, to the detriment of their poorer kinsmen. This process was assisted by the fact that, often, many of the poorer families were unable to uphold their claims to portions of the communal land as their menfolk were absent in the towns, or in other parts of the 'zone', hoping to support their immediate families by finding regular employment there. For it was generally the less well-off who tended to abandon their land in favour of opportunities elsewhere, (often even leaving the 'zone' altogether to work in the French Protectorate or in Algeria). This was especially true in the late 1930s and the 1940s, when the Spanish recruited extensively among the Moroccans for troops to assist Franco during the Civil War (Friedlander 1964), and when many small peasants and landless farmers fell into debt to their fellow tribesmen during the famines and economic difficulties of the war years, between 1939 and 1945 (Kelso et al. 1967: 39–43; Naval Intelligence 1942: 125, 159). The growing importance of the towns and villages as commercial centres, military camps and the loci of administrative control, together with the hope they provided of employment, contributed greatly to the development of a considerable rural exodus and of a new floating urban population of casual workers and 'penny capitalists' (Tax 1953; Frank 1969b).

For the growth of 'urban centres' was associated with an increase in trade and commerce, most of it on a very small scale, rather than with the development of industry. What industrial development there was centred on the Nador–Melilla region and served to increase the differences between the north and the south of the province (Troin 1967). There was relatively little development of 'modern, mechanised agriculture', the majority of Spanish farmers in this area being themselves relatively poor and what was produced was exported to Spain through Melilla. The exploitation

[14] Some land was 'privately owned' (*melk*) during the nineteenth century among such groups, but this was rare.

of the countryside was limited to cotton production on a relatively small scale, in the northwest of the region, a number of orchards, also in the northwest, and the fairly systematic denudation of the low hills in the southeast to produce firewood and charcoal for export to Spain. (Cattle, eggs, poultry and hides were also exported, largely to Spain.) The area of land actually appropriated by the Spanish in this region was quite small compared with the western end of the 'zone', and much of that land remained unexploited throughout the colonial period. Nevertheless, the introduction, between 1913 and 1927 (Morocco 1; 2817, 1175), of a number of laws relating to the registration of privately owned land made it possible for Spanish buyers of tribal land to confirm the legality of such purchases, and also for a number of privileged locals to appropriate for themselves large areas of grazing and agricultural land.

Imports to the 'zone' as a whole consisted for the most part of supplies for the Europeans, both military and civil, and fell into four main classes: food-stuffs (including cereals, refined sugar, edible oils, flour, semolina and wines), manufactured goods (such as cotton textiles and candles), machinery (iron and steel goods, motor vehicles and spare parts), and petroleum. Expenditure on Public Works was relatively substantial (although apparently insufficient to develop more than a very small road and rail network), but spending on social services, including medical services and education, was minimal, what services did exist being confined largely to the 'urban centres' for the benefit of the Europeans. Of the Europeans in the towns, the Spanish and French were mainly skilled workers, shopkeepers, or proprietors of cafes, while the Italian immigrants tended to be unskilled labourers. Throughout the period of occupation European earnings from unskilled and skilled work were at least double those of Moroccans doing the same jobs; the decline in the value of money and a general rise in prices, especially after the Civil War, emphasised the gap between these two sections of the 'working' population. (Naval Intelligence, 1942: 159–65). Nevertheless, despite the clear, and probably growing, inequalities both between the European and Moroccan sections of the colonial society and within the Moroccan population itself, social inequalities appear not to have been as great or as striking as in the more 'developed' French Protectorate.

It has been argued that the present poverty and 'backwardness' of the north as a whole, and of the central and eastern Rif in particular, is due almost entirely to its physical isolation and its lack of development under the Spanish. Such commentators point to the orientation of the northern 'zone' towards, and its dependence upon, Spain—itself a poor and underdeveloped country (Frank 1969a; Davies 1965)—and suggest that 'the major obstacles to the integration of the ex-Spanish region [after independence] are obvious' (Ashford 1961: 209). These 'obstacles' were the existence in the north of Spanish administrative, educational and financial systems, which meant that all the special training of administrators, all public notices and regulations, and all communications were in Spanish, while the poverty of Spain meant that the level of general education and economic development was markedly lower in the north.

THE POST-COLONIAL PERIOD IN NORTHEAST MOROCCO

In the years between 1956 and 1958 a certain amount of relief was distributed in the northern zone and a special commission initiated to consider the development of the northern provinces, but 'the new government seems to have gone as slowly as possible with the integration of the north..' (ibid.: 210), and there was a significant hiatus between independence and the completion of the merger between the two 'zones' in the early part of 1958 (ibid.: 209–10). When the administrative and financial merger was finally brought about, and the north at last 'integrated' into the newly independent Moroccan nation, a whole new set of controls and regulations came into operation in the north, introducing new taxes, licences and fees, and aggravating existing difficulties. 'Within a month there were petitions for relief and special controls to keep down the cost of living' (ibid: 211; Waterbury 1970a: 238–42), workers were laid off and strikes occurred, producing extensive unemployment throughout the zone. In other words, closer 'integration' of the less-'developed' north with the more 'developed' south worsened, rather than improved, conditions in the north, as the northern provinces' dependence on Spain and the Spanish economy shifted to a dependence on the more 'developed' sectors of the Moroccan post-colonial economy.

Local officials in the northeast, (and elsewhere), were probably aware of the growing difficulties and dissatisfaction throughout the countryside, but no sign of this appeared in official government statements, although, as has been pointed out, 'Rabat could hardly have been ignorant of the depletion of tribal food reserves over the summer [of 1958] so that many areas were at a near starvation level by fall' (Ashford, 1961: 212). When dissatisfaction grew so bitter that the tribes in many of the poorer parts of Morocco rose up in arms, the uprisings were quelled with a careful mixture of promises, threats and military force. The most serious trouble was in the northeast (in the provinces of Al Huceimas, Nador and Taza) and in January 1959 the King's son (later King Hassan II) led an expedition of 20,000 Royal Army troops into that region to subdue the insurgents.

A royal commission established to discover the nature and extent of the tribesmen's grievances reported in December 1959 that the major problems appeared to be:

(1) A feeling of frustration and abandonment arising from the realisation that independence had not brought the north what it had brought other regions.
(2) Unemployment. (The difficulty of labour migration from the eastern Rif to Algeria was now considerable, and it was pointed out that many former soldiers in the Spanish army were without work.)
(3) Fiscal injustice.
(4) Lack of hospitals, schools, roads and agricultural credit.
(5) Poor or corrupt administrators from outside the region (Waterbury 1970a: 240).

The suppression of the various tribal uprisings throughout Morocco during 1959 marks the end of a transitional post-independence period (of three years) during which mass participation in the process of 'nation-building' had been encouraged verbally at least, and the beginning of a period of increasing control over the nation's political and economic life by the King and his *makhzen*. Control has been achieved by means of a complex and extensive system of patronage, supported by a number of hierarchical formal institutions, such as the Ministry of the Interior and the Army. After May 1960, when the King became prime minister, all governmental posts of any importance were filled by royal decree, and by March 1961 the King (by this time Hassan II) was prime minister, minister of defence, minister of agriculture and minister of the interior. In June 1965, after riots and demonstrations associated with the economic crisis of 1964-65, the King suspended Parliament and declared a state of emergency.

Despite hopes, in the early years after independence, among certain sections of the population, for a genuine programme of decentralisation through the creation and encouragement of the rural commune system, interest in the commune as an institution for the promotion of social, political and economic development was first overshadowed by increasing party competition and political turmoil and then, after 1963, replaced by attempts to bring about limited social and economic development from above (Ashford 1967: 23-59; Ben Bachir 1969; Bencheikh 1968).

It was considered necessary, however, to maintain some appearance of democratic participation, and in May 1960 the first elections were held throughout the country for the councils of the newly created rural communes. That the local commune system is a mere façade for the maintenance of control over the rural population and serves only to perpetuate existing inequalities—whether social, political or economic—has become increasingly clear to the rural population over the last decade, but no official alternatives now exist. Ambitious men in the northeast, as elsewhere, have come to realise that virtually the only source of local power and of wealth lies in the maintenance of good relations with the local authorities, or, if possible, with persons in the provincial, or even national, capital. The political parties provided little in the way of alternative avenues to power or of alternative sources of wealth and prestige, for the vast majority, even before 1963, and now it has become inadvisable to admit to having any political interests at all. The strength of the *makhzen*'s grip on the countryside is exemplified in its relation to the supposedly democratic rural commune (Cherkaoui 1968).

The commune councils have little power, for the control exerted by the local authority (the *qaid*), over the agenda, the direction of the discussion and even the conclusions and decisions of the council meeting was from the beginning, and remains, considerable. Much of this control over the actions and deliberations of the commune council appears redundant when it is appreciated that the elections for the council are strictly controlled by the local authorities, and that those elected are rarely other than the candidates approved by the administration in the first place.

CONCLUSION

A system of patronage, in which each individual is dependent on others whom he considers better placed than himself to obtain favours or desired goods, and from whom he expects to receive favours for himself in return for services of some kind, is seen to extend from the poorest rural inhabitant to the Palace in Rabat. Apparently running parallel to the system of patronage, reinforcing its effectiveness at all levels, is the chain of economic relations that extends from the ultimate exploited, through innumerable 'middlemen', to the final exploiters within Morocco. Both economic and political relations in Morocco today are confined within essentially hierarchical and pyramidal structures involving systematic inequality throughout and the existence of greater and greater monopoly power (both in economic and in political terms) the higher up the structure one goes. These structures depend for their continued existence upon a general, explicit recognition by the lower members of the hierarchy (at each level) of their dependence on the higher members and upon the ability of the higher members (at each level) to maintain their monopoly of economic and political power.

Since independence social inequalities in the northeast, as elsewhere in Morocco, have become sharper and clearer; gaps have visibly opened up within the pyramidal structure of Moroccan society and the underlying emergent class structure is becoming more apparent as the tribal ties and the relations of kinship and friendship which serve to mask the essential structural inequalities generally lose their strength. At the lowest level, the mass of the population, both urban and (although to a lesser extent) rural, is beginning to chafe at the perpetuation and systematic promotion of social, economic and political inequality, blaming first the *makhzen* (the 'government') and then the local notables and rich peasants.[15] In the specific case of the areas directly affected by the

[15] This is what is happening in that part of the northeast where my research was carried out. I worked in the rural commune of Zaio between March 1968 and December 1969, my work in this region being part of a longer-term project directed by Professor R. T. Holt of the University of Minnesota. A brief, preliminary report appears in Seddon, 'Social and Economic Change in Northeast

Lower Muluia irrigation project the introduction of 'development' schemes which are seen by the local inhabitants as likely to produce 'development' for the few and insecurity and relative poverty for the majority (and which may well do just this) are accentuating existing conflict and tensions, both between the mass of the people and the *makhzen*, and also within the local population between those most likely to benefit from the 'development' of the region and the rest, and thus clarifying the structure of social inequality in the northeast.

Any development project which increases the degree of exploitation and inequality and fails to improve materially the general standard of living and the productivity of an area for the benefit of all its inhabitants is not merely inadequate but also likely, sooner or later, to generate precisely the kind of social and political conflict that the present power elite wishes above all to avoid. Furthermore, while it is clear that the present political structure in Morocco affects the nature and scope of economic development, it is equally true that the stagnation of the economy, unemployment and associated social and economic inequality will, increasingly, put pressure on the fragile political balance, and produce violence whether on a limited or on a larger scale.

Morocco', *Current Anthropology*, vol. 12, 1971. My acknowledgements to Professor Holt and to my friend and colleague Raymond Jamous, for their assistance and support.

9
Land tenure and 'room for manoeuvre'*

ANNE SHARMAN

INTRODUCTION

African systems of land tenure have been studied extensively (Mair, 1948c, 1956; Biebuyck 1963; Colson 1971). In many cases these studies have been carried out by social anthropologists, such as Professor Mair, who have been concerned with the contribution that social anthropology can make to the formulation of government policy. Not surprisingly their emphasis has often been on the way in which traditional systems of land tenure were misunderstood by administrators, and changed as a result of colonial rule and a variety of associated influences, such as more advanced technology and availability of durable goods; the introduction of cash crops and a market economy; increased population density; and limitations on geographical mobility and expansion.

This paper presents another case study of how and why a system of land tenure has changed. But it has a particular emphasis, the way in which individuals today manipulate new institutions for dispute settlement to acquire rights in land.[1] The process is examined largely through analysis of written records of government court cases. Men and women do not participate equally in such cases, a fact which is also discussed. The policy implications of the analysis are considered in the conclusion.

It is not a paper about 'individualisation' of land tenure,

* See Mair 1969c: 120–35. I wish to thank the Editor, Beverley Brock, Rayah and David Feldman and Graham Fennell for reading and commenting on earlier versions of this paper.
[1] The fieldwork on which this paper is based was carried out at different periods between February 1965 and July 1967 in West Budama county, Bukedi District, Uganda. Discussion relates only to events prior to July 1967.

although it will be clear that changes are taking place both in the rights claimed by individuals or small family groups and in the size of the group within which there is reallocation of surplus land. Analysis of directions of change is important, but the situation at present shows a complex mixture of continuity and change. Conflict and uncertainty at the local level over rules of land tenure is not simply the outcome of a situation in which changing circumstances are giving rise to conflict between the group and the individual over clearly defined rights in land, particularly the right to alienate land. It is also the outcome of confusion regarding rules regulating rights in land, and their application.

Following the incorporation of small autonomous political units into large, centralised states, customary systems of land tenure have in most cases been recognised and retained. But the effectiveness of customary rules regulating land ownership (i.e. security against eviction),[2] use and transactions depended on their association with a particular form of social organisation and particular institutions for the settlement of disputes. New institutions introduced for the settlement of disputes, working with foreign concepts of property and rights in land, have had difficulty in applying customary rules regulating land tenure. Rules that are anyway changing and uncertain are further distorted and confused by being interpreted and applied by government courts. This lack of clarity in the rules and their application is found at the local level in countries with very different national policies (whether or not these are clearly formulated) and views as to the desirability of encouraging 'individualisation' of land tenure by issuing freehold title to land. This can be seen, for example, by comparing the situation described in this case study from West Budama county, Bukedi District, Uganda, and Feldman's case study from Tanzania (Feldman 1970).

POLITICAL ORGANISATION: PAST AND PRESENT

West Budama is occupied by the Adhola, who generally present themselves as members of a single tribe and as collectively descended from their ancestor, Adhola, although they do acknowledge that a few clans have recently come from Busoga District, and changing circumstances have led some to claim membership

[2] For this distinction between three different aspects of land tenure see Apthorpe 1968.

of neighbouring tribes, such as the Teso, previously repudiated.[3]

The traditional political organisation appears to have been based on the clan system, together with co-operation on a territorial base, cutting across clan organisation, for certain ritual activities and warfare (Sharman 1970). Below the level of the clan, localised clan sections were the most important units of organisation. Although localised lineage groupings of various sizes were sometimes recognised, segmentary division of the clans into lineages was not stressed. Localised clan sections were the largest land holding groups. Rights over land were established by clearing or conquest, and passed to the sons and later male descendants of the original occupiers.

The distribution of clans and size of local clan settlements varies in different parts of West Budama. The largest clan settlements are found in the original areas of settlement. In other areas clan settlements are smaller and in the most recently settled area, although agnatic groupings are still localised, each one is very small and many clans are represented in one settlement. This is partly the result of the way in which Adhola clans used to expand. The clan segments did not retain the same spatial relationship to each other, while pushing outwards to take over new land.[4] Adhola clan segments had rights in particular pieces of land and expanded by dividing and planting clan colonies some distance from the original settlement, where there was land available for clearing or land successfully taken from other tribes.

There were ritual officers in each clan, keepers of ritual drums and other emblems (Sharman & Anderson 1967), and those who performed rituals at local or central clan shrines, all of whose positions were inherited patrilineally. There was, however, little differentiation of secular political authority. Each extended family had its own head, who regulated day-to-day affairs and settled disputes within that unit. Settlement of disputes between more distantly related or unrelated people depended on arbitration by elders.

The Adhola were conquered at the beginning of the century for

[3] In fact settlement in the area took place over a period of about 400 years, probably starting some time in the fifteenth century, with conflict and intermixture of different tribes. See Ogot 1967.
[4] This is the type of expansion described by Southall 1952, for the Kenya Luo and by Bohannan 1954, for the Tiv. Adhola expansion was closer to that practised by the Ibo, as described in Jones 1949.

the British by a Ganda general. A hierarchy of county (*saza*), sub-county (*gombolola*), parish (*muluka*) and sub-parish (*mutongole*) chiefs was established, similar to those in Buganda, but not corresponding to any traditional Adhola positions. This administrative hierarchy is still found today.[5] It is distinct from the judicial system and the chiefs are not generally concerned with land disputes and matters relating to the use of land. However, they are expected to ensure that the requisite amounts of cassava and sweet potatoes are grown as a famine reserve, and to this end sometimes arrange for a person with a lot of land to lend some to neighbours, particularly for small plots of sweet potatoes. The judicial system consists of courts at three levels, the sub-county courts, the district and sub-district courts, and the High Court of Uganda.[6] Land cases, except for second appeals,[7] are heard in the sub-county courts. However, such cases may never reach the courts but be dealt with by the clans, although these do not form part of the official judicial system.

With the imposition of colonial rule basic changes were also made in the clan organisation. As was so often the case in uncentralised African societies, the British created authority positions where none had previously existed. In the past dispersed sections of the same clan probably had infrequent contact, since communications were poor and the need for large scale co-operation limited.[8] But after the area had been conquered the Ganda and British tried to persuade the Adhola to elect officials for the whole clan and this they finally began to do in about 1935. In 1945 the government requested clan leaders to attend a meeting of the council and most clans did then elect leaders (Southall 1957: 10;

[5] In 1967 a new constitution was introduced in Uganda and, as is well known, further drastic changes have taken place since then. The administrative and judicial organization described is that used under the old constitution, which was in use when I was in the area.

[6] Until 1964 there were two court systems, the native courts run by the local government and the courts run by the central government. There were also local government police and central government police. These two systems were integrated in 1964.

[7] The sub-county courts are served by both Grade III and Grade II magistrates. First appeals are from Grade III to Grade II magistrates and are heard in the same courts.

[8] External threats do seem to have begun to lead to more widespread co-operation. About twenty years before the arrival of the Ganda general who first occupied the area for the British, there is some evidence that centralisation of authority had begun to develop. See Burke 1964: 193 and Southall 1957: 15.

Oboth-Ofumbi 1960: 16–17). Today there is not only a leader for the whole clan but a hierarchy of clan chiefs and other officials, which mirrors the administrative hierarchy, although having no official place in it. This hierarchy follows the territorial distribution of the clan, but the exact area in which a clan leader has authority over his clan members does not necessarily coincide with the official local government territorial unit. The head of the clan for the whole of West Budama is called the *saza* chief, and for local settlements of decreasing size, *gombolola*, *muluka* and *mutongole* chiefs are chosen.

The *saza* chief works in conjunction with a council of about four to eight members and at each level there is a clerk and treasurer. Some clans also have their own magistrates. The clans are important in the settlement of disputes. Disputes may be heard by the clan chiefs or dealt with in the clan courts. Court fees are paid for hearings and cases may be heard in these courts which can also be heard in the government courts, such as disputes over land. Thus the clans have been transformed into hierarchical organisations with recognised central officials, responsible for co-ordinating activities throughout West Budama, although such co-ordination is not necessarily effective. While they have acquired new judicial and administrative functions, the widespread relevance of their ritual functions has declined.

AGRICULTURE AND LAND TENURE TODAY

The kind of agriculture found in an area will affect the pattern of holdings in land, use of land and transactions in land.

In West Budama the main staple is an annual crop, finger millet, although bananas have spread into the area and are of considerable importance in parts that are suited to their cultivation. Cassava and sweet potatoes are also grown, together with a variety of relishes. The main cash crop is cotton, while groundnuts may also be sold in bulk and there are opportunities for marketing of other food crops. A variety of different sorts of livestock are kept, including cattle, sheep, goats and chickens, and these may be important sources of food and income. The numbers of cattle kept are relatively small, but they are still highly valued as a deposit of wealth, and some rich householders have herds of twenty or more head of cattle.[9]

[9] In my sample of 188 consumption units (randomly selected from all those

Most cultivators grow some cash crops, required at least in order to pay tax, and participate in the market economy. Casual wage labour is used in production and there are numerous new possibilities for the use of cash and food resources. These latter include expenditure on new farm equipment and other farm investments; a great variety of consumer goods; education of children; and new enterprises such as trading.

Land has become a scarce resource and with the development of a market economy has acquired a commercial value. There is now the possibility of selling it, and although this market in land is sometimes opposed by clans and clan leaders, it is not so opposed by the government. The significance of the market in land lies not in the supposed greater facility with which rights in land can change hands,[10] but in the fact that rights in land might change hands without reference to the status of the parties in the transaction in relation to each other and to the community.

That there is a shortage of land in West Budama can be shown in a number of different ways. Thus, for example, Othieno (1967: 60) showed that of the thirty-one farmers with whom he worked in Gwaragwara, only fifteen had enough land to enable them to follow the recommended crop rotations allowing a fallow period which would prevent deterioration of soil fertility and maintain existing crop yields. But in this paper I am not concerned with attempting an objective assessment of the seriousness of the land shortage, but with showing how land shortage is leading to pressure on land, as demonstrated particularly by conflicts over land and by migration. Pressure on land has also contributed to fragmentation of holdings.[11]

Conflicts over land can be taken as an index of pressure on land. It is sufficient to say that from a total of 523 civil cases brought to

consumption units with children of five and under) 110 had no cattle; 34 had 1–2; 29 had 3–6; and 15 had 7 or over.

[10] Apthorpe (1968: 5) has pointed out 'In most societies in East Africa it is perfectly normal rather than abnormal for land rights—or rights in cattle or in water, depending on what the basic mode of livelihood is—to be changing hands frequently, in different ways and for different purposes, however isolated or near subsistence economically a particular society may be.'

[11] Fragmentation of holdings may also be related to the original division and allocation of land on the basis of its suitability for different crops, but I do not have evidence for this as a factor today. Table 1 gives the number of holdings held by male householders. Clearly holdings are fragmented, but as there are no earlier figures for the area it is not possible to tell to what extent this represents an increase.

Mulanda sub-county government court in 1964, 1965 and up to June 1966, 203 were land cases. Of these 74 were heard in 1964, 72 in 1965 and 57 before June in 1966. In addition there are many land disputes which are settled by clan leaders and never reach the government courts. Threats of violence are often used during land disputes and violence may finally be used where agreement cannot be reached. For example, after lengthy litigation in which he finally won his case, a sub-parish chief was murdered. The murderers were said to be the people who brought the case against him.

TABLE 1. Number of plots used by a sample of 183 cash-budgeting units in Mulanda parish

No. of plots	No. of householders	Total No. of plots
1	68	68
2	53	106
3	35	105
4	14	56
5	6	30
6	4	24
7	2	14
8 or over	1	10
Total	183	413

The population of the area and migration into rural areas of other districts also indicate pressure on land. When I was working in the area the most recent census available was that taken in 1959, but an estimate of total population for each district in 1963 was also made by the Census of Agriculture (Uganda Government 1966). In 1959 the Bukedi District population was just under 400,000 and the average density was 280 people per square mile. This was the second highest in Uganda, exceeded only by Kigezi District.[12] The estimated population for 1963 for Bukedi District was 467,119 which gives a rate of increase of just over 2 per cent per annum, so that the average population density rose from 280 to 300 people per square mile in the four years between 1959 and

[12] See Kerr 1967. However, habitable areas of Bugisu have a higher population density, the overall population density for the District being reduced if uninhabited areas of Mount Elgon are included.

1963. Since the 2 per cent rate of population increase is well below the national average of 2.5 per cent it seems likely that there was a net population movement out of the district. Information specifically for West Budama has been given by McMaster (1966). In discussing the period from 1952 to 1958 he points out that there seems to be a fairly large-scale continuous movement of people out of the heavily populated parts of Uganda into the more fertile and less densely populated parts of the country. That West Budama is an area from which there is movement into other areas is suggested by the fact that during the period with which McMaster was dealing there was an annual increase in population of below 2 per cent.[13]

My own material also gives evidence of considerable movement out of Mulanda parish into certain sparsely populated parts of Buganda and Busoga, where land is cheaper to rent or buy and is more fertile (see Table 2). The reason generally given for moving to Buganda or Busoga is that of wanting more and better land on which to grow cotton to earn money, but this recognised route

TABLE 2. Migration of a sample of 183 householders and their relatives from Mulanda parish

	Relatives farming in Buganda or Busoga	*No known relatives in Buganda or Busoga*	*Total*
Householders who have farmed in Buganda or Busoga	55	17	72
Householders who have not farmed outside W. Budama	36	51	87
Householders who have not farmed but have been otherwise employed outside West Budama	14	10	24
Total	105	78	183

[13] Other factors, such as the occurrence of a low birth rate and/or a high death rate, could be significant. Data on comparative birth and death rates is not available, but there is no reason to suppose that they are markedly different in this area. See Kerr 1967.

out of West Budama may also now be taken for other reasons, such as elopement, avoiding witchcraft and so on. There is movement both to and from these areas, and some people cultivate fields both in West Budama and outside, so that patterns of migration are complex.

There are a number of reasons for this pressure on land. In the past when settlements became too large and conflicts over land developed pressure could be relieved by groups of people hiving off to form new colonies on uncleared land or land taken from other tribes. There is now no unoccupied land in the vicinity. Grazing land is cultivated and even the forest land around the central shrine of the Adhola, which for a long time people were afraid to clear, has been almost entirely opened up for cultivation. Colonial rule and the Pax Britannica reduced the possibilities of driving groups of people off their land by force. Force may still be used in stealing other people's land, but it is more subtly applied by individuals against their immediate neighbours and relatives, and the pieces of land involved may be relatively small. It is a case of small-scale internal politics, not external relations.

Individual migration to other, more distant areas, has not been on a scale sufficient to prevent a steady increase of population in the area, caused by the familiar pattern of improved medical facilities and prevention of large-scale famines. Also improved technology, introduction of cash crops and the possibility of new patterns of consumption has made it both possible and desirable for increasing numbers of people to cultivate larger areas of land.

Land tenure today

Until Independence in 1962 all land in Bukedi District was technically vested in the 'Crown', after which it was transferred to the District Land Board. The constitution introduced in 1967 provided for all public land to be vested in a Land Commission, which in each District would work through a District Land Committee. Although in West Budama all land is technically public land there has been little explicit government interference with customary land tenure, the only exceptions being the requisitioning of land for road, rail, township and other developments. Prior to the introduction of the 1967 constitution a specific request had been made in the District Council for the area to be surveyed and legal titles issued to individual holders, a move which would have been consistent with general government policy.[14] However, the fragmentation and extreme conflict over land, already described, made the Department of Lands and Surveys reluctant to embark on such a hazardous venture and no plans had been made by the time I left.

Rules regulating acquisition and use of land by customary land tenure

Rights in land in West Budama are generally rights in specific pieces of land, not rights to a farm as Bohannan (1963) described it for the Tiv and Plateau Tonga. Different kinds of rights are held by different groups or individuals. Changes in the traditional system of land tenure have already occurred as a result of changes in clan organisation and the development of a market in land, among other things. Thus what is described here is what might be called a contemporary form of customary land tenure, which has incorporated these changes but is still not written down.

The right to alienate land. Land is now a saleable commodity and by the right to alienate land is meant the right to sell it to people outside the largest land-holding unit. Today this is the clan or sub-clan, although traditionally the largest land-holding unit was probably a smaller, localised clan section. Sale should not occur without referring it to the clan head and his committee. If sale does occur without the knowledge of the officials the offender may be brought before the clan leaders or court and attempts made to get the land back. It is said that land is held in trust for future generations and it is the responsibility of the clan or localised clan section to see that the rights of the growing generation are protected. Sales also occur between smaller land-holding units within a clan, but since they are within the largest land-holding unit this procedure is not alienation in the sense that it has been used here. Sales outside the extended family or local lineage group may, however, be resisted by senior members of these groups and may be seen by them as alienation of land. Some young men claim that they can sell land to people outside the clan without reference to clan leaders, but this is generally an assertion of independence, and not a statement that the clan would not try to interfere if they tried.

[14] This was the case at the time I was working in the area. What policy there was based on East African Royal Commission 1953–5, Uganda Protectorate 1955 and International Bank for Reconstruction and Development 1961.

However, an individual is sometimes considered to have the right to sell his land when he has not inherited it or bought it from a clan member, but bought it himself from an outsider.

The right to administer land (allocate land for cultivation). This right can be held by a localised clan section, or by the head of an extended or nuclear family. The former is unusual and only found in the case of old grazing land which has remained undivided after becoming cultivated. In this case any member of the clan, or even an outsider, can ask the head of the localised clan section for permission to use the land. Usually allocation of land is controlled by the head of the family. A father may allocate land annually to his son, or on his son's marriage may pass on the right to administer the land. Where he retains the right to administer the land until his death, his widows (or widow) may, if they are not remarried, in turn continue to control the land allocated to them for their children and administer it in their own right until their death. In this case the land may still not be divided after the parents' death, and may be allocated annually by the senior brother or administered jointly by the brothers. Control over the use of a piece of land is also sometimes acquired from maternal relatives or from a wife's relatives, where the wife's parents have no sons of their own and treat their daughter's husband almost as their own son. Nowadays land may also be bought.

The Adhola say that in the past the basic domestic unit was the patrilineal extended family, consisting of a man and his wife or wives, their unmarried children, their married sons and their wives and children. For ritual activities, allocation of land and settlement of disputes they sometimes co-operated with members of a larger, localised agnatic segment. Ideally a man and his sons had houses on the family land. The father retained control of it until he died, sometimes holding it jointly with his brothers, and allocated land annually to each of his wives and their sons. Today there is a generally accepted tendency for the father to divide his land before his death, and when he dies his land is more frequently divided between his sons and not left under joint control or under the control of the eldest son. Furthermore, in some cases the residential contiguity of the extended family has broken up as a result of migration to Busoga, Buganda and other areas in search of land or employment (Sharman 1970).

TABLE 3. Acquisition of use of land by a sample of 183 cash-budgeting units in Mulanda parish

Acquisition of land	No. of plots
Allocated annually (patrilineally)	33
Allocated annually (other)	1
Given or inherited (patrilineally)	208
Given by other than patrilineal relatives	1
Borrowed[1]	115
Rented	37
Bought[2]	18
Total	413

[1] Land is said to have been borrowed when there is no explicit agreement that payment in some form will be made for the use of the land. Gifts in kind may be given.
Forty-one of these are small plots borrowed for sweet potatoes.

[2] Of these transactions five were between members of different clans, six were between members of the same clan, and seven were between people whose relationship was not specified.

Rights to use land for cultivation. Rights to use land without rights to allocate it might be acquired in a number of different ways. As described above, rights to use land may be allocated annually by the head of the extended family. Wives and married sons have rights of use and younger children may also cultivate separate fields. This does not mean, however, that wives and unmarried children have complete rights over the crops which they grow on the land. Control and use of subsistence crops is generally left to the women, but control and use of cash is generally regarded as the men's responsibility and the majority of women leave the sale of their cotton and the administration of the cash received to their husbands (Sharman 1970; MS).

Also land may be borrowed from paternal or maternal relatives or friends without paying rent. These arrangements are generally made between individuals, but as there is a bye-law requiring farmers to grow some sweet potatoes government chiefs sometimes arrange for a person with a lot of land to let neighbours use a section of it for planting small amounts of sweet potatoes. Finally land may be rented from paternal or maternal relatives, friends and neighbours. Rent varies not only according to the size and conditions of the plot, but also depending on such considerations as the length of time the plot has been used and the relationship of the people involved. Since both the main cash crops are annuals, cotton and the less important groundnuts,[15] there are not the same problems as those found in other areas where large acreages of perennial cash crops are grown on land which has been borrowed or rented or is regarded as being held jointly, so that it should be available for the use of people other than those who are growing the cash crops. The only perennials grown in any quantity are bananas, and these are never grown on borrowed or rented land as far as I know.[16] Where the land of a banana plantation is held jointly by otherwise separate domestic units use of the plantation is divided up between the different consumption units. Small plots or patches of land are often borrowed for sweet potatoes (see Table 3). Otherwise borrowed and rented land is generally used for rotations or part rotations of cotton, millet and cassava and sometimes groundnuts. Other crops may be interplanted.

Rights to grazing land. Rights to areas of land for grazing used to be held by localised clan sections, any members of which could use it. These areas are all cultivated today, but rough, unused areas of land, such as that near the swamps, may be grazed by anyone's cattle. Fines are imposed when cattle damage crops.

This discussion shows some of the opportunities and difficulties a householder might encounter in trying to obtain additional land for cultivation. In addition it must be emphasised how the system of land tenure limits the possibility of women farming independently. Women generally only have rights to use land allocated to them by their husbands or other men under whose jurisdiction they come, except in the case of active widows who are not remarried. They can on occasion borrow land from their close relatives, but mostly land transactions are carried out by men. However, small patches of sweet potatoes, generally the sole concern of women, are freely lent by the women to one another.

[15] Coffee is not an important cash crop in the area. All coffee in the district is of the lower quality variety, Robusta, since conditions are unsuitable for the growth of Arabica. Even Robusta is marginal in many areas because it is susceptible to the fairly intense dry seasons which occur periodically. Planting of coffee is discouraged by the Department of Agriculture.
[16] None were grown on borrowed or rented land by the farmers in my sample.

LAND TENURE, CLANS AND GOVERNMENT COURTS[17]

The means by which land is allocated and disputes over land are settled in customary tenure have already been described. This section is concerned with showing the consequences of contradictions between these processes and the functioning of the government system and difficulties in applying the latter. Separate spheres within which conflicts are settled by the clans and by the government courts respectively are not found in West Budama, as they are in some other areas.[18]

The largest unit involved in the allocation of rights to use land for cultivation is the localised clan section. There is no government body which regularly allocates or registers rights in land, although all land is technically vested in the government Land Commission. On the other hand, disputes over rights in land are dealt with not only at a number of levels within the clan, but also in government courts, and only decisions in government courts can be enforced officially. The clan officials can still, to some extent, be said to be concerned with the welfare of the group; with the protection of what might be regarded as their common interests and the maintenance of clan land. The lesser clan officials live in the area over which they have jurisdiction and so are relatively familiar with the area and its inhabitants. And they are said to question all the neighbours of the litigants in order to arrive at their decisions,[19] although witnesses are used at the hearings.

In contrast the government magistrates are often outsiders, with no position in the local community and relatively little know-

[17] After 1964 court records were kept in English, so that the precise meaning of kin terms is not always clear. Prior to 1964 records were kept in Luganda.

[18] For example, the Lugbara of northwestern Uganda, Middleton 1966. In West Budama there is no obvious distinction between the sort of cases heard by the clan officials and in the government courts. It would take more detailed analysis of cases heard by clan leaders only, those taken directly to government courts, and those taken to government courts after an unfavourable judgement by clan officials, to understand the conditions which lead to some cases being heard by clan leaders and some by government courts.

[19] The effectiveness of clan leaders in arriving at equitable solutions to conflicts over land should not, however, be exaggerated. Records of court cases heard by clan officials are sparse and incomplete and give no indication of the fairness or general acceptability of the decisions arrived at. I did not have the time myself (since this was not my main research topic) to study either the procedures at these hearings or the extent to which more influential men could determine the final judgement. Opportunities for manipulating the system were probably fewer, but nevertheless there.

ledge of the area. In arriving at their judgements they rely on inspection of the area under dispute and the statements of the litigants and their witnesses, who may be supporters rather than neighbours or people who know how the land under dispute was allocated. The magistrates may be easily deceived or easily encouraged to leave the straight and narrow way in arriving at their judgement. Furthermore, although land is supposedly held according to customary tenure, the principles to be applied in deciding a case are not always clear. It is sometimes the traditional norms which are in dispute rather than their application or abuse in a particular situation. The government courts uphold the right of individuals to alienate land over which they have rights of allocation, and to allocate land without reference to their traditional obligations.

This has led to dissatisfaction amongst clan leaders. One clan *gombolola* chief, who had also been a court assessor in Mbale,[20] argued that clan officials, not government courts, should be reponsible for settling all land disputes.[21] Government courts, he said, are always taking land away from its rightful users, because they know so little about the local situation. He also gave two examples of the sorts of cases in which the judgement of the clan officials would not be upheld by the courts. First, he described the case of a man with two sons. He disliked one of them and refused to give him land. Traditionally a father has the obligation to give his sons land to use during his lifetime, and to pass his land on to them at his death. The clan *gombolola* chief acted to assert the son's right to use some part of his father's land, and to protect the son against the old man trying to sell the land before his death. He gathered members of the clan together, and in their presence took the land from the father and gave it to the son. This case was not taken to court, but had it been the clan chief was convinced that the son's claim would have been rejected. The court would have recognised only the right to allocate the use of land for cultivation, not rights of use in themselves.

However, the court is not consistent. Sometimes it supports

[20] There is provision for magistrates, when applying customary law and taking down evidence, to summon two assessors from the area to assist them in evaluating the evidence. They are not bound by the assessors' opinions.
[21] This could lead to more literal and rigorous application of rules of customary land tenure and greater emphasis on the exclusiveness of the clan, as has been the case in some areas. See Brock 1969: 19.

those who have the right to administer the land and sometimes those who have rights of use. In its judgements it does not distinguish between rights of alienation, rights of allocation and rights of use,[22] so that where rights of use are upheld they are transformed into rights of administration and alienation. If the court recognises that it is rights of use which are at issue in a dispute then the case is dismissed or the right of administration of a person other than the litigants is confirmed. Four cases can be used to demonstrate these points: one between men who claimed to have borrowed the land from the same person; one between brothers who only held rights of use; one between a man and his brother's son, who had been allocated land by his father (i.e. the plaintiff's elder brother); and one between brothers whose father had died.

(a) Civil Case 17/1966. Mulanda Sub-County Court
The plaintiff (A) sued the defendant (B), both of whom were farmers, for encroaching on his land and calling the clan chief to demarcate the boundary, without his permission. A said that another man (C) had left him the land when he went to Buganda. He asked the court to order B to leave his land and refund Sh. 24 court fees. He further, rather confusingly, claimed to have bought the land from someone else in 1951. Possibly he was suggesting that it was he who had originally lent the land to C. B denied the claim, and said that he would not dispute the case since the land was not his but belonged to C. He added, however, that he had sued A before the clan officials and won the case. B called one witness, C, who said that he had given the land to B and that A should pursue the case not with B but with himself. Judgement went against A and the land was left to C.

(b) Civil Case 27/1965. Mulanda Sub-County Court
The plaintiff (A), a farmer, accused the defendant (B), also a farmer, of encroaching on his land and destroying his foodstuffs and demanded that B leave his land and pay Sh. 12 court fees. A and B are brothers. A brought five witnesses to the court, but none of their evidence supported his case. B denied the accusation and said that he was simply cultivating his father's land and that the crops there belonged to him. He brought only one witness, his and A's father (C) who said that he had not yet

[22] It may be true that, as Apthorpe (1968: 3) has written, '..usually any land law reform calls for some over-simplification of the realities of rights and obligations because of the difficulty that would otherwise be presented of consulting absolutely all interested parties.' But this does not mean that prior to land law reform simplification should necessarily be allowed to develop in a haphazard and irregular manner.

divided the land between his sons and only allocated them land to cultivate. He made no mention of A's claim that some of the crops on the land were his. But the court did not rule that the land belonged to C and that the only point at issue was who the crops belonged to. Judgement was against the plaintiff and specified that the land should remain with the defendant, although it was recognised that A had some finger millet on the land, which he was to be allowed to weed.

Thus in this case the defendant in effect established boundaries and registered his right in the land even before his father had given it to him.

(c) *Civil Case 90/1966. Mulanda Sub-County Court*
The plaintiff (A) and the defendant (B) were both farmers. A accused B of encroaching on his land, which had been left to him by his father, and asked the court to order him to leave the land and refund Sh. 24 court fees. B is A's elder brother's son. B said that he would not plead the case, because the disputed land belonged to his father. A said that B had planted cotton there and that he now intended to sue his elder brother for allocating the land to B. Judgement was against the plaintiff, with instructions to sue his brother not his brother's son.

In this case the right to allocate land was the one emphasised, but the defendant had himself defined the case in these terms. In civil case 27/1965 the litigants did not define the case as one involving rights of use rather than rights of administration.

(d) *Civil Case 35/1965. Mulanda Sub-County Court*
The plaintiff (A) and the defendant (B) were both farmers. A sued B, his elder brother, for refusing to give him some of the land left to them by their father, and demanded that he be given some land. The defendant pleaded guilty. The judgement was against B, with instructions that A be given a piece of land.

In this case the younger brother obtained rights of administration over the land where traditionally he might have had only rights of use. In this case B recognised his obligations and defined the situation in such a way that A could easily claim rights of administration. There are no cases in the court records which I studied of an elder brother claiming the right to retain control of the family land. Possibly court decisions promote the already existing tendency for the extended family to divide into nuclear and polygynous domestic units for purposes of land allocation.

178 LAND TENURE AND 'ROOM FOR MANOEUVRE'

This discussion of the way in which rights of use and rights of administration may be confused and distorted by court judgements, and consequently manipulated in the courts, arose from one of the situations described by the clan *gombolola* chief. The second situation he described, in which there would be conflict between clan and court judgements, was that of a man selling inherited land to a member of another clan. In such a case the clan could not get the land back by sueing the offender in court. The case would be dismissed and the land left with the man who had bought it. This point is illustrated by the case given below. Thus other methods have to be used to retrieve the land. The clan *gombolola* chief said that in his particular area the clan had always found it possible to get the purchaser to return the land and accept a refund of the money paid. He suggested that people were afraid to be uncooperative, in spite of the lack of officially recognised sanctions. But not all clans are so efficient in retrieving their land.

Civil Case 136/1965. Mulanda Sub-County Court
Both litigants were farmers. The plaintiff (A) said that he had bought the piece of land in question from the defendant (B) for 2 head of cattle and Sh. 100 and planted *burowa* trees to mark the boundary. He had built a house and cultivated crops on the land. Then B wanted A to return the land in exchange for the cattle and money, in spite of the agreement they made. A still owed B one head of cattle, but said that when he tried to pay it B refused to accept the payment, uprooted A's cassava and brought someone to build a house on the land. A wanted the court to order the defendant to leave the land and refund Sh. 19 court fees. In reply B said that he did not himself wish to exclude A from the land, but the clan elders demanded that he should. He pleaded guilty. A and B brought one witness each. One was present at the time when the agreement was written. The other was B's son, who had written the agreement. The judgement was made against the defendant, who was also asked to pay Sh. 19 court fees.

In this case the court is supporting the validity of contracts between individuals without any particular relationship to each other: contracts which have not been recognised by the local leaders who would traditionally have had the final say in the management of land. It should not be thought that in the past clan land would never have been given to someone from another clan, such as a sister's son seeking assistance or a stranger wishing to settle in the community. But the land would have been given with the person's status in mind and the agreement of those with the right to administer the land.

So far I have discussed cases where there has been conflict over interpretation of the kind of rights held in land. But in many of the cases which come to the courts the kind of rights held in the land are clear and conflicts then arise for different reasons. These cases are concerned with boundary disputes and encroachment on land over which rights have been established by inheritance. Cases may be brought directly to the government courts or following a judgement by clan officials. In the latter instance the case may be brought to the court to ensure that the original decision is enforced, or with the aim of reversing the clan decision. If it is established that a judgement by clan officials has indeed been made previously, between the same litigants and in respect of the same piece of land, then the court generally supports the clan judgement, taking it as evidence of the validity of the claim of the successful litigant. Two cases will serve to illustrate this point, the first brought to ensure reinforcement of the clan decision and the second to change the clan decision.

(a) *Civil Case 87/1966. Mulanda Sub-County Court*
Both litigants were farmers. The plaintiff (A) sued the defendant (B) for cultivating his land and uprooting the markers (probably elephant grass), which had been used by the clan officials to demarcate the boundary. He asked the court to order B to leave his land, replace the markers and pay Sh. 24 court fees. B denied the claim. A continued that the land was originally given to him by his father (C), and that he had a boundary with B. They previously had a dispute over the boundary, which was brought before the clan officials. B was defeated and the boundary was demarcated earlier in the year. B still has crops on the land, but A's brother and mother both have houses there. A brought three witnesses, all of whom supported his claim, and provided additional information on the crops A had on the land and the fact that B had also built a house on it.

B argued that the land was left to him by his father (D). Before he died D had divided his land between B and C and demarcated the boundary. B argued that he had various trees and crops on the land and four houses! B said that A had previously had a dispute with B's son over the land, which was settled by the clan leaders; that A's mother and brother were living on the land; and finally that he did not want the land! The defendant brought one witness who confirmed the claim that B had received the land from his father. Judgement was against the defendant, who was asked to pay Sh. 24 court fees, and the old boundary was confirmed. Throughout the case it was uncertain who had what crops, trees and houses on the land, but in the final judgement B was granted permission to harvest four plots of cassava and some millet.

(b) *Civil Case 143/1966. Mulanda Sub-County Court*
The plaintiff (A), a tailor, sued the defendant (B), a farmer, for refusing to let him use the land which had been left to him by his father (C). A is B's father's brother's son and B had looked after the land for A while he was in Busoga. A asked the court to order B to leave the land and refund Sh. 24 court fees. B denied the claim. A continued that when he returned from Busoga in 1966 B refused to let him build on the land. They took the dispute to the clan officials, who gave a small portion of the land to A. A brought two witnesses, one of whom did nothing but swear! This man had a boundary with the land under dispute and had previously had a dispute over the same land with B, in 1958 when A was in Busoga, and lost. The other witness confirmed A's claim.

B said in his defence that he had been left the land by his father (D), A's father's brother. C had in fact been in Buganda for some time and when he had returned D had given him some land, demarcating the boundary between B's and C's land. When C died A and his brothers migrated to Buganda (there seems to be some confusion about where they actually went) and B used the land. On A's return B gave him back his land in the presence of the clan leaders and they signed the clan book to this effect. B has a permanent home, banana plantation, various trees, cassava, finger millet and his father's grave on the land. B brought as witnesses two of the clan officials who had judged the previous dispute between A and B, and they supported his case. The judgement went against the plaintiff and the old boundary was confirmed.

The case shows how a man may attempt to push claims in the government courts which have not been accepted by the clan officials. It also shows the variety of evidence which may be taken as indicating legitimate control over land, and the complexity of cases which involve the maintenance of rights in land during periods of migration.

Under these conditions people may be deprived of what the clan officials regard as their legitimate rights in land not because the clan officials and government courts disagree on the principles to be applied in settling the dispute but simply because there is considerable scope, as procedures stand at the moment, for litigants to misrepresent the situation successfully. Two cases will serve to illustrate this point. In one case it is in dispute which piece

LAND TENURE AND 'ROOM FOR MANOEUVRE'

of land had been sold to whom. The other case is lengthy and confused and shows a number of ways in which deception may be practised in land transactions.

(a) *Civil Case 85/1965. Mulanda Sub-County Court*
The plaintiff (A), an assistant inspector of police, sued the defendant (B), a farmer, for encroaching on his land, cultivating it and demolishing his house. He asked the court to order B to leave the land and refund Sh. 24 court fees. A claimed that the land was sold to him by C for Sh. 400 in 1963, that the boundaries were demarcated by the government *mutongole* chief and that the agreement was written by D. B denied the claim. A brought C and D as witnesses. D confirmed that he had written the agreement. C said that he first sold a piece of land to B for Sh. 150 and then another to A for Sh. 400. He claimed that no one had been cultivating the land before the dispute.

On the other hand, B claimed that the land in dispute was that sold to him by C in 1962 for Sh. 300. The agreement was written by E, whom he brought as a witness. E confirmed that he had written the agreement. No further evidence is recorded, but the judgement went against the defendant, who was ordered to pay Sh. 24 court fees. The land remained under the control of the plaintiff.

Whatever the actual basis of B's claim to the land, this is a case in which the haphazard recording of land sales and lack of systematic registration of rights in land, which need not necessarily mean individual freehold rights, has provided considerable scope for misunderstanding and possibly profiteering.

(b) *Civil Case 3/1965. Mulanda Sub-County Court*
Both litigants were farmers. The plaintiff (A) sued the defendant (B) for cultivating his land and refusing to leave it. He requested the court to order B to leave the land, refund Sh. 12 court fees and pay compensation for preventing him from growing cotton. He said that the land under dispute was left to him by his father. He lent the lower portion to his 'niece' (C) in 1943 and the upper portion to his 'uncle' (D) in 1950. The exact nature of these relationships is not indicated. D's wife died while he was using the land and her grave is there. Later he moved to another village, and A lent the land to his brother's son (E). As regards the lower portion of the land, C was joined by her husband (F) and they cultivated the land together. In 1959 C died and her grave is on the land under dispute. After C's death F sold the land to B without A's knowledge, but when E tried to cultivate the land B refused to let him. A named those who had a boundary with the land under dispute. When cross-questioned he said that he had no receipt for having lent the

land to C, because traditionally receipts were not given in such transactions. But, he said, various neighbours witnessed the transaction, who were members of the same clan as himself. When he first gave the land to C he lived adjacent to it. He denied that there had been a previous case over the disputed land in 1964. A called two witnesses, both people who had been present when he lent the land to C, and who were said to be using adjacent land. They supported his claim with their evidence, but one stated that there had been a previous court case in 1964, which had been dismissed for some reason.

The defendant's case was as follows. He bought the land from F, his 'personal' uncle, for Sh. 250 in November 1960. The graves on the land, he said, are those of F's wife and son. F showed him the land and the government *mutongole* chief (G) and *mutake* chief of the area were present, together with B's brother (H) and neighbours whom G called as witnesses. A was not present because at that time he was not living on adjacent land, although his brother still farmed nearby. B produced the note of sale as evidence. He also said that A had sued F in respect of the same piece of land in 1964, but the case had been dismissed, because they could not trace F. No one in the case knew where F was living. He had moved from the land in dispute in 1962. B gave the names of those with land adjacent to the land under dispute, only two of whom were the same as those mentioned by A, namely E and another man (J). Neither of these men were called as witnesses by either litigant. However, B said that in 1963 he had had a case with E over the upper portion of the land, which was settled in his favour. This case was not mentioned again by anyone. B called two witnesses, G and H, both of whom witnessed the sale in 1960. H said that when F first came to the area he stayed at J's house, together with his wife C, and that J gave him the land under dispute. The conditions under which the sale is thought to have taken place were explained by G. In 1960 G arrested F for not paying poll tax and took him to the *gombolola* headquarters. F arranged to sell the land to B to raise money to pay his tax, and to this end G accompanied F and B to the site and called the neighbours together as witnesses to the transaction. None of these witnesses was called in this case, but they are reputed to have included both E and J. G admitted that he had not known A's father or D and did not know there was another grave apart from C's on the land. A had earlier claimed that he had paid F's tax when he was arrested.

Judgement was against the plaintiff, who was also asked to pay the court fees. The plaintiff subsequently appealed to the second-class magistrate on the grounds that:

1. The receipt upon which the third-class magistrate based his judgement had not been proved to have come from F, since F was not in the court.

2. All B's witnesses had agreed that C was buried on the lower portion of the land in dispute, which had been given to her by him.
3. The grave of D's wife on the upper portion of the land had been mistaken by the defendant's witnesses for the grave of F's son.

When the appeal was heard the judgement was reversed on the grounds that the receipt of sale produced as evidence in the case did not fulfil the requirements of documentary evidence that 'if a document is alleged to have been signed or to have been written wholly or in part by any person the signature or the handwriting of so much of the document as is alleged to be in that person's handwriting must be proved to be in his handwriting.' The magistrate said that during the previous hearing B had said that F signed the alleged agreement while he was on remand. In his view F was forced to sign the so-called agreement if he signed it at all, but in fact on the basis of the evidence before him he did not think that F had signed it!

This case illustrates clearly the difficulties encountered in arriving at accurate judgements under existing conditions, and the insecurity of rights in land, particularly where a person lends land to another or acquires rights in land by purchase.

Evidence of rights in land can easily be manipulated. Three sorts of evidence are acceptable: physical evidence, such as graves on land and boundary marks; eye-witness evidence; and written evidence of a transaction having taken place. This last was obviously unknown traditionally, when reliance was on members of the local clan section acting as witnesses to a transaction and ensuring compliance with the agreed terms. If land was used for many years by the person who borrowed it, he might subsequently be allowed to pass these rights on to his son. But today there is a shortage of land, so that no one wishes to let his rights lapse. Agreements to lend land are still often made only verbally before witnesses, and depend on the knowledge of clansmen and neighbours, but this knowledge is often not made available to the official body, the government court, responsible for the settlement of disputes. As can be seen from the last case, important witnesses to the agreement, or neighbours involved in the transaction may never be brought to the court. The separation of the court from the local community requires that they have accurate written records on which to base their judgements. But in a situation where the government is not responsible for regular registration and allocation of land and the majority of people are still illiterate, most transactions go unrecorded. Written receipts may anyway be of dubious validity, with an uncertain cross or untraceable thumbmark (as in the last case) the only sign left by the signatories.

The courts are regarded as places where all relationships can be denied. One example which was described as particularly despicable was that of a government chief. He was having a dispute with his young brother, who wanted some of their dead father's land to cultivate. During the court hearing the chief is reputed to have denied not only his relationship with his brother but also that with his mother. However, such abuse of power acquired through the new administrative system does not always go unchecked. The hearing of land cases often provokes violence and extreme sanctions may be applied by those who regard themselves as wronged, as in the case referred to earlier where a chief had been murdered.

The only means of registering any rights in land is through court cases, but even when there is no appeal following judgement there may be a series of cases over the same piece of land, between the same or different litigants. Even an unappealed judgement does not end disputation or the possibility of losing the land.

As can be seen, most disputes are over use or ownership of a land site, or loss of crops on the site. There were, for example, no cases over whether or not a payment had been for rent or for sale.[23] However, there were one or two cases where compensation was demanded for the cost of ploughing land which had been encroached upon, although there were no cases where the value of other land improvements had been taken into account. Such requests for compensation are for reimbursement of a cash expenditure, rather than a recognition of the value of the improved land.

WOMEN, GOVERNMENT COURTS, AND LAND TENURE

In the cases I have presented so far the litigants are always men, although, as has been discussed earlier, women may hold rights in land. In some cases brought by men, the rights women hold may be important in the claim they are making. For example, in Civil Case 3/1965 the case partly rested on the plaintiff's claim that he had originally lent the land to his 'niece' rather than to her husband. But only very occasionally do women defend their rights in court. Only five cases were recorded, among those heard in

[23] This is in marked contrast to the situation found in some other areas. See, for example, Feldman 1970.

1964, 1965 and 1966, in which one of the litigants was a woman. Three of these women were defending their rights to the land which had been left to them by their dead husbands. Traditionally this land was held for the dead man's sons to inherit when they were old enough. If the dead man's wife was inherited or remarried the new husband did not gain control of the land, but was expected to use it to support the dead man's children and held it in trust for them. Sometimes these men abuse the trust put in them and refuse to pass on the land to the dead man's children when they are old enough. But no such cases were brought before the government courts during the period studied. These were all cases of encroachment onto the land by others. The other two cases recorded were of women defending their rights in land which had been given to them by their dead fathers. It is not clear in these cases whether the rights the women were defending were originally rights of use which would revert to the patrilineal males when the women died. In terms of the rules of customary land tenure this is most likely to be the case, but this does not mean that in practice their sons would not have been allowed to continue cultivating the land after they had died. In one of the cases the woman was asserting her rights against those of her husband, who had sold her land without her permission.

Civil Case 69/1966. Mulanda Sub-County Court
The plaintiff (A) sued the defendant (B), her husband, for selling her land without telling her, and asked the court to order B to return her land and refund Sh. 24 court fees. The land had been given to her by her late father. The defendant pleaded guilty to having sold the land, which was not his, for Sh. 140 and the judgement went against him. He was ordered to return the land and pay Sh. 24 court fees.

This case shows that women can win cases in the government courts, even against their own husbands, so why are so few cases brought to the courts by them?

Traditionally women were very limited in their sphere of action.[24] They were confined to what Fortes (1958) calls the 'domestic domain', and within that domain all major decisions concerning the organisation of the domestic unit were taken by

[24] In this area, where no detailed studies have been done before, in commenting on aspects of social organisation in the past, all that can be presented is the conscious model of the local people. This will represent an ideal view of the past, but the extent to which it represents an ideological model today will vary for different members of the community.

the husband. The changes which have occurred in this century have had far-reaching effects on the position of women. The introduction of cash crops, marketing and the possibility of employing labour to perform male tasks; Christianity, and education have all contributed to these changes. Other factors which may affect the actual freedom which a woman has in performing activities are her husband's economic status and her participation in earning money; her husband's occupation; the number of wives he has and their seniority and place in his affections; and his attitude towards the position of women and women's activities. For a few, the changes which have taken place have enabled them to participate fully in the 'politico-jural' domain, even attaining the status of District Councillors. But in some respects the activities of women have become more limited than in the past and most women are still effectively limited to the domestic sphere (Sharman 1970; MS). This does not mean, however, that they do not attempt to manipulate their opportunities for acquiring rights in land. But the goals of the women themselves, which are related to the situation in which they find themselves, affect the form which their manipulative activities take, and they seek to acquire rights in land and crops for limited purposes. They hanker after more clothes and other modern consumer goods, and want more say in the allocation of cash resources to ensure the satisfaction of their needs as they rather than their husbands see them. But in many cases, even when they do acquire their own cash income, they do not buy goods very different from those bought by their husbands. Nevertheless, by asserting themselves and gaining some more control of resources they are beginning to establish some 'room for manoeuvre'. For example, even a little money for transport enables them to visit the town and attend the hospital with their children. The significance of these initiatives on the part of the women for bringing about more far-reaching changes in their social position makes Fortes distinction between the 'domestic domain' and the 'politico-jural' domain appear inadequate for the analysis of changes started by minor shifts in control within the domestic domain.[25] His

[25] The inadequacy of Fortes' distinction between these two domains was first suggested to me by Beverley Brock. The distinction needs to be looked at again in more detail, I think, given the current concern with analysis of relationships between the sexes and within the family in terms of sexual and family politics.

LAND TENURE AND 'ROOM FOR MANOEUVRE' 187

emphasis is on the way in which the politico-jural domain and the domestic domain are related in particular societies, and how the unchanging cycle of the domestic group, which varies only within given limits, serves to perpetuate the existing system.[26]

For those women who are still constrained by traditional and local patterns of social control their aim is to quietly outwit, rather than directly oppose, their husbands. For example, one woman whose husband spent a lot of time with a second wife, borrowed land from her mother, on which to grow groundnuts, without her husband ever finding out and demanding the money which she had earned. This is but one example of the fact that women often maintain close ties with their natal family and close kin and may obtain rights in land and assistance from them. A reason sometimes given for separation is that the wife is always going to visit her parents or her brothers (Sharman 1969, 1970). But even in this case, access to land often depends on a woman's relationship to the men who control it. And women are accepting secondary rights in land, which, as has already been discussed, may not be recognised in a government court.

There are some women who have the means, both economic and educational, to compete with men in the wider economic and political arena. Nevertheless, there are few of them, and the land they require for the farming activities which form the basis from which they work seems generally to be obtained through traditional channels, with the co-operation of the men. Where there are conflicts and attempts to sanction their behaviour these may take a variety of different forms characteristic of the society. Thus, for example, one woman, who had been a District Councillor for about seven years prior to the Bukedi riots,[27] had her numerous granaries and house burnt down during the disturbances. Up until

---

[26] This is not, of course, true of his analysis of the Ashanti in Fortes, 1948. But even in that article, his analysis is largely in terms of changes brought about by the initiatives of men rather than women.

[27] There is a long history of conflict between Protestants and Catholics in the area, and while the majority of the population was Catholic many of the chiefs were Protestants. Toward the end of the 1950s there were many complaints that the chiefs were abusing their power. The dissatisfaction with the chiefs reached a climax in January 1960, with riots throughout Bukedi District. These riots were ostensibly against the tax assessments, but in West Budama they were also an expression of the resentment felt by the Catholic population against the chiefs and others, such as Councillors, in some cases Catholics, whom they felt were supporting the government and therefore favouring the Protestant minority. See Burke 1964, and Uganda Protectorate 1960.

that time she had been farming her husband's father's land, although she had long been estranged from her husband. During the riots she was forced to hide and, receiving no help from her husband, her only chance of maintaining the position she had built up over the years was by acquiring new land in another area and concentrating for a while on commercial farming. Her brother had died and she decided to farm his land. There seem to have been no immediate heirs and her brother's wife married again and moved away. In the past, and to some extent today, final separation was frowned upon. A woman might use some of her father's or brother's land after her marriage, but should not return to her parental homestead and inherit her father's land. If she returned to her father's homestead she was thought to endanger the well-being of unmarried girls living there and if she died there her spirit might kill them. Divorced women do in practice sometimes return to live at their natal home, but when this woman sought to take her brother's land the ancestors are said to have opposed her move. After her brother's burial they occupied the house for some months, while she camped outside.[28] To overcome opposition she had to seek assistance from outside the area in which she lived, in the form of mystical power, and is said to have had recourse to a local practitioner in Busoga. The medicine he gave her drove the ancestor spirits from the house and she took up residence. Following this move she was successful in farming, employing labour and obtaining assistance from government departments, and became a progressive farmer,[29] but she continued to be the subject of considerable criticism and hostility, which she put down to jealousy. This hostility was expressed in two ways, through the use of *juok*[30] and through gossip. After the riots she was ill for some time, and again after she had moved. She said that her illness was the result of poisoning/sorcery. To recover she underwent a long period of treatment in hospital and

---

[28] However, this might also have occurred in the normal course of events. In the past houses were destroyed after the death of the owner, during the course of the burial ceremonies, in part to avoid just such an occupation by spirits. This is still done with poorer houses today.

[29] A progressive farmer is defined by the government as '..a farmer who actively follows the advice and puts into practice the instructions given to him by the Department of Agriculture, or the Department of Veterinary Services and Animal Industry, for the proper management of his farm.'

[30] *Juok* is the term for both poison and mystical power. A sorcerer is *jajuok*, a person who uses *juok* to harm others.

also made use of other medicines obtained from the practitioner in Busoga. And her neighbours gossiped. They said she had stolen their land and, because she farmed alone, said that any man she cooked for took the place of her husband. They described her as a famous prostitute, because she had travelled to distant places. Such gossip appeared to leave her unscathed. Her position and influence did not depend on the support and approbation of her neighbours and relatives. But because of this jealousy and hostility she had to limit her local activities so as not to provoke violence and sorcery or poisoning. When she subsequently became active in the organisation of women's groups, as she had been in the past locally, she was asked to help at higher levels and participated relatively little locally.

CONCLUSIONS

In Padhola today most people rely on farming for their livelihood, so that acquisition of land is of major importance. This paper has described the current system of land tenure and availability of land for both men and women. It gives an example of the effects of leaving rights in land to be defined by 'customary law' when firstly all aspects of social life are changing rapidly, so that 'customary law' is itself changing and cannot always be easily applied in settling land disputes; and secondly new institutions have been set up to administer 'customary law', which are unsuited to this purpose.

The material presented is relevant to current policy issues. The form of land tenure best suited to the social and economic conditions existing in East Africa is a constant subject of debate among those concerned with various aspects of land law and land reform.[31] What reforms should be made is ultimately a political question, since choice of reforms will depend on the social and economic goals of the reformers. But consideration of the validity of the assumptions made about the relationship between systems of land tenure and specified social and economic goals; the urgency and need for reform; and the implementation of reforms must rest on detailed knowledge of the local situation.

[31] Colson (1966) has distinguished three different aspects of land tenure: rules regulating acquisition and use of land; patterns of holdings existing in the area; and the distribution of rights in land among the population. Changes in land law do not necessarily lead to changes in the other two aspects of land tenure and vice versa.

The material presented here is particularly relevant to such questions as the need to clarify and register rights in land, the importance of establishing an accurate method of recording land transactions and the necessity of systematising procedures for settling disputes. To evaluate these issues comprehensively would require another paper,[32] but one or two points can be made. It has been argued that insecurity of tenure discourages farmers from carrying out improvements on their land, because they can never be sure that they will reap the benefits of such improvements.[33] I do not have the material to evaluate this argument as applied to conditions in West Budama, but it is true to say that boundary disputes may inhibit the work of the agricultural extension workers for another reason. Where there is a dispute they cannot measure the land and give advice on its cultivation without provoking a quarrel, because showing the land to an official is regarded as effectively registering the boundaries described. Thus they avoid working on farms where the boundaries are in dispute. On the other hand, it is extremely difficult to bring about the possible changes mentioned above and the costs of doing so may be prohibitive. Also, as Apthorpe (1968) has pointed out, weaker rights may be neglected in registration. One set of rights which might be neglected are those held by women, making them even less independent and able to show initiatives in following new patterns of behaviour. Yet it is recognised that improvement of family welfare depends to a considerable extent on women, and they often need independent control of resources if they are to improve the conditions under which they and their children are living.

[32] See, for example, Allott 1971, for a brief introduction to some of the issues raised by the question of registering rights in land.
[33] See, for example, Kamarck 1967. In this connection it is often mistakenly assumed that security of tenure must be and is associated with recognition of individual freehold rights. See Brock 1969.

10

Cause, knowledge and change: Turkish village revisited

PAUL STIRLING

In 1949–52 I spent a total of about fifteen months in two villages near Kayseri in Turkey, and rendered an account of them—an account necessarily deeply influenced by the common-sense constraints which I brought from my own social background. In June 1971 I was able to visit these villages, only for a few days each; but because of my warm reception, I was able to record, observe and to infer very considerable and striking changes.

These changes are not in themselves surprising; they are like the changes described in peasant societies from all parts of the world. Yet I personally found them striking, because of the impact of these differences on villages and people I once knew well. I have read about and seen social change in peasant societies. Yet I was surprised; which reinforces my conviction that there is a profound discontinuity between words in sociological books and what people actually do.

This experience led me in two directions. First, it strengthened my dissatisfaction with the way social change is described, discussed and explained by sociologists: second, brief as my visit was, I wanted to put my observations and impressions on record, since I am able to offer direct comparisons with 1950–52.

The differences from 1950–52 are many, closely interconnected and, taken together, fundamental. Nevertheless, the villages are very much the same villages as in 1950, and possibly some 'salient' things about them have not changed yet, and may never do so, or not for a long time. How can I communicate my perceptions of what has changed and what has not?

My difficulty is not peculiar to myself. Much of the language which sociologists use—and I include social anthropologists—is bedevilled by emptiness and imprecision, and not infrequently by a mystification which suggests religious cult rather than scientific analysis; while the attempt to convey the facts in more descriptive and common sense language, even given the necessary degree of literary skill, is hardly less selective and misleading, and perhaps more so. If the task of discussing social change in one village is so difficult, small wonder that sociology and social anthropology are baffling and confusing disciplines.

THE EMPTINESS OF CONCEPTS

This whole article illustrates my point. But perhaps it is worth briefly defending this pessimism. The term 'social change' itself suggests almost no boundaries and no specific core of meaning. What is it that changes? Or is it more appropriate to make the question plural? What are the things that change? All things change all the time, including people and communities and societies. How much change then, and in what, do we need before we talk of 'social change'?

In an article with a title highly relevant to my theme, 'How small-scale societies change' (1969c), Professor Mair offers one answer. 'When we speak of changes in society we mean changes in the rules that govern social relationships—rules about the ownership and transmission of property, the right to exercise authority, the duty to co-operate with particular people in particular circumstances' (p. 121).

Professor Mair puts this definition forward in the course of an important argument. She is contending that 'explaining' social change is not a special and separate sociological (or anthropological) activity requiring its own special theories. Sociologists —and their audiences—live themselves amongst bewildering social changes, and it is absurd to talk as if we all expect societies normally to remain unchanged, so that change is exceptional and needs *explaining*. A little later in the article she defines *social relationships* in terms of statuses or roles, and proceeds to argue that the concept of *role* as a set of rules of behaviour for holders of named statuses is very far from excluding personal choice in social life. She mentions as normal human aims, power, wealth, prestige, comfort and enjoyment. 'The significance of the act of choice is that in making it a person may have to weigh the proportions in which either choice will gain him these different goods' (p. 127). Choice then is between ends as well as between means. It may also include choosing to break, interpret or even rewrite social rules. Such choices have always been present in all societies.

'Every society then offers to its members opportunities of succeeding in life by various criteria of success, and the different criteria are I would say in essentials the same in all societies. It is the opportunities that are limited by the scale of the society and its technical possibilities, and what has happened to the small-scale societies in the last hundred years is an immense widening of the field of opportunity' (p. 128).

Although her examples are not directly relevant to peasants in a modern European state built out of an ancient imperial Islamic society, most of what Professor Mair says with such clarity makes excellent sense in the context of Turkey. People's reactions to new opportunities are in terms of perceived advantages. New relationships involve new obligations which conflict directly with the old ones. Roles in new situations have to be learned not as people normally learn them, from other people who know them and take them for granted, but in odd and perhaps strange circumstances, at times where no consensus about the new situation has yet emerged.

But even so the concepts are still empty, in the sense that they do not tell us what is involved. To make sense of them, we need to be able to provide examples from our own experience and reading. They are also vague in that the boundaries implied are not clear, that is, we cannot be sure what is included and covered, or what is not. (They also carry theoretical assumptions, implications, and exclusions, which are not easy to spell out clearly; but that is not my main point here.) Social anthropologists will recognise Professor Mair's emphasis on specifiable rights and duties which can be summarised as 'rules'—rules for 'defining' social situations, and rules for acting according to the 'definition' reached.[1] But this use of 'rules' is considerably wider than that in common English. Outside anthropology people would think of some numbered, written list, perhaps rather formally worded;

---

[1] Compare the notion of property as a 'bundle of rights',—by which is meant a list specific to a given type of situation in a given society. Or Leach's attempt to compare marriages by listing the specific rights involved (1955).

and many sociologists, not in the anthropological tradition, might find surprising the implication that the totality of social action of the society studied can be adequately described in terms of rules for specific role relationships.

Social anthropologists use 'rules' to cover major moral principles; formal political and juridical procedures; expected behaviour between spouses, kin, neighbours and members of groups and organisations; etiquette, ritual and formal occasions; recognised ways of evading or circumventing other more formal rules; and even regularities observed by the ethnographer but not made explicit or even admitted by the people themselves. Indeed, to make sense of Professor Mair's definition we must include all these since she implicitly but clearly is talking about social life in general.

The point I am making is not a criticism of Professor Mair, but a general difficulty of social science. Professor Mair's lucid article summarises both a massive detailed knowledge of Africa and its recent changes, and wide acquaintance with writings on 'social change'.

But this erudition and lucidity is only obvious to those who also know at least in part what Professor Mair knows, and know that she knows it. To others, her background knowledge is obscured by her clarity—by what I have called the emptiness and vagueness of sociological language—a difficulty with which she copes better than most of us. Like all of us she is using words which are in current use in English, and many of which have other special meanings for other academic communities, so that her full meaning is clear only to those who share both the cultural world of social anthropology, and the wider world of educated users of English.

FOUR KINDS OF CHANGES

The difficulty is a general one, because we cannot write or talk without words. Like others, I, too, felt I needed some kind of classification or summary or framework in terms of which to think out the changes I observed. The scheme that follows arose directly from attempts at description; it is an extension of Professor Mair's definition. I propose four types of changes. The four types are not mutually exclusive; and they each imply the others: (i) changes in social relationships; (ii) changes in knowledge and beliefs; (iii) changes in values; (iv) changes in the general characteristics of the society.

(i) *Social Relationships*
By social relationships, I mean the role relationships between people living in the village and in nearby villages, and also those with people outside the rural area—with officials, employers, fellow workers, bank managers. Since 1950, the content of many relationships have changed, many new relationships have been added, and the relative importance and frequency of relationships have also changed. As Professor Mair makes clear, since social groups imply relationships between their members, this heading includes *a fortiori* changes in the size, purposes, degree of specificity, strength, and distinctness of social groups, both old and new.²

(ii) *Knowledge and Beliefs*
Knowledge and belief are much more difficult. I include here relatively simple bits of information—who is Prime Minister, what voting is about, how much fertiliser to use in specific circumstances, how to find a cheap bed at night in Ankara, what a German social security child allowance is worth. But I also include changes in ideas and assumptions of a much more radical kind—about the nature and consequences of sin, the nature of illness, the essence of femininity and masculinity, the uses, reliability and consequences of money, and much more.

First, the word *knowledge* normally implies truth. But a large amount of what people in any society regard themselves as knowing would not be regarded as true by me, nor by most of my readers, nor by at least some people in their own society. I do not want to expand this point here, but in all kinds of ways what all of us think of as *knowledge* is normally either inaccurate or simplified or false—for example, a temporary theory, a rumour, or a patient's account of his own illness. The expansion of information, through word of mouth, formal education, mass media, official statements and so forth does not necessarily involve an increase in the proportion of truth in what is known in the village. Indeed, most of the new *knowledge* is also partial, misleading, inaccurate, biased, foreshortened or just plain wrong. In what follows, I use *know* and its derivatives sometimes *subjectively*, that

² I have consciously refrained from using both *structure* and *system* in this context.

is, with the knowing subject's assumption that what is known is true; and sometimes *objectively*, that is, with the implication that though the knowing subject takes the truth of his knowledge for granted, I as observer do not.

Secondly, the word *belief* has different implications from those of *knowledge*. We normally use the word *believe* when the certainty is not absolute. It may imply that the believer lacks conclusive evidence—'to the best of my knowledge and belief'—or that an element of judgement or opinion is involved. Alternatively it may imply a moral commitment to maintain a proposition or set of propositions, for which common sense hard evidence is tacitly or explicitly admitted to be weak or non-existent. In very many contexts—in both Christianity and Islam, for example—faith and orthodoxy are moral virtues, and doubt a sin. What people *believe* is therefore extremely difficult to state accurately. Yet to describe social change, we must make the attempt, since beliefs certainly change; and change more than people are normally willing or able to make explicit.

(iii) *Values*

Plainly, if people's knowledge expands greatly, then there are likely to be changes in the notions of what to aim for, what is desirable, what is right and good, what is tolerable, what is acceptable and what is unacceptable. In other words, their values change. Besides new opportunities, and new knowledge and skills for exploiting these opportunities, they have new objectives. They may use old opportunities or break old rules for new purposes. Here again, I include things which are very different; the evaluation of desirable qualities in nubile girls, the evaluation of occupations, preferences for the form in which wealth should be stored and accumulated all directly affect immediate aims and conduct; but ideas about honour, sexual propriety, obligations to kin, piety and sin also may change; these are 'values' in a much more general sense. The accurate reporting of changes in values is at least as difficult as the accurate reporting of beliefs.

(iv) *General characteristics*

The fourth heading is a mixed bag. There are a number of changes in the overall character of the society. In the village, homogeneity of knowledge and of values declines, the sanctions of informal interaction become less effective, defiance of accepted rules and norms increases—with a further decline in homogeneity. The introduction of money and market principles affects social relationships, moving them away from traditional reciprocities towards bargaining and profit taking. The possibilities of acquiring knowledge, skill and wealth are greater, so that the slow changes which take place in the hierarchical structure of any relatively closed village community are accelerated, and some of the poor, the weak, and the young acquire power, wealth and even authority. The introduction of state and commercial institutions and procedures—schools, the judiciary, credit co-operatives, banks, agricultural improvement schemes, health officials and doctors, public works officials—into the day-to-day life of the village not only alters village society, but also shifts and blurs the boundary between village and the outside.

CAUSE

What is clear from the examples I have just chosen is that notions of cause are implicit in any description. It is impossible to eliminate from our thinking and writing a whole series of phrases like *gives rise to*, *means* (in a causal sense), *stems from*; or particles like *since*, as and *for* in weak causal meanings. Such covert causal statements are worth attempting to make explicit.

It is of course important to sort out cause from logical implication. For example, I myself have written 'This increase in migrant labour alters social relationships..' To be precise, an increase in migrant labour implies change in social relationships since more villagers now have relationships with employers and fellow workers that they did not have before. But they also bring back new information, objectives, ideas and resources which alter existing social relationships in the village—causally. In this case, as often, logic and cause are both involved.

I would like to be able to present a description of changes in which these causal connections were made explicit, and accurately weighted, with clear indications of both the reliability and the general validity of the implied causal statements. But if societies are as complex as I have suggested, then a causal analysis even of a 'stable' society is fantastically difficult. To describe such a set of causal connections when they are changing is far more difficult.

Yet I see no easier way out. So I have attempted to describe at least some of the changes, and to suggest some causal connections between them. But some background seems to me essential before I discuss these in detail.

BACKGROUND: TURKEY AND THE WATERSHED

All countries described euphemistically as developing, on closer inspection turn out to be special cases. Turkey is unique in many ways. She is a European country; a member of various liberal democratic capitalist western clubs—the Council of Europe, OECD, NATO—and by commitment a future member of the European Economic Community. Yet the cultural roots of the Turkish people lie in pre-Islamic Central Asia, and in Islam. And they are conscious of having run a great empire for some five centuries and know they have never been ruled by outsiders.

The new Turkish Republic of Turkey, under Mustafa Kemal, later called Ataturk, set its face towards Europe long before most of the 'developing' nations. In 1923 he initiated an astonishing series of legislative reforms including a new system of education (1925), a new system of law and judicial procedure (1926), and a new alphabet (1928), which in time cut most educated people off from the literature of their Islamic imperial heritage. In 1932, the government announced a Five Year Plan for industrial development, and Etatism became part of official policy. Ataturk died in 1938 and after the Second World War his successor, İsmet İnönü, allowed a parliamentary opposition party. In 1950 he held and lost the first genuine general election in Turkey, and inaugurated a multi-party system of parliamentary government.

The dramatic legal, institutional and formal changes belong to the pre-war years. But the real social changes in Turkey in many ways date from after the War, and the time of my first fieldwork around 1950 has arguably turned out to be a watershed.[3]

Both economic and population growth accelerated very sharply around that time. Official government estimates of national income per capita show no increase from 1938 to 1950; but in this year it began to rise and by 1968 the national income had roughly tripled and the income per capita increased by around 75 per cent. Official population figures show an increase from 13.5 million in 1927 to all but 21 million in 1950. Some of this increase is simply

[3] I owe this point largely to conversation with Professor Mübeccel Kıray, but see Stirling 1965: 290ff.

an increase in the efficiency of counting people, and it is in any case less than 2 per cent per annum. Moreover, even with the total of 21 million in 1950, there was still more or less enough land to support the traditional way of life at standards of living acceptable to most villagers.[4] After 1950, growth accelerated, with serious pressure on rural resources. The annual population increase rose to 2.5 per cent per annum (1950–55) and then to 2.9 per cent (1955–60) and the total grew by 1970 to 36 million. Up to 1950, official figures of the national proportion of the village population gave it as very close to 75 per cent, over some twenty years. Since then, this proportion has been falling and in 1970 was about 60 per cent of a very much larger population. The urban population doubled between 1950 and 1965 from 5 million to 10 million, and the population in cities over 20,000 rose from 3 million to 8 million; the rural population rose from about 15.5 million to about 20.5 million in the same period.

Other economic and social indicators tell the same story. Between 1948 and 1968 value added in agriculture rose from T.L. 12.5 thousand million to T.L. 21.6 thousand million, even though agriculture fell as a proportion of the national product from 45 per cent to 28 per cent. In the same period, value added by industry increased 3.5 times, steel consumption 4 times, electricity consumption 5 times and electricity generating capacity 7 times. In education and medicine also expansion accelerated after 1950.[5]

The year 1950 is also a watershed politically. Ataturk's own political party, the Republican People's Party, ruled autocratically. It worked on the assumption that the educated and westernised knew what was good for everyone else, and in particular took secularism and State control of the economy seriously and rigidly. The opposition Democrat Party won the election and remained in power until 1961; they had learned to play for village votes, partly by a more permissive attitude to Islam, partly by a conscious policy of giving villages specific benefits such as feeder roads,

[4] I owe this point also to Professor Kiray, who argues that 21 million is very little above the carrying capacity of Anatolia in times of peace under the Roman, Byzantine and Ottoman Empires.
[5] The quantities in this and the previous paragraph are available from Turkish official statistical sources, such as the 1965 Census, the provisional results of the 1970 Census, and the Five Year Plans. They are given here simply as approximate indicators of the scale and timing of changes.

fountains, schools and so on, and partly by abolishing direct taxes on agriculture. It also claimed to encourage private enterprise, though without in any way dismantling state enterprises. The military junta which took over in 1961 soon restored civilian government, under a constitution more firmly democratic than before. Formal planning for development became normal from 1963; in 1965 the Justice Party, the successor to the Democrat Party, won a clear mandate, and the expression of political opinion and protest was, for a while, freely permitted. In the late 1960s civil disorder increased and in 1971 the army imposed a government to restore order and carry out reforms, which did not materialise. Martial law remained in force until September 1973, a few weeks before fresh elections; and many people are in prison for political offences. In October the Republican People's Party, declaring itself social democratic left of centre, topped the polls in an indecisive election. I have no doubt that Turkey's political difficulties are directly related to the effects of rapid national economic growth and the accompanying social changes. But these connections are not easy to specify, nor are they the point of the present article.

THE TWO VILLAGES REVISITED

The two villages which I studied were in the province of Kayseri, roughly in the middle of Turkey. I set out the main basic data about the two villages in 1950–52 and in 1971 in Table 1 (p. 201).

I visited both villages for one day each in 1970. In the summer of 1971 I spent two months in Turkey: eleven provinces out of 65 were under martial law. I was granted permission by the Turkish Government to visit the villages for seven days with a Turkish colleague, a most helpful and knowledgeable museum assistant from Kayseri. I spent three days in Elbaşı and four in Sakaltutan, and was able to write down from assorted informants a census of all Sakaltutan households, and one in three of Elbaşı households. I met old friends informally and asked and listened as much as possible. I also had a chance to talk for a few hours with village friends while in Adana.

If the data are reasonably valid, are they generalisable? Three points are relevant here. First, in many areas of Turkey there have been striking developments of very different kinds; new crops, large scale capitalist farming (Hinderink and Kiray 1970), new industries. Nothing specific of this kind has happened in these villages—but then nor has it in most parts of Turkey.

TABLE 1. Some basic village data

	Sakaltutan		Elbaşı	
	1950	1971	1952	1971 (based on 1 in 3 sample)
Population	633	852	1,200	1,700 (?)
Number of households	105	134	216	253
Average household size	6·0	6·4	5·6	6·7
Percentage of households with more than 1 married man	24	32	23	26
Skilled migrant workers	40	150 (?)	10 (?)	100 (?)
Households permanently migrated to town	6	65	6	114
Date of migration from Sakaltutan:				
1950–57	0			
1957–64	18			
1965–71	39			
Not known	8			

Secondly, Kayseri has a very old tradition of skilled building labour, and in 1950 villages near Kayseri were full of established migrant craftsmen—masons, carpenters, painters and so forth—who worked in towns and cities. These skills were already spreading rapidly to the more remote villages. For example, by 1950 Sakaltutan had acquired some forty skilled men, mainly plasterers, in, allegedly, about 10 years. This tradition made it possible for most men migrating for work to earn roughly three times as much a day as unskilled labourers. Although other areas have other specialities, there must be many villages which send mainly unskilled labour to the cities, and the large difference in earnings must have considerable consequences on the processes of change.

Thirdly, this area had another ancient speciality—carpet making. Bünyan in particular is famous for its carpets, and Kayseri itself and many Kayseri villages contained women who knew how to weave carpets (Stirling 1965: 59). In the last twenty years, carpet making in Elbaşı has been transformed by the commercialisation of production on a 'putting out' basis, and the skill has spread to other villages, including Sakaltutan. In 1950, people made carpets or *kilims* for their own use or for weddings, and only casually for the market; they used village wool, and bought dyes and other materials. Now carpet merchants provide all capital expenses including looms, and girls work in their own homes on pre-determined piece rates.

These two villages are then exceptional only in that both women and men have been able to benefit from a traditional craft.

THE DIAGRAM—FACTORS AND PROCESSES

The main diagram (p. 203) summarises some of the ideas that occurred to me while I was in the field, and afterwards while going over my notes. I can weight neither factors nor causal links; the factors are not mutually exclusive, nor are the boundaries around them always clear. These 'factors' indeed are not even things of the same general order of existence. Equally the causal connections for which the lines and arrows stand are not of the same kind, and do not reflect similar 'efficacy' or similar processes. Even the double boundaries which I use to emphasise certain factors as crucial are selected on my own judgement.

Any two-dimensional diagram must simplify reality. Even so, the point of the diagram is to illustrate complexity, and these misgivings I make explicit in order to add weight to this emphasis. In what follows I shall not discuss all thirty-one boxes, for some hardly need comment; nor will they always be discussed in serial order, but rather in the order which best suits the development of my argument.

Boxes 1 and 2—National Changes

I have already (pp. 194ff.) sketched some of the kinds of national changes which affect villages. I only wish here to agree warmly with Professor Mair that most rapid and important changes in small-scale societies originate outside them. Of course, local internal factors and processes are what external factors affect, so that uniform external causes do not have uniform local effects, and it is these internal processes in which I am interested here. But of course the changes in the villages of Turkey are a response to

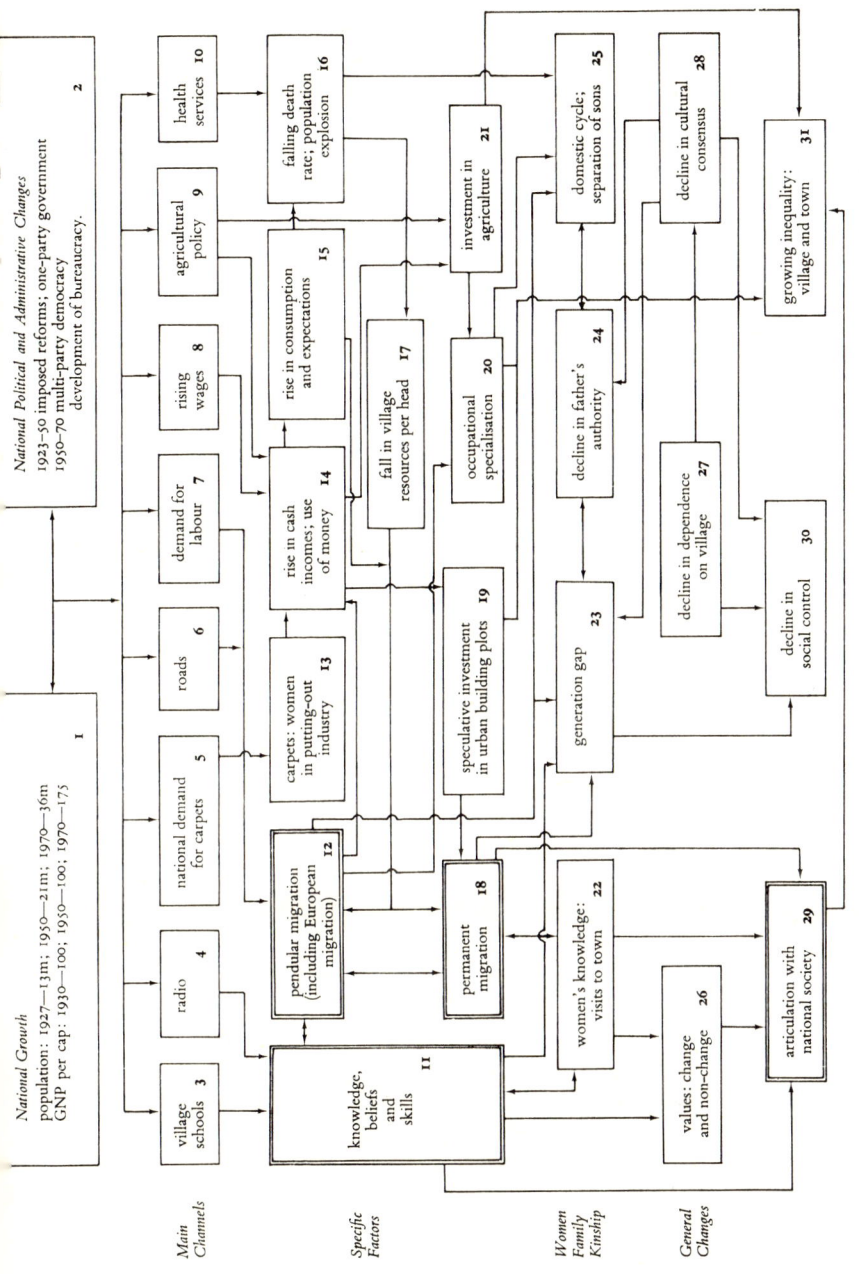

events, policies and changes in Turkish cities and governments, and beyond these in the world at large.

Boxes 3 to 10

I have named seven general ways and one local way in which the two villages are affected by national society. Although I have not joined these eight boxes to each other with arrows, it is obvious that they are not all independent factors, but affect each other. The order in which they appear is purely one of convenience.

Five of them, schools, radio, roads, agricultural policy and health services involve direct official government action: three— the rise in labour demand, the rise in real wages, and the growth of the demand for carpets are the result of economic growth.

In general, they are all self-explanatory; but I comment on the relation of each to these two villages.

Box 3—Schools: Up to the summer of 1950 Sakaltutan had only a minimal school; a local literate villager taught one arbitrarily selected group of children for three years, concentrating on the three 'r's' exclusively. He had been doing this for about five years. In 1950, as we left, the first trained teacher arrived; in 1971 there were four.

Elbaşı had had a school for very much longer, and in 1951 had three trained teachers; now there are six.

In both villages, school enrolment is now virtually total, for girls as well as boys.

Box 4—Radios: The government provides the programmes, the people themselves buy the radios. In 1950, there were none in Sakaltutan, and in 1951 one or two had just arrived in Elbaşı. Now most households have one, and everyone who wishes is able to listen frequently. Everyone knows the national news; but neither village had regular newspaper readers even in 1971.

Box 6—Roads: Turkey's national road building has been one of its most successful enterprises. Elbaşı already had in 1951 an efficient feeder link to a good main road to Bünyan and Kayseri. But in 1951 the road from Kayseri through Sakaltutan to the small town of Tomarza had only been passable to lorries for two years. It was still a village cart-track, deteriorating rapidly, and restricting speed to 15 kilometres an hour. A few irregular lorries passed through Sakaltutan into Kayseri in the morning and returned in the evening. The road did not touch Talas, Sakaltutan's administrative centre. By 1955, a new route had been opened from Kayseri through Talas to Sakaltutan, and by 1970, a decently engineered and metalled road carried regular minibuses and buses, reaching Kayseri in little over half an hour, against eight hours in 1947 and two hours in 1950.

Box 9—Agricultural Policy: Since around 1930 a government agency, the Office of Soil Products, has bought wheat and other cereals directly from the producers at fixed prices. The price each year was, and still is, decided by the Cabinet and has been consistently above world prices. This policy removed the producers' recurrent problem of fluctuations in price from harvest to scarcity within one year, and from glut to famine between years; and probably did much to encourage cash cropping and thus increased production of cereals. Secondly, through the Agricultural Bank, founded in 1878, the Government also provided substantial credit, even to relatively poor farmers.

Box 10—Health Services: The sharp decline in the death rate in Turkey is, as it is everywhere, largely the result of the availability of world improvements in medical techniques, through national improvements in medical and health training and organisation.

Box 7—Demand for Labour: The growth of Turkey has created a vast and continuing boom in building, with a large demand for building labour. The villages of this area have helped to supply this demand on a large scale. Building provides an unstructured casual labour market with, so far, no State imposed formalities. The men pay no tax, have no insurance, work when they choose; they are subject only to their contracts with employers which in turn reflect the informal arrangements sanctioned by custom and the economic balance of power. This system provides no security; but it has great advantages of flexibility for a peasant labour force whose members have their minds on wives, children and fields back in their villages.

Box 8—Rising Wages: Even in 1950–52, skilled building workers, so long as they could find regular work, seemed well-off compared with a middling or small landholder. Moreover, most villagers have considerable periods during the year when they have relatively little to do. Thus a skilled migrant labourer, especially if he had some land and a family prepared to work it, was decidedly better-off for cash than other villagers, except the few who controlled relatively large amounts of land or relatively large herds of animals. Earnings were said to be about 10 T.L. a day, against 3 T.L. for unskilled labour; village rates for both were half as much.

Since then the real return for a day's employed labour has risen faster than that for a similar input in village agriculture. Hence, quite apart from population pressure on local resources, the absolute amount of cash brought back to the village from this source is vastly greater and still growing; and the proportion of the total village income from non-agricultural sources has risen even more sharply. According to my casual enquiries in 1971, skilled workers could earn from 60 T.L. to 100 T.L. a day, against the unskilled labourer's 25–30 T.L. a day. (Summer 1971: roughly, 15 T.L. = U.S. $1.00, 35 T.L. = £1.00.)

Box 5—Carpets: The growth of carpet making as a cottage industry in this area would provide a fascinating study in itself: twentieth-century putting-out (p. 201). This industry is long established in Bünyan and Kayseri. (Geray 1967: 49). The entrepreneur provides the loom, and all materials, and the weavers provide a workshop in their own home and the labour. The conditions are tough. Girls may work long hours in cramped conditions and poor light, which can damage their health. They often work on a large carpet in groups of two or three. For a solid month's work—thirty days in the villages—a girl was said to earn about 600 T.L., or around 20 T.L. a day. People put the annual maximum at 6,000 T.L. for ten months' work, but I doubt if many girls did as much as 300 days a year. A potential 6,000 T.L. compares favourably with the 2,000 T.L. a year which both Kiray (1970: 11) and Kapil and Gençağa (1971: 15, 16, and Table III), give as a minimum family annual income.

People said that carpet making had been the salvation of the villages, since many households derive a steady extra income from it. Except that people say a girl will ask her father for a watch and more new clothes, which he cannot refuse, the income involves no cost and no risk, and goes straight to the head of the household. For the first time, adolescent girls are a direct cash asset to their fathers. It is highly convenient since it involves no problems of morality or new ideas; indeed it keeps vulnerable girls suitably busy. Since it goes on in the home, it is not necessarily full time; indeed it is infinitely flexible. Households short of woman power can easily fit the weaving into domestic and farming routines.

Girls often begin at a very early age, but an untrained adolescent girl is said to be able to pick up the basic skill in about two weeks. A really skilful girl is one who can weave fast and with great evenness; her skill may earn her a wide reputation, and become a factor in her eligibility for marriage.

Apart from increasing the village cash income, and giving women a small lever against male dominance in the household, the carpet trade does not appear to have wide ramifications for the village; largely because it requires no new relationships or sources of knowledge for the women, and very few for the men.

Boxes 11 to 21

Ten of these eleven factors (all but Box 11) are in principle more or less definable and measurable. They have of course symbolic, cognitive and affective aspects which are hard or impossible to measure, but all have measurable dimensions.

Box 11—Knowledge, Beliefs and Skills: People can only operate with the knowledge, beliefs and skills which they have. New opportunities (Mair 1969, Ch. 10) only change behaviour if people know about them; and they may know about opportunities which do not exist but which all the same change their behaviour.

This box therefore cannot be omitted, and I spell out again (cf. p. 195) some of the difficulties of including it. In the first place it is not distinct from other boxes in the way in which say the rise in cash income is distinct from the rise in consumption in the village. This is not simply because of indefinite boundaries; but also because every change must have intrinsic symbolic and cognitive aspects.

In the second place it is vast and heterogeneous yet it cannot satisfactorily be sub-divided. It includes skills of a general kind—

for example, reading, writing and counting; it includes detailed everyday information about bus routes, rents, prices, law, hygiene; it includes occupational skills and information about the building industry, how to get jobs and how to recruit labour; it includes social skills—shopping, dealing with landlords, walking into and doing business in a bank; and it includes items of general knowledge essential for the encounters of social intercourse in a new range of casual acquaintances in cafes, buses, jobs, shops.

Thirdly, it is extremely difficult to gather and report accurate data about it either from informants or from general observations and impressions.

Fourthly, it follows that it is extremely difficult even in principle to give a meaningful quantity for this box, or for any important sub-section of it; any measurement in this field is likely to be at worst seriously misleading, and at best highly specific.

Knowledge changes individuals; that is, quite simply, someone who for example has become a skilled tile layer through a visit of several months to Adana is specifically different from a cousin of similar abilities, origin and personality who has not. Knowledge also changes societies. The villages in 1971 stored different kinds of information, and vastly more of it, and with much more range of individual variety than they did in 1950-52. *A priori*, such great changes in stocks of knowledge modify people's basic assumptions or major beliefs about their metaphysical and social universe—about man, about God, about good and evil, about suffering and about moral rules. Cognitive changes on this large scale may be gradual or traumatic; unconscious or explicit, understood, partially understood or misunderstood.

Since the 'universe' is almost invariably perceived as absolute and unchanging, people are very often unable to see that the 'universe' of their society is different from what it used to be; and their perception of such changes as they do perceive is seldom clear, articulated or easily checked.

Some causal chains

To follow exhaustively through the causal model box by box and connection by connection would take me beyond the data available and the scale of this occasion. Some of the suggested connections—all open to the high sounding label of 'hypotheses'—

are left to the diagram. Instead I comment at varying length on some of the boxes and on some of their causes and consequences. But before doing so I draw attention simply as illustrations to three out of many causal chains which could be extracted from the diagram.

Causal Chain 1

Falling death rate
↓
More people
↓
Less village resources per head
↓
Pendular migration
↓
Higher incomes
↓
Better nutrition and better medicine
↓
Falling death rate

The falling death rate causes increases in the number of mouths to feed, in people to share land resources and in people available for work. Thus population increase has been one major factor in stimulating labour migration, and its net effect is not therefore a fall but a rise in village income, a rise in standards of living, including nutrition; the new income also makes possible a sharp increase in the use of medicines and medical services. Thus the falling death rate stimulates factors which further reduce the death rate.

Causal Chain 2

Sporadic pendular migration
↓
Higher incomes
↓
Higher minimum standards of living
↓
Aspirations for higher incomes
↓
Regular migration for all young men

This model simply shows that, given other factors, once sporadic pendular migration has begun, it causes a rise in village expectations, which in turn causes migration to become a normal and regular part of village life.

Causal Chain 3

Pendular migration
↓
Permanent migration
↓
Increased pendular migration
↓
Increased permanent migration

Permanent migration to towns is perhaps the single most important result and the single most important cause in the chains of change in a village. It certainly is one of the most dramatic both for the nation,—for the growth of cities,—and for the individual, —his emotions, 'cognitive structure' and identity. It deserves some discussion.

Box 18—Permanent Migration: The number of people who had left the two villages permanently in 1950-52 was very small indeed, if we exclude a large number of women and one or two men who moved between villages for reasons to do with marriage, kinship or property (Stirling 1965: 30, 202, 203). The pattern was clear: if a man left the village he did not take a village wife with him, but married a woman of the town to which he moved. It did not occur to me at that time to check carefully the reasons why these few who left had done so; on the whole, those who had left did not keep in close touch with their village kin. Of course, the obligations of kinship may simply be dormant, ready to be reactivated if occasion arose. I only heard of about six men of Sakaltutan origin who were permanently resident in towns. Only three women in the two villages had ever lived in town, and of these only one intended to return. No village household or married couple had ever left Sakaltutan. Most men said firmly that they personally and villagers in general could not migrate permanently because village women could not and would not live in town, so that a married man could not migrate permanently unless he abandoned wife and children.

Even in 1952 some of the younger migrants were already showing signs of preferring town wives and town homes to a poor village which was growing rapidly more crowded. Yet in fact, I have no record of any departure from Sakaltutan between 1949 and about 1957. Details on those leaving after 1957 were gathered hastily. Only ten of those for whom I have information left before 1961, and most of these are in some sense special cases. Two or three belonged to very poor families. Three went to Europe as bachelors, one of whom is married to a non-village Turk in Germany, and the other two are now married in Turkish towns; and another went to Saudi Arabia for two years. But from 1961, more prosperous and successful villagers began to join the exodus. Of sixty-five adult men reported to have left Sakaltutan altogether, eighteen were said to have left between 1957 and 1964, and thirty-nine between 1964 and 1971. Although the details of years of departure were not carefully checked, the number increases steadily, and more were talking of making the move during my stay.

I discussed the problem of moving to town many times with many people in my brief stay. Naturally, the arguments are complex; they can be grouped under two heads,—economic, and those concerned with personal and social satisfactions and comforts.

Few men in Sakaltutan have jobs outside the building industry. In 1950-52, I recorded five men working in the State cotton mill in Kayseri, and returning to the village every weekend. Of these, at least two had moved their families permanently to Kayseri by 1971.

In the building industry daily earnings depend on personal output, through an individual contract system. Employment was still in 1971 inherently casual, and there was no official control, no insurance scheme, and no use of labour exchanges. The pendular migrants have two advantages over permanent migrants. First, by keeping their wives and families in the village they can continue to use patrimonial land, escape rent, and feed their families very cheaply; though they have to meet their own expenses in town, even when unemployed. Second, they can seek work anywhere in Turkey where their friends and contacts report a favourable opportunity; though if they spend two to three months in the village each winter, and work in different cities, they are less able to keep a warm and active personal network of friends and fellow workers to find them work when they need it.

People said that a good and reliable craftsman has a lot to gain from living in one town all the year round. He can establish permanent ties and mutual obligations, he can move rapidly from job to job, and by becoming known for reliability will find himself in demand.

This argument is even stronger for the contractors. The building industry largely consists of small contractors, who through subcontractors parcel out the tasks of building to craftsmen, who may in turn employ their friends and kin as colleagues or apprentices. Quite a number of men from Sakaltutan managed to rise to become small contractors or subcontractors. The advantages are great,—a profit on the deal, and the ability to offer work to kin and friends, and thus like a traditional 'ağa', establish a following. But obviously this kind of success depends on maintaining a reputation in one town.

One major factor is economic security. A pendular migrant with land keeps a firm eye on his village possessions, and stays and eats in the village if no work is available. He does not starve. Some permanent migrants also retain rights to village house and land. Many allow kin to use land or houses, and in fact could not exercise the rights they think they have without a dispute. Obviously, if many migrants returned at the same time, they would not be able to survive as farmers. Yet many of them go on believing that if the worst came to the worst they could return to their village property. But a man who has lost his village rights by sale or long neglect faces the prospect ultimately of destitution if the town cannot provide an income. The economic balance obviously varies from case to case. A man with adequate village land and a successful town career must choose between advantages; a man with no village resources and little success in town must choose between evils.

Economics apart, a man also has to weigh the advantages of having his wife and children in the village, secure against destitution, cared for, and watched over morally by parents or other close kin, against the advantages of living with wife and children in his own home day in and day out, at his place of work.

The women in 1950 were unanimous: they could not live in town. Many had never been to town at all, and none went regularly. By 1971, all village women as far as I could judge had some close neighbours or kin living in town, and many older women now pay regular annual visits to daughters or son's wives to see their grandchildren. In 1950, they said life in town, with unknown cooking techniques, no store of home-grown food, and no close kin and neighbours, would be impossible. Some still prefer the village, but many are only too keen to be shot of the grinding village chores, and long for the amenities of a town house. Girls are beginning to want town husbands.

The danger of dishonour does not seem to trouble town-based husbands. Village women resident in town are not allowed to go out to work. Indeed, they are not allowed to go out at all, not even shopping, and it is my impression that although the new situations in which women find themselves vary enormously, mutual observation and gossip relationships between women neighbours develop very rapidly. I was struck by the fact that village-born women with village-born husbands are more restricted, housebound, segregated and socially isolated when they move to town than they were in the village.

Permanent migration to town is accelerating. Once again, it is simple to suggest plausible causal factors which promote the movement.

The village population is still rising, and in Sakaltutan is now far beyond the carrying capacity of the village land. Many see themselves as having little to stay in the village for. Secondly, with the rise in the national income per capita, town wages are rising relative to the income to be earned by working the village land, even if a man has enough land to work. Thirdly, the arrival of agricultural machinery decreases the number of men needed to work the village lands.

Experience and knowledge contribute enormously to this process. The regularity of pendular migration gave all young men first hand knowledge about how to survive and earn in towns. Once a few village wives had moved to towns without breaking their village ties, the same kind of information became rapidly diffused among the women, radically altering their attitude to moving to town, and removing one of the main barriers to permanent urban migration. This stock of town experiences, knowledge and values is constantly reinforced by the ever-growing intimacy between the village and its own urban residents, who for many purposes, especially economic co-operation and marriage, remain in many ways part of village society. The greater the number of permanent migrants, the easier it becomes for others to follow.

Migration also stimulates migration in a more directly economic way. Most villagers had very little cash to spare, and savings normally took the form of investment in animals. In 1950–52, a few had begun investing in lorries, mills and even an Ankara hotel. Now that they have much more cash people with savings are looking for investments. One new profitable form of investment has turned out to be urban real estate, especially building plots. Villagers become land speculators, and with the current rates of urban growth and of inflation they can hardly go wrong. One profitable use for an urban plot is to build two or more dwelling units on it, and live in one whilst renting or selling the others. The villagers say that to be secure in town it is necessary to own property, not only to avoid paying rent, but also to receive rent to tide over periods of unemployment. A man who sells village property without acquiring town property is, they say, foolish and reckless. The sight of kin, recently neighbours in the village, now living as urban rentiers is plainly another 'feed-back' factor, stimulating others to do likewise.

To sum up, the permanent migration of whole families to town is new to both these villages. From a trickle in the late 1950s, it has grown in 1971 to a still accelerating flow. Its causes include the growth in urban real wages, the fall in rural resources per head, the fall in labour needs per unit of land, the educational opportunities of the town, the vast and continuing improvement in road communications and the still accelerating growth of the villagers' knowledge.

Box 21—Investment in Agriculture: In 1950 the Sakaltutan headman reported on an official form that all villagers were, by occupation, farmers. This summed up the village view in both villages. The basic skills were agricultural skills, and in this virtually all adult men were the same. Other skills and crafts were seen as extra, supererogatory, and therefore not worth official mention. A proper adult man should own land and farm it; if he had none, he farmed or herded for someone else.

At the traditional technical level for the village, farming required very little operating capital. The greatest needs were oxen and seed, and in a normal year every normal household had these; landless households were few and even these sometimes owned oxen and seed and took on land as sharecroppers.

Since 1950 yields have increased. In Sakultutan people spoke of a rise in an average year's yield from 5 for 1 of seed in 1950 to 8 for 1 in 1971. Similarly in Elbaşı people spoke of an increase in yields of from 10 to 1 to 15 to 1. These crude measures at least indicate some increase in yields per hectare for cereals; and by implication in productivity per unit of labour. The increased yields have been achieved by using selected seed, by more fertilisers, and by the use of machines, making for better timing, more effective ploughing, and less wasteful harvesting.

One interesting effect of the increase in the use of machinery is the decline in the village population of draught animals. In Sakaltutan I was told that oxen have declined from about 200 to about 80; people have switched from oxen to cows, which yield milk to improve diets, to sell as cheese, and to produce more calves for sale as meat. In Elbaşı, work oxen have disappeared, though the number of horses remains high.

These changes in agriculture have two consequences. First, since the necessary operating investment in each year's crop has risen, the disaster of a crop failure is more serious. If a man has spent cash or credit on ploughing, fertiliser and good quality seed, then if the crop fails not only is he hungry, but he has also sustained a loss in money terms, and has nothing for his next year's investment. Second, as costs increase, the emphasis switches steadily away from growing the family food supply, with cash income perceived as almost incidental, to a business enterprise with costs and income carefully calculated, and some food for the household perceived as almost incidental. With soil as poor as that in Sakaltutan, people will one day discover that even with the most efficient techniques, farming does not offer a return on a year's work comparable with work in the other sectors of the economy; but that day is not yet.

Thirdly, the pattern of farming and land use has already begun to change, and I see this change too as likely to accelerate.

In Elbaşı, several households own tractors, and one man owns two. All have fairly sizeable holdings. In Sakaltutan, although the largest holdings are much smaller, two households have managed by complex manoeuvres and by investing earnings from household members migrant in Turkey and in Europe to acquire a tractor and the relevant equipment. In both villages households with machinery are willing to buy or rent land, to take on sharecropping, or to work their neighbours' lands for a fixed fee. This last arrangement is rapidly becoming the most common. The owner is responsible for harvesting. Thus for one brief sojourn in the summer of three or four weeks each year, he derives full benefit (less the fee) from his land.

Box 20—Occupational specialisation: A few households thus commit themselves to agriculture, enlarge their operations, and become specialists. The enlarged operation enables them to mobilise resources to face higher costs and higher risks, and by yielding higher average profits enables them also to keep up with rising consumer needs. It requires of them new skills; knowledge of fertilisers, varieties of seed, marketing, machinery, and farm management.

Many village household heads have consequently given up working on their own land, except perhaps for harvest. Instead, migration enables them to earn wages, and agriculture becomes a side line. Thus a basic new division of labour is growing up in the village between farmers and the rest. So far, this division is not conspicuous, because all older men still regard themselves as competent to farm whenever necessary. But many boys no longer learn farming from their fathers and already many young men live by their crafts and cannot and do not wish to farm.

This trend, accentuated as the old die and the non-farming young grow older, suggests a prediction. As this division of labour grows, the non-farming households will have little stake to keep them in the village, and perhaps quite soon permanent urban migration will overtake the village population growth and these villages will become depopulated.

One extremely interesting development in Elbaşı is likely to provide a temporary brake on this process. In this whole area, village land is allowed to lie fallow every other year (Stirling 1965: 48). For the first time in 1971, in Elbaşi some of the land due for fallow was planted, allegedly with success. Such a development—resting of course on crop rotation and the cropping of animal feeds,—could greatly increase the demand for labour in the villages, the productivity per hectare of village land, and the animal carrying capacity of the land. But with the rapid growth of mechanisation the cropping of fallow will accelerate the process of agricultural specialisation in the villagers, which must eventually end with some rural depopulation.

The changes in agricultural organisation I have been describing are changes in the organisation of production and in the distribution of resources in the village. But once again they are linked causally to changes in knowledge. The importance of technical, commercial and financial knowledge is relatively obvious; but changes in more basic assumptions are also involved. Most people in 1950–52,—and surely even more so earlier,—saw the village as home, and its land and its crops and animals as the indispensable moral and physical centre of their lives; relations with the outside world were ultimately temporary and dispensable. Wages and commercial profits were directed to the village household in its village social arena. At the other end of the process, by no means yet reached, agriculture becomes a business like any other, a source of income to buy manufactured necessities which come from town; home and land are merely assets to be sold for cash if and when it pays to do so; and resources are directed to power and status in a national or at least regional arena.

Boxes 22 to 25: Household and kinship

At first glance, changes in household and in kinship are unimpressive. The same or apparently similar people live in the same or similar houses with very similar arrangements. Nevertheless, the changes that have begun are fundamental, complex and accelerating.

I have selected four points which seem to me crucial. Box 22 (women's knowledge) concerns the effect on women of a whole new segment of experience, and thus the relations between men and women in general. Box 23 (generation gap) concerns the new modes of socialisation and the results for the relation between young and old in general; Box 24 (decline in father's authority) concerns control and power in the domestic group; Box 25 (separation of sons) the structure of domestic groups and the working of the domestic cycle.

These changes are so far no more than adjustments to the basic pattern which I described for 1950–52 (Stirling 1965: Chs. 6 and 7). Very briefly, domestic units were agricultural production units as well as consumption units. Income and property were pooled under the direction of the household head, and cash incomes were still subordinate to subsistence farming. Every man aimed by late middle age to become head of a household consisting of his wife, his married sons and their wives and children, and his unmarried children. In practice, mainly for demographic reasons, relatively few households at any point conformed to this ideal; the few sons who had separated from living fathers were objects of explicit disapproval. Within this unit, the head's authority was in theory absolute. Within it also, men and women experienced the only social and sexual intimacy permitted. Women were segregated as far as possible, and markedly subordinate; their sexual propriety was important not only to themselves but to their whole household; a man was judged on the fair name of his mother, sisters, wives and daughters, and even a threat to their reputation called for violence.

Box 25—Separation of Married Sons: I found one striking change in this pattern. It is now perfectly acceptable for a married man to separate from his living father and set up an independent household. In Sakaltutan, I was given a new set of rules. A man should still bring a new bride to live in his father's household. He may then separate in a year or so without disgrace or gossip, but he ought not to do so unless his parents have other sons still at home. One son must keep his wife in the paternal home to take care of the old people, though no rules say which it should be. Once therefore one son has married, at least one daughter-in-law is likely to be living in the house. I do not have the data to test either how widely this new formulation of the rules is accepted or how far it is observed.

Demographically the average size of the households has increased, and the proportion of joint households (households containing more than one married man) has also increased, in both villages. This is surprising, since the formal rules have changed in the opposite direction. In *Turkish Village* I explained that the paradoxical gap between the universally stated ideal of the large three generation patrilineal household and the actual preponderance of simple one-marriage households was due to demographic factors. Similarly, the present inverse paradox is also due to a reversal of demography. Once it was relatively difficult to produce living adult children. Fertility was a problem, and the child death rate very high: in Elbaşı perhaps as high as one third or more of all children born. Now most children survive and grow up reasonably healthy. But the unqualified village assumption that children are desirable is only now beginning to change. Men expect to have more than one son, and most young married couples have several children each. At the same time, the life expectancy of adult men is also rising dramatically, so that most fathers live long enough to see their sons marry and beget children. Great grand children are not uncommon.

This demographic change has two results. Far more of the surviving older couples have one, or several, living married sons, which increases the number of joint households. At the same time, overcrowding becomes a major problem for many households, and a major factor in the change which I have just reported in the explicit rules. Moreover, the new division of labour between agricultural households, and those which simply harvest their patrimony, or let it out altogether, has diminished the number of households with land resources sufficient to hold together and employ an agricultural joint household.

Two further changes seem predictable. The genuine old-fashioned joint households with sons and grandsons under the control of an older man will persist only in those households which specialise successfully in agriculture, need a large labour force, and can offer economic resources to members. On the other hand, a new household type will emerge in which, effectively, the income from a pendular migrant supports unproductive old parents, so that households with two married couples are likely to continue to be common, but with a reversal of their traditional internal economic and authority structure.

Box 24—Decline in Father's Authority: Traditionally, fathers commanded, sons obeyed. Sons did not speak publicly, nor smoke in their father's presence. The whole weight of village morality was behind a father. Sons were watched, gossiped about, and reminded constantly of breaches of the rules. A father's prestige, wealth and power depended on retaining control of sons as a source of labour, income and fighting power. Loyal adult sons were, and perhaps decreasingly still are, a man's greatest asset.

Father's authority rested not only on the informal sanctions of village morality, but on two other powerful sanctions. First, by controlling land he controlled virtually the only resource which could provide a son with work and income. Secondly, every young man needed a respectable wife to bear him respectable sons on which to build his own position in the village; father provided the necessary resources and reputation; and indeed ostensibly chose the bride.

Migrant labour undermined the strongest of these sanctions. It has become increasingly simple,—and is now customary,—for young men to provide their own income by learning a building skill. In moral theory, all earnings should still go to the household head, for his disposal in the overall interest. But once a son is not working as a member of a household team under his father's orders, but earning cash from an employer outside the village, he can decide both what he tells his father, and what proportion of what he says he earns he is willing to hand over. A father can no longer starve a son into submission.

Men, especially young unmarried men, spend freely in town and resent paternal pressure to save and hand over their earnings for the household. Fathers resent their sons' fecklessness and insubordination, and suspect them of deceit. This theme recurs constantly in reports of tension and open quarrels between fathers and sons.

The second sanction,—the arranging of a marriage,—remains. The values surrounding female modesty and purity have changed little and it is impossible even in town for a man to court in person a respectable and eligible girl. Honourable marriage, which gives the essential status of head of a respectable family whether in town or village, must still be arranged for a man through someone else, preferably through his father. Young village men, even those now resident in town, want to marry village girls whose background they know to be pure. Marriage is expensive, costing around a year's earnings. For social respectability and for the necessary cash a man still depends on the support of his father and his household.

A father will sell animals and contract debts in order to marry a son, and will do so as prestigiously and as lavishly as he possibly can. He equally wants a respectable daughter-in-law and grandchildren. But he also expects an earning unmarried son to contribute to the household resources, that is, to his own wedding in advance. I discovered one father who refused to help a son, resident in town, with his marriage as a punishment for the son's failure to contribute during his adolescence. Others, I suspect, faced with the dilemma may be more lenient.

Even this sanction is likely to weaken, partly because the strict rules of rural sexual morality seem virtually certain to be relaxed in practice in urban conditions—some evidence supports this guess,—and partly because men can acquire new networks which provide them with urban-born wives of acceptable respectability.

I cannot measure quarrels between fathers and sons in 1950–52 against those in 1971; but I can assert that fathers have decreasing control over sons, that both illustrative instances of and village comments on the change are common.

Box 23—The Generation Gap: This decline in the control of fathers over their own sons is clearly part of the wider field of relationships between young and old. Traditionally, village society exacted a high degree of deference and of specific obedience from the young. Children began to work for their households as soon as they were able. As sons obeyed and deferred to fathers, girls obeyed their own mothers at home, and their husbands' mothers after marriage. So long as the total stock of highly valued knowledge in the village consisted of traditional religious knowledge, and traditional agricultural techniques and skills, the old people did in fact know best. In 1950–52 this monopoly of knowledge, respect and power by the old was already under attack, and changes were under way, but the formal rules remained and the conspicuous exceptions were seen as breaches, as any social rules are sometimes breached. By 1971, the situation had changed radically.

I have already written of the new and heterogeneous flood of knowledge and skill into the village between 1950–52 and 1971. This knowledge and skill was so to speak stored not like traditional knowledge in the elders, but in the young. 'We', one man remarked, 'are like our fathers were, but our sons are not like us.' What I have said about the decline of father's authority applies more generally. The young are less deferential, and less obedient, because it is they who are able to exploit the new opportunities. But what is important is not only that they are able to reject the power of their elders, but that they are different from their elders.

The differences are superficially conspicuous. They dress in town-bought clothes, some go bare-headed, and their mannerisms, conversation and consumer habits are different. Two differences are fundamental. First, as I have said (p. 216) they are no longer committed to the land. They do not want to emulate their farming fathers. Secondly, they have been to school, and are literate in the new secular script. What is important about literacy in this context is not merely individual competence; the village is becoming a literate community, aware of and able to draw on the vast stored memory of the written word. Such a community must in time come to make new and different assumptions about the sources, nature and use of knowledge. This theme is vast and complex; for example, truth rests not on the oral authority of the elders inside village society, but on written authorities from the modern urban world. Modern discovery and invention rivals eternal revelation as the source of truth.

The generation gap then is not only a matter of conflict and relative power; for the first time ever, the young are radically unlike their predecessors. They are not therefore recruits for replacing and reproducing the statuses of the elders as they die off; village society is no longer self-reproducing.

Box 22—Women in town: A parallel revolution is taking place in the still separate world of women. In discussing permanent urban migration I have already remarked on the opening of the village women's world to information about and from the towns, through the growing number of daughters and daughters-in-law who live or have lived in town, and through the now customary visits of village women and girls with their urban kin.

Three effects are already noticeable. First, teachers reported that most villagers are eager to send daughters to school. One elderly villager expressed his continued opposition to schooling for girls above eleven years of age, but clearly already most young girls are literate. Secondly, as I have said, some girls want to marry town husbands. In 1950 a wife shackled a man to the village; wives may soon be driving their husbands out of it. Thirdly, almost all informants reported that within the village women are already less submissive and actively demand more comfort, more consumer goods and more personal freedom.

In Elbaşı, girls moved about with more freedom, and for the first time I saw village girls with bare heads and wearing clothes noticeably though not strikingly different from the once strict village traditional costume. I was told that population growth and family planning are now discussed in the village by men and by women.

So far, these changes are mere beginnings; but then urban contacts and literacy for girls are very new. Changes are bound to accelerate as the young grow older and the new influences grow. Mothers with less village-bound beliefs and customs will in time treat their babies differently, and transmit different rules and assumptions to their growing children.

Boxes 26 to 31

I have already covered implicitly much of the contents of the last six boxes. My six labels are—abbreviated—changes in values, decreased dependence on the village, decline in village consensus, increased articulation with the national society, a decline in village social control, and an increase in inequality both within the village, and, for villagers, in the towns to which they migrate.

Box 29—Articulation with the National Society: The village is drawn into the national society. State intervention has increased steadily since the foundation of the Republic. All men serve in its army. Teachers live in the village, bringing national curricula and national values to the children. The numbers and effectiveness of visits from police, agricultural officers, bank and co-operative officials, judges, health officials, road engineers and so forth have increased steadily. The inflow of cash has vastly increased economic transactions with people outside the village. And now people living outside the village in a different kind of society are accepted by the villagers as part of village society. Sakaltutan has planted urban colonies. In 1950, the village boundary was sharp; it was clear who belonged and who did not. In 1971, it was no longer clear; the boundary was blurred.

Box 28—Decline in Cultural Consensus: The inflow of new information and of alternative ideas and values provides people with a whole set of alternatives for discussing and interpreting the events of other villagers' lives, and their behaviour. Once again the differences are not yet conspicuous. But while explicit statements of certain values, and metaphysical and religious assumptions are virtually unaltered, in a large number of ways people do not share as they used to do the same socially created reality. Alternative models for action and for judgement of actions are known to exist; rules and customs become less specific and less mandatory, breaches of them more defensible; and the area of tacit disagreement grows, that is, increasingly the more sophisticated simply ignore or avoid areas of potential confrontation or argument.

Box 30—Decline in Social Control: A decline in dependence on village society and a decline in normative consensus must diminish the effectiveness of village social control. The empirical evidence rests largely on statements by the villagers. Wedding customs are more easily attenuated; older men can evade their obligations; young men are less assiduous in their religious duties; boys are less respectful and obedient and much more likely to turn dissolute; even girl are more demanding and less demure. *A priori* also, sanctions from which people can escape are less effective, and rules which they can dispute are less easy to enforce. The sight of some fellow-villagers successfully evading, defying or ignoring customary morals and obligations encourages others to do likewise when it suits them. Decline in social control stimulates decline in social control.

Box 31—Growing Inequality; Village and Town: It is a commonplace that 'development' and 'modernisation' at a national level bring vast increases in the division of labour, and radical changes in the distribution of national resources and in the structure of occupation and income. Opportunities for personal upward mobility must increase sharply, and are perceived to do so by the villagers; but we cannot reliably measure the increase, nor the village perception of it; still less any gap between perception and reality.

We do know that migrants to the cities move in at very different points in the social hierarchy. On the evidence from Sakaltutan, Elbaşı and their neighbouring villages, I distinguish, with of course overlaps and complexities, four main groups. A fifth group is not typical of these villages, but is well documented for Turkey,—and other countries.

First the very poor move in to escape village destitution. Very few come from these two villages, but those who do become the urban unskilled—labourers, shoe blacks, porters, street vendors. They are partially employed, the bottom of the town hierarchy.

But as has recently been shown even at this level they are likely to enjoy higher incomes in the town than in the villages (Kiray 1970: 11).

Secondly, the bulk of the migrants from my villages are skilled men in the building industry. Most of these have some standing in their village, and some land (Stirling 1965: 227), and they move because they find that their urban employment offers in their specific case a better way of life or a more satisfactory future than staying in the village.

With these, I include a slightly different group, the factory workers. Some nearby villages had far more of these than did Sakaltutan.

Thirdly, I distinguish from the craftsmen the successful entrepreneurs, though the boundary is not sharp. Two or three men from Sakaltutan have established themselves in Adana as building contractors. One man claimed—and I believe him—to deal in hundreds of thousands of Turkish lira (thousands of pounds sterling). Another ran a business for the machine polishing of new stone mosaic floors. A man from a neighbouring village now builds and owns apartment houses in Ankara. Such families can afford to, and sooner or later will join the prosperous urban professional and business classes. But in 1971 those I met were still basically villagers with village loyalties, village friends, and a village style of life and thought. They were very much self-made men.

Fourthly, there are the educated villagers, those who succeed in continuing their education outside the village through middle and high school, teacher training school, or university. They may end up as clerks, civil servants of various levels, or in the professions. Their education commits them to town and middle-class status, imposing a whole set of social relationships, knowledge, assumptions and ways of behaviour radically unlike those of the village. Even those who retain ties with the village no longer see themselves as villagers, and consciously adjust their behaviour for visits to their less educated kin.

Finally, in some areas elsewhere, by acquiring land and using new economic opportunities, villagers have built up an agricultural income which provides the means for an urban middle class way of life (Hinderink & Kiray 1970). Some of these move out into town, either switching their capital resources into an urban investment or becoming absentee exploiters of their village property.

By and large it is still true, even in Elbaşı, as I wrote of 1950-52, that villagers treat each other as fellow villagers. Though they are not equals, yet neighbours acknowledge each other; the newly rich cannot escape their poorer past, and the rich and the poor are often linked in kinship through those of middle rank. Rich and poor share a common culture and a common loyalty.

In towns and cities, by contrast the rich and the poor live apart. Between residentially distinct social classes, the whole pattern of consumption, etiquette, routine behaviour, knowledge, skill, and assumption is different. Sociologists working in industrial societies have recently highlighted and explored a whole range of social mechanisms which tend to reinforce the perpetuation of social disadvantages. People born to poor parents normally live in poor housing, with poor neighbourhood schools, poor public services, high unemployment and poorly paid jobs. Their children suffer in turn. In newly developing countries where the urban proportion of the population is still relatively low and growing very fast, it might be difficult empirically to prove the operation of such mechanisms. But it seems certain that most children born in the poorest sections of the new cities will be seriously disadvantaged.

The position at which a village migrant finds himself in the urban hierarchy is chancy. It depends on his health, his family's health, his wife, how many siblings he has, where he comes in birth order, what resources in the village his father has and what resources if any he has himself; sudden disease among sheep or oxen for example might cripple a family. One set of brothers may in one generation contain a successful contractor, an educated civil servant, a plasterer, a farmer and an unskilled labourer. Brothers may keep in touch with each other, but in the next generation the differences of income, and of domestic style, residential area, schooling and status are bound to hamper the effective maintenance of kin ties; and the social distinctions set up in the migrating generation seem likely to persist, as the urban structure brings its barriers down around the newly settled families.

The changes I have been discussing upset also the internal hierarchy of the village. Two examples illustrate the point. First, one man who was a poor shepherd in one village was one of the first men to migrate to Germany, and invested his savings in sheep and land. He is now one of the better off men in the village, and employs his brothers to look after his animals. Secondly, households which have specialised in agriculture by machinery may in time achieve a dominant position in the village.

Neither change is unprecedented. I have argued (Stirling 1965: 146) that changes in the relative fortunes of village families from generation to generation were always common and largely fortuitous; and certainly Elbaşı had one dominant self-made man who died in 1951. But the rate and scale of the changes have vastly increased. In general, the number of people who have managed to move fairly sharply from their established position in the village rank order is much larger; and secondly, the general range of income in the village is wider. These changes are both a result of and a contribution to the increase in the gross national product of both village and nation. But they also contribute causally to the decline in village social control.

Box 26—Values: Change and Non-change: On my brief visit of 1970, the great changes in the two villages struck me forcibly. The slightly longer visit in 1971 brought a more sober assessment. The men who were my close friends and rough co-evals in 1950 were still there, grandfathers in most cases, but the same people with the same values and beliefs, if with rather wider knowledge. At what for want of a less overworked cliché I might call 'deeper levels', many 'values' are much the same. To illustrate what I mean, I take three examples: marriage; socialisation; and religion, or 'world view'.

I was struck by the strength of assumptions and attitudes and customs surrounding sex and marriage. In spite of the changes I have described, and the opportunities migration offers the men, people still hold the same general view. No one courts a girl directly and openly; all marriages are arranged because young men are still keen to have chaste and reputable wives to give them honourable and healthy sons. Most men in the towns seek girls known to them through the village; that is, girls chosen by father, or failing that by other close kin from the village network. A few are beginning to marry girls from other backgrounds; but the emphasis on wifely respectability is as characteristic of most of the townspeople as of the village. A recent national survey of all

Turkey including the urban elite, reported 90 per cent of village respondents as saying that a son ought to begin married life in his father's household, a 'value' which surely is an intricate part of the values about sex and marriage (Timur 1971).

I argued (p. 223) that children growing up in a village with so vast an increase in available information and ideas, not least among their mothers, must grow up different from their elders. But the visible change in child-rearing so far is slight. People do not yet consciously recognise major differences in the treatment of children. In a society where the adult women are still mostly illiterate, and where neither mass media nor government officials have successfully begun to influence motherhood and babycare beliefs and practices, parental assumptions and roles are those which the parents learned from their own parents. Child rearing practices, the related moral and cognitive assumptions, and the 'values' implicit in and passed on by them change only slowly.

Similarly, the village remains committed not only to Islam but to its own particular interpretation of Islam. There are certainly some changes. People know much more about alternative dogmas and interpretations of dogmas; ideas of causality, especially in relation to agriculture, medicine and mechanical technology, are changing; the young are less traditional in religious observance. But far from declining, formal religion is booming. Increased village economic resources are spent on mosques: societies for religious education of children flourish and increase. Equally, the number of villagers who have made the pilgrimage to Mecca,— the number that is of *haci* (haji)—is now in double figures in both villages, and still growing. (This religious duty is less arduous than it once was, now that travel agents arrange package tours.)

All the same, the society is becoming more secular in the long term. The large areas of new knowledge which I have discussed are not, unlike most of the old knowledge, related to religious authority or guarantee, and do not fit into the traditional religious universe of the villagers. Equally, people are constrained by the changes to act in a host of new ways which have no connection with religion, not only in new and old occupations, in using fertilisers, tools and techniques, and institutions such as banks and co-operatives (into which for example interest is built without question),—but in formal education, in health practices, in travel, areas where religion was once highly relevant. And while the young have always been less attentive to religious duties than their elders, it seems obvious that the present generation ignore the ritual duties and moral precepts of religion on a new scale. None of this, as far as I could judge leads the villagers to religious doubt or to reformism. Religious dogma and practice are still absolute and eternal. But their centrality and their relative importance have already been by-passed by the addition to village culture of new areas and new activities which people simply do not relate to religion. This situation cannot be stable, and though it is barely beginning, the processes of change here too must feed on themselves and gradually accelerate.

I have argued that in three main areas of explicit values, marriage, child-rearing and religion, there is so far no admission of change, and plenty of evidence that change is resisted. In one sense, the society is in concrete terms still the same society. The villagers in each village are the same people (or their children and grandchildren) with a recognisably stable system of social relationships and of social values and assumptions. The fact that this ostensibly contradicts the rest of what I have been saying,—that social relationships, knowledge, information and skills, values and important general characteristics of the society,—this time 'society' as an abstract concept,—are changing radically at an accelerating speed—illustrates my initial point; that to convey the situation even as I understand it is extremely difficult. So the village is the same village, yet it is also undergoing rapid irreversible and fundamental changes.

11

Status and the innovator

SANDRA WALLMAN

INTRODUCTION

Lucy Mair has written of the 'gallons of ink..spilt in the discussion of the..relation between scientific research and social needs.. between, "pure" and "applied" science' (Mair 1957a: 9'. She has dealt with the pitfalls of prediction and the applied anthropologist's dubious reputation for 'social engineering' and 'human manipulation', and has, perhaps more explicitly than any other writer, considered what the anthropologist can and cannot do, should and should not do in the practical sphere.

While the dilemma of this doubly marginal position remains unresolved, the nicest problems in anthropology are still those which combine effort to solve widely recognised practical problems with the 'pure' intellectual exercise of testing and so furthering social theory. From this point of view the present topic must be near ideal. On the one hand, the practitioners' literature in administration, agriculture, medicine etc. regularly and frequently discusses innovators, and anyone who has been at all concerned with planned change or economic development in the field will have grappled, more or less successfully, with the enigma of the innovation process. On the other hand, the perception, interpretation and differentiation of status and role—i.e. of the social person—continues to underlie sociological analysis at individual and structural levels.

The concepts of status and role are peculiarly subject to conflicting definition, but the fact that the usefulness of a particular version in one analytic context does not carry over to all others is embarrassing only if we are inexplicit. In this context it is useful to begin with T. H. Newcomb's statement: 'The ways of behaving which are expected of any individual who occupies a certain position (in society) constitute the role..associated with that position' (quoted in Banton 1968: 24),—the position itself constituting a status.[1] This version allows recognition of the element of situation clarified by Nadel (1957); of the possibility of conflicting definitions and interpretations of situation—perhaps most readably described by Goffman (1959, 1968); and of efforts made to classify and differentiate roles and role systems handily discussed and developed in Banton's recent exegesis (Banton 1968).

Uses of the term innovator are curiously limited. The innovator is more commonly analysed in terms of his own motivation than of his effect on others. Disincentives to innovation, the impediments that may be entailed by other apparently unrelated roles that the innovator plays, are neglected. And although it is clear that the recipient or adopter of an innovation may, in another situation, become the advocate or innovator of it, the importance of the 'folk' interpretation of particular incumbents of the status has been underplayed.

A classic exception is Dunning's (1959) paper concerning the way in which marginal white men—i.e. marginal to white culture —become *de facto* innovators when their behaviour is imitated by Eskimo in Northern Canada. Rogers (1962) describes a comparable intercalary status,[2] and concludes that (all?) innovators perceive themselves and are perceived by others as deviant. Normally however, when the marginality of innovators is noted (as, *inter alia*, Barnett 1953: 380; Barth 1963; Voget 1950), it is either marginality as the observer's verdict of an innovator's status in the 'scientific' system that is stressed, or marginality as a subjective assessment, a self-image of the innovator. Sometimes the two levels are usefully—if unexpectedly—contrasted. A brief exchange in the (then) Journal of Farm Economics concerning the social and economic characteristics of farmer-innovators highlights the possibility of difference between the innovator's self-image and the way he actually behaves (Hildebrand & Partenheimer 1958; Rogers 1959).

For my purposes, the related concept of innovator-as-hybrid is

[1] At the risk of protesting too much, let me say that I am *not* here using Merton's status=role set equation. The array of roles associated with a particular innovator's status (the role set) is not consistently associated with that status (cf. Banton 1968: 23).
[2] Rogers writes of 'conflict or discrepancy between the role expectation of the local client system, of the bureaucratic boss and [the innovator's] self-definitions of his own role' (Rogers 1962: ch. VII, The role of the change agent).

particularly useful. Ben-David (1960) in a fascinating historical analysis of innovators in medicine indicates that they have rarely been wholly within science *or* medical practice, but 'role-hybrids' straddling the two. This conforms to Gilfillan's (1935) assertion that the innovator (in his context, the inventor-innovator) is always a relative outsider with connections within the field in which the invention/innovation/discovery is made. Ben-David sees this hybrid role as having not only technological significance ('Practice is an invaluable guide in locating real problems rather than finding illusory ones', op. cit.: 558), but also as a potential means of communication between two reference groups; the successful innovator must be both inside and outside the recipient or acceptor sphere.

In the following discussion of innovators in Lesotho I shall hope to demonstrate three propositions:

(1) The successful (i.e. acceptable) innovator is invariably some kind of hybrid, part inside, part outside the 'ordinary' system.
(2) This favourable hybrid position can be clearly distinguished from positions of role conflict or confusion, whether subjectively or objectively felt, that frequently confound the efforts of individuals cast in the innovator role.
(3) The status of innovator is not an independent status (cf. Banton 1968)—i.e. it is not, at the level of interaction, separable from other statuses which the innovator is known to occupy.

The evidence has implications for planned change and for role theory and allows some encouraging speculation on the hybrid role of the applied anthropologist.

LESOTHO[3]

Lesotho is a newly independent territory surrounded by and inescapably dependent on the unsympathetic Republic of South Africa. The country's situation is therefore peculiarly insecure, both politically and economically, and the Basuto themselves exceptionally chary of change. While the persistent failure of development projects in Lesotho cannot be attributed to the

[3] Lesotho was, until October 1966, the British dependency of Basutoland. I refer to it by its pre-independence name only where it is clear that certain conditions pertain to the pre-independence period only. (It was always called 'Lesotho' in the vernacular.) The observations made here pertain to periods shortly before and shortly after independence—roughly 1963-9.

innovator factor alone, the conservatism of the rural population does entail that people are extra-sensitive to individual status—their own and everyone else's—and that status disqualifications are regularly made the excuse for inaction. While the example may not be typical, the effect of status on innovation is usefully underlined.

The discussion deals first with the disqualifying effect of regularly opposed pure or non-hybrid statuses, then with the contradictions inherent in certain status combinations, and finally with a small number of successful cases.

DISCUSSION

(a) Dichotomies

(i) *Insider/Outsider*. In the language of community development the innovator is normally described as 'inside' or 'outside' the community (Du Sautoy 1958 *passim*). This dichotomy conceals the fact that the two statuses are not conceptually equivalent. Basuto villagers refer explicitly to insider innovators as such, but the opposite attribute of outside-ness is too widely applied to be informative. In some contexts, anyone not a member of the narrowest local group is an outsider; in others the dividing line is drawn around a village or district area, a political or racial group. Each 'we' has a corresponding 'they'; each kind of outsider-innovator is ascribed a different status and excites different prejudices. The local rejection of insider-innovators is, by contrast, unambiguous:

Old people say in Sesotho 'He who dies in his own place is not eaten' (*Moshoela ha habo ha a jeoe*). Equally, 'A warrior is not praised in his own place' (*Mohale ha a bokoe ha habo*). . If you live as and where I live, you cannot know more than I. .

The proverbs can be seen to operate in fact. Three examples are suggestive:

(a) M. is an agricultural prophet and one of the most colourful and controversial figures in Lesotho. He is by origin Zulu, but was born in and has married into the Basuto community in the Leribe District:[4] he is said to be 'of Leribe'. And of the several Districts in which he has worked, he has had least success in Leribe. Some

[4] Leribe is one of nine administrative districts in Lesotho. The others (some of which are referred to in this discussion) are Berea, Maseru, Mafeteng, Mohale's Hoek, Quthing, Qacha's Nek, Mokhotlong and Butha Buthe.

explain this by the fact that his past failures are known best in that area: he did several other jobs before starting his development movement (as trader, teacher and farmer successively) and achieved no marked success at any. But the comments of his immediate neighbours suggest that their reservations would apply equally to any 'home boy'..

(b) The senior nutritionist in the Department of Agriculture, a Mosuto woman from Berea District, finds her home area the only place in which people are openly sceptical of the information she brings: 'They saw me grow. Why should they listen to their own child?' The fact that she is known to have studied abroad now gives her some compensatory kudos, but innovation at home is particularly uphill work..

(c) Field Organisers of the Mafeteng Tractor Scheme are expected to sell the tractor services and to liaise between the Scheme and the villagers. Only one—perhaps the most successful of the group—comes from outside Mafeteng District: he is a native of Mohale's Hoek some thirty or forty miles away. Unlike his locally (Mafeteng) born colleagues, he says that he is never asked who his father is. He insists that he would be were he doing the same job in Mohale's Hoek. But once people have established that he is not from Mafeteng there is apparently thought to be no point in trying to place him in 'my' structure:

..If you are from my place, I must know whose child you are and all about you to see where you touch me. If you are from another place I need not bother because I do not know your people well. I do not work the fields with them, share boundaries with them, attend feasts and funerals with them. They are not involved in my life..

The insider is suspect because, as the proverbs indicate, he can know no more than we do, and also because *his* doing something abnormal (which includes, *inter alia*, something new) will disrupt the pattern of our lives more than the same thing done by an outsider. He is involved with us. Not only will the innovation itself change things, but the innovator too will be changed. His structural position will be altered by the fact that he brought the idea.

(ii) *Special/Ordinary*. Although an imprecise dichotomy, this is especially illuminating. Anyone who has new ideas and makes

STATUS AND THE INNOVATOR

some attempt to implement them is no longer ordinary. The innovator is therefore, by community definition, special in some way. This specialness may make him a leader, but it may also make him an outcast. If a man is admired, is he necessarily emulated? When someone looks over the innovator's fence does he identify with him and say to himself 'I can do that too',—or does he think of all the reasons why he cannot do it, all the things that make the innovator different?

A conservative, suspicious and probably lethargic peasant is primarily concerned to find excuses for *not* doing something new. That is to say that the reasons for not doing something weigh more heavily than the reasons for doing it. The excuse of specialness weighs very heavily indeed:

..It's all very well for *him*. He is rich/educated/well connected. He has twenty acres of land/a loan from government/a job in town. I am not so lucky. I cannot do what he does..

This kind of thinking is certainly not peculiar to Lesotho, but is pertinent wherever innovation is made to depend on the 'demonstration effect' of certificated progressive farmers, or of local school teachers, ministers and the like.[5] There is no doubt that the 'special' man or village is worthy of encouragement or that encouragement pays greatest dividends in an already going concern. It is understandable that agricultural agents should concentrate development effort (in the form of loans, grants-in-aid, advice) on individuals or in areas which have already shown that they are exceptional in some way—even if only in willingness to take advice from the government. But it is inevitable that assistance of this kind will separate the recipient still further from the ordinary man and so curtail his innovator role. While he may improve the overall state of the country as he improves his own lot, it cannot be assumed that his ideas will diffuse through the community,—certainly not by direct example.

(iii) *Chief/Commoner*. The administration and control of Basuto villages is the right and responsibility of the Chieftainship. Without at least the tacit approval of the headman or chief of a community it would not be tactic even to begin to speak of change. It

[5] While the attitude is not peculiar to Lesotho, I have subsequently argued that the 'demonstration effect' of South Africa is such that economic development as a whole is peculiarly limited (Wallman 1972).

would, in any case, be very difficult: no village meeting[6] may be called without his permission and, although this is largely a formality, he is by no means obliged to give it. Without it, the aspiring innovator will not get a hearing. While chiefs are the source of rewards and punishments in the villages, no new idea can be 'safe' if the chief rejects it.

It follows that a progressive commoner must somehow carry the chief with him. This is not unknown but is, given the present political structure of Lesotho, extremely unlikely. The Chieftainship forms one of the most powerful and defensive factions in the country; for a chief to support the innovation of a commoner would be to concede leadership to some other faction and tantamount to putting oneself out of business. Nor is the innovator role of the unaligned, faction-free commoner very feasible. To have any chance of effect the innovator must be somebody with influence. What gives him influence? The present political climate entails that any such person belongs to or is claimed by one 'side' or another. Even Civil Servants, though necessarily apolitical, are branded 'Government' (*Muso*) as though members of some competing political faction and are received accordingly—first by the chiefs and so by the people.

(iv) *Official/Unofficial*. Does this indicate that a government employee is unacceptable as an agent of change? Closer definition is necessary: one must know what kind of government is in power and what sort of image it projects. Colonial government in Basutoland was not, even legally speaking, popular government. It was not 'ours'. When a colonial government suggests that something must be done, the peasants' habit is to let 'them' go ahead, remaining as uninvolved as possible, impotently resenting the inconvenience brought—or maybe sabotaging what is done just a little because this is the only way to assert the fact that it is, after all, our land and life and lassitude that is being affected.

Nor has actual government policy helped. Until relatively recently it was the recognised duty of technical departments (notably the Department of Agriculture which is most concerned with innovation at village level) to enforce what it took to be essential change; agricultural field officers, for example, came to

---

[6] For an analysis of the structure and function of these meetings, see my paper on Lesotho's *pitso* (Wallman 1968).

be described as 'a kind of policeman who came with news and promises that later brought you into court'. Towards 1960, as a result of both political pressure and departmental enlightenment, this policy was changed: agricultural services became 'advisory' and emphasis was shifted from regulation to extension. But the department's unsympathetic reputation was—and is—too firmly established to be changed overnight, and politicians cannot be expected to wait patiently and silently for its change of gear to show results on the ground. Many of them have made political capital out of necessarily unpopular measures to save the soil, improve stock or whatever—even where these measures are no longer enforceable in law.

In sum, where the colonial government was seen to be the innovator of a particular scheme, the general reaction to it was not favourable. It is tempting to assume that this antipathy towards government disappears with independence (cf. Du Sautoy 1958, pp. 178-9). But if legal status and policy image have altered in Lesotho, two crucial questions remain: Firstly, has local-central communication improved to the extent that even villagers can call the government 'ours'? Secondly, is the new government unified or does it continue to be emasculated by inter- and intra-party friction?

The first question is still unanswerable. While independence brings an upsurge of enthusiasm and energy on which the government innovator may ride for a time, this enthusiasm cannot feed indefinitely on itself: it demands results, it needs to see things happening. A pre-independence lack of efficient machinery to get information to and opinions from the villages does not automatically disappear; there is no reason to suppose that people know more about and are more involved in a black government than in a white one, nor does independence of itself create a dialogue between government and people or reduce the social distance between 'us' and 'them'.

The second question is already more acute. Although abysmally undeveloped economically, Lesotho has an elaborate political structure and a correspondingly large number of political factions (Wallman 1969a ch. 2). Apart from the much-ramified network of chiefs and the long-standing complexities of the Administration, there are several relatively well-organised political parties. If politicians are sincerely concerned about the welfare of the people, they are also aware of the need to win elections,—particularly where the majority of elected District and National Councillors have no alternative means of income (Wallman 1969a: 30–2). Politicians are nowhere entirely scrupulous in their electioneering. Both before and after independence there have been instances in which the apparently disinterested effort of a group or an individual to start something in the way of development has been set back or totally spoiled by the 'sabotage' of another faction. If the innovator is, say, a Congressman, or some members of a village improvement committee are known to be Congressmen, those who are members of another party or who oppose Congress *ipso facto* will do everything to ensure that the project fails, the idea is discredited.

While this is not the place to discuss the pros and cons of a one party system in a newly independent African country, the essential importance of strong leadership cannot be overstressed. From the point of view of local effort and innovation it is vital that the innovator is considered respectable, that at least the social risks of change are minimised. The degree of factionalism still existing in Lesotho makes any attempt at innovation socially dangerous— with or without official backing. It is probable that only an unambiguous government prepared and equipped to respond to local initiative could foster rural development on any significant scale.

Without political security the non-government innovator also lacks the necessary respectability. In Lesotho certainly, no 'unofficial' effort to stimulate change has left any great mark on the country to date. There are numerous voluntary associations— women's clubs, church clubs and youth clubs which are indigenous in membership if not in inspiration—but these are ill-coordinated and jealously reluctant to pool their resources of funds and people. Their aims are exclusive and usually conservative—'safe'. A limited but more important contribution has been made by a small number of individuals, working as individuals outside any institutional framework that they have not themselves created incidentally. Although pervasive political tension makes it difficult to compare the relative acceptability of official/unofficial status as such, these individual cases do allow an assessment of the advantages and disadvantages of official backing.

The most cogent example is that of the prophet M. (see above) who has evolved his own highly individual system of agriculture and runs a school for good citizens-*cum*-community development workers that are bonded to him for five years in the way of lay missionaries. The (government) Department of Agriculture maintains that his methods are technically unsound, but there is no doubt that he is able to inspire people to change their habits of work and living. It is obvious to anyone who meets him that his personality contributes importantly to this success, but a number of structural points are as relevant to his status:

(a) He is bound to no plan, scheme or timetable, but can adapt method, spending and phasing *ad hoc*;

(b) he gets no policy instructions from 'above' which must be carried out whether or not he thinks them appropriate;

(c) he is not identified with the past failures or misdemeanours of government.

M.'s position therefore allows him maximum flexibility. In stimulating change at village level this is clearly an advantage. On the other hand, he would be the first to recognise how useful official backing could be:

(d) only the government has resources of staff, money and transport, and access to a wide range of personnel and information outside of the country;

(e) only the government is—or could be—in a position to follow up something it has started by placing field staff, and by testing and assessing the results of an innovation;

(f) only the government can combine the efforts and advantages of several technical approaches.

Potentially, the official innovator has the advantages of the continuity of the government machine behind him. Equally, he may be handicapped by administrative red tape. The solo innovator by contrast cannot rely on bureaucratic backing, but has a flexibility that allows him to respond to a local situation as it develops. In Lesotho the characteristics of continuity and flexibility appear to be mutually exclusive: each innovator is handicapped on one ground or the other.

(v) *Black/White*. In Southern Africa the matter of colour is seldom ignored. Nor is it entirely unequivocal. Lesotho was taken under the 'protection' of Queen Victoria in the time of Moshesh—the founder and first Paramount Chief of the Nation. In the Sesotho idiom, the arrangement was made between allies, 'equal chiefs' (*Marena a lekane*), and Britain is still widely regarded as the protector and teacher of Basuto, the agent of safety and progress:

..If the Queen in England could hear our voice, we would be alright. The troubles of Basutoland would be mended..

But while the line of Victoria is remote enough to be idealised, the representatives of Victoria with whom people have had some contact tend to be held in less affection:

..They are not like her: they have been talking to the Boers..

Virtually every adult in Lesotho has had experience, at first or second hand, of South African *apartheid* policy. Not a few expatriate members of the Administration are recognised to suffer what is referred to as 'a South African attitude'—i.e. a propensity to belittle, exploit or at best to ignore 'natives'. In Southern Africa even a handful of diehards are enough to make every white man suspect, racist unless shown otherwise,—and how, without special circumstances, effort and conviction is he to prove himself otherwise? Many whites thus become 'South African' by default: it is too difficult not to be.

The attitude of the average villager to the average white man is therefore extremely ambivalent. On the one hand whites are the necessary source of progress (after years of colonial dependence at home and second-class citizenship abroad, an unsophisticated black man tends to assume his own inferiority); on the other there is a deepseated mistrust of anything that whites do or suggest or undertake. Reaction to a white innovator is compounded of a conviction that he is more knowledgeable and more powerful than 'us', and a suspicion that he is after something—land for the Republic for example.

During the last few years this negative race prejudice has become increasingly articulate and, in a sense, more courageous. There are now times and places in which any white man is automatically ill-received—contrary to Basuto traditions of hospitality and cautious friendship, and despite the capital of nineteenth century goodwill that Britain had accumulated in the territory. Innovators suffer accordingly.

(b) *Contradictions*

Not all the problems of the innovator are a function of Basuto attitudes to his status: some he carries with him as personal tensions. Several stereotypical patterns recur often enough to warrant attention.

(i) *The Idealist-in-Africa.* A 'liberal' white man can be as race conscious as Vorster—particularly in Southern Africa where so much of life is geared to the recognition of colour. Pre-Africa experience of British universities or South African experience of the evils and anomalies of *apartheid* (or perhaps a combination of both) sometimes create an inverse racism which insists that all black men are nicer or cleverer or more honest than all whites. Clearly this cannot be so, and when inevitably the idealist comes into contact with an ordinary bloody-minded human being who happens also to be black, his reaction is a special form of resentment:

..This man is letting down the side and spoiling the picture that I see and fight for..

Akin to this is an uncritical and rosy acceptance of the doctrine of the equality of men: 'equal' is taken to mean 'the same'. On this basis the idealist—perhaps in reaction to South Africa's insistence on the innate differences between races—cannot countenance the fact of different ways of thought, attitudes, ideals between peoples for fear that this is tantamount to racism and the support of its corollary Bantustans and Tribal Colleges. He is unable to cope with personal and cultural inequalities because in his mind they are confused with race; the recognition of them is felt to be as reprehensible as *apartheid* itself.

Such romantic confusion is not well suited to the innovator role since its first effect is inflexibility. This may take various forms. The idealist may decide that a certain project must be organised exactly as it would be under ideal English conditions. He will then institute complex systems of organisation and bookkeeping—anything less would be an insult. He will insist that everything be subordinated to the 'proper' running of the project including political and, most drastically, familial obligations—as in the case of an employee who was refused permission to attend his brother's funeral on the grounds that it was not good commercial practice (see Wallman 1970). He will set impossibly 'western' timetables and schedules of progress. And he is more likely than most to assume that local concepts of time, space, integrity and machinery are the same as his own because not only does he run the common risk of being unaware of the differences,[7] but he will be determined not to take account of the differences he sees.

There is no doubt that this class of innovator is especially well-intentioned and hard-working. He is as often the most unpopular and the least effective—being thoroughly misunderstood by Africans and whites alike.

(ii) *The Tired Reactionary*. A generation ago colonial and missionary service and their separate but similar ideals were considered both noble and fashionable. No one minded being called paternalistic because very few people—neither the subjects nor the objects of colonialism—denied that the motives and effects of paternalism were positive and commendable. A man joining overseas service at that time looked forward to a lifetime career of benign superiority, a high standard of living and respect, an eager appreciation of any effort made or job done. Possibilities of diminishing Empire and independent Africa were remote—certainly in time and probably in imagination. One could expect change, but it would be slow and gradual, not in 'our' time. Certainly it was nobody's duty to accelerate it.

But of course the change accelerated itself. After years of apparently mutually satisfactory dealings with one's colonial charges, the fashion 'suddenly' changed. At the end of a long and maybe arduous career a man finds himself required to justify his being and his actions, to roll to the punches of politicians at home and abroad, to tolerate if not to accept fundamental changes in class and race structures, to direct his own training and the administrative machine into which it once fitted so well away from 'peace and protection' towards 'rapid development':

..In the old days the Basuto were polite and friendly. *They* greeted *you* first. They called you 'friend' and 'father' and your judgement was law. Now there are accusations of malice and exploitation, demands for independence and houses next door. Sometimes small boys throw stones at your car and shout 'White man go home'..

[7] For a discussion of the differences and their practical implications, see Wallman 1965.

The scope and role of overseas service have changed so much in the last few years that the social and professional orientation of the 1940s is no longer appropriate. But numbers of men now high in the administrative hierarchy joined the Service at that time. And a man cannot change himself to suit. It is safer and more comfortable not to get involved, to do one's job according to the letter of London's law, to mark time as unobtrusively as possible until the golden handshake comes with independence or—if that takes too long—until one can decently retire to a cottage in Devon or Durban. While the structural position of the high level administrator makes him the prime instigator of development, the changes of a generation have often completely unsuited him to the innovator role.[8]

(iii) *The Careerist*. The careerist is best defined as a man who always puts his career before his job. Everybody does so sometimes; the careerist never stops. A real careerist has no special interest or involvement in any one project or area. He will go where promotion is and regards one post as a step on the way to the next.

The obvious way to further one's career is to impress the man in charge. Where the Colonial or International Services are concerned, there is not one man but a pyramid of men; not one office but a succession of offices—widely dispersed, impersonal and never very communicative. How then does one impress the boss? Necessarily on paper and by report. And what makes the best reading? Size and the expansion of size; fast and visible results.

As an innovator the careerist is likely to favour big projects which demand more establishment and immediate execution. In a small, poor, markedly unresponsive territory, properly startling results are not easily achieved. But the careerist can neither wait for nor 'use' the slow, usually unspectacular process of rural change which cannot even be directly attributed to the efforts of one innovator. He will therefore have to emphasize those aspects of his work which lend themselves to the biggest, fastest and most promotion-worthy effect—however spurious and unenduring they may turn out to be.

It should be noted that the same distortion can occur without

---

[8] African civil servants in the pre-independence era suffered different tensions but to the same effect (see Wallman 1969a: 15).

any careerist intent: In a territory like Lesotho which depends on foreign aid for all its development schemes, a fair proportion of the time of any government department must be spent in trying to attract money into the country. Here too the most saleable projects are big, fast and visible—ostensibly because this is what the overseas taxpayer demands. Individual officers cannot always be blamed for wording their applications and doing their jobs accordingly.[9]

(iv) *The 'Expert'*. (Inverted commas are used to indicate disbelief and to distinguish this category from the genuine expert able to concentrate, adapt and apply his expertise during a relatively short stay in some strange country. The 'expert' often travels in this disguise.)

The 'expert' is akin to the careerist in that he lays more emphasis on what his job looks like than on what it actually achieves. He may or may not be itinerant and transient, but he always manages to cover wide areas of professional ground in an astonishingly short time. He knows 'it' and all about 'it' because he is expertly qualified or has done the same thing somewhere else and is able to assess the local situation entirely and unerringly in three days or months or years. He cannot, clearly, be expected to listen to the local view, the junior officer's opinion, the villager's own analysis of his own situation: by definition he knows more than they.

But it is not the sublime confidence of the 'expert' that is most perturbing—it is the tenacity of the title. Once a man is so labelled no one is prepared to contradict or demote him, neither his employers nor the recipients of his advice. He needs only to write a report and to recommend things; where he gets his information and whether his recommendations are implemented (or, indeed, whether they *can* be implemented) does not affect his status. 'Expert' advice has been had—and if we don't like it we can call in somebody else who is bound to produce different ideas even if only to assert his own 'expertise'.

In a territory which probably suffers every development problem ever defined, the government is anxious for 'answers'. An 'expert' has 'answers' and these are always tempting. Coming from an internationally, nationally or professionally sanctioned source

[9] See Appendix: the Administration of Colonial Funds (ibid.: 165–70).

they are irresistible, both because everyone says they are right and because it is not your fault if they are wrong. It also happens that to ask for and receive the recommendations of experts is profitable to the extent that money is attracted by their word. This combination of fashion and necessity ensures that the 'expert' is seldom challenged or persuaded to test his assumptions with any care. His innovator role must therefore be inefficient if not diastrous.

(v) *The Technician*. For the technician, unlike the careerist and the 'expert', the job counts above all. He sees in it the cure for the country's ills—at least regards it as the only feasible starting point. But in a country with a surfeit of pressing problems, one could reasonably look for solutions in any one of many fields. And given scarce national resources, each specialism must compete for support against every other. Lacking a clear statement of priorities, much of the country's available specialist energy is dissipated in rivalry between the different professional approaches championed by different government departments. In the villages innovation is set back by the confusion of successive—or concurrent!—technicians each implementing or trying to persuade others to implement his preferred form of development.

This problem of organisation aside, the technician's greatest handicap as an innovator is his own impatience. He can see what he intends and can cope effortlessly with the complexities of his job; he knows exactly what technical move could produce the desired technical result. But knowing something so well he tends to lose sight of the assumptions that made it valid.

For example: To the ecologist trying to save the soil it is 'obvious' that certain areas are unsuited to the growth of certain crops, that certain lands must be rested if they are ever again to yield a fair harvest, that ordinary habits of living are accelerating the loss of topsoil beyond redemption. It is not so obvious to the peasant—nor, very likely, to the non-technical officer in charge of administration. The villager sees what is happening 'with the eyes' well enough, but he does not necessarily see the connection between what is happening and the way he lives; between soil erosion and the way he farms. He does not share the technician's assumptions. And if he did the difficulties of change would be much more immediate than the need for it: How can he close his lands or reduce his stock or move his village? What about ploughing and bridewealth and..?

The technician cannot help but regard these as secondary matters. As his impatience grows he begins to see them as 'mere' excuses that are exaggerated deliberately to annoy him. Inefficiency always makes an efficient man impatient—the more so where his own specialism is concerned. Must his technical role be sacrificed to local expediency?

While it is arguable that efficiency cannot be the first criterion of success in an innovation process, it should be clear that the technician is bound to fight for it every inch of the way. His impatience will, in its turn, antagonize the rural people with whom he works and may eventually place him in a state of defensive isolation such that communication—and so innovation —is impossible. Perhaps the only help for this is to insulate the technician and the villager from their mutual irritation and work some compromise of their separate needs. Here the role of the intermediate extension agent becomes crucial. In Lesotho the extension arms of government are still rudimentary and not entirely convinced of the validity and urgency of the technician's case: extension is apparently conceived as the passive antithesis of the regulatory approach. In effect the technician's vision is neither communicated nor adapted to the local setting, and his plans seldom materialise as innovations.

(c) *Successes*

The picture is not wholly negative. Three examples are cheering:
(i) A man who had attended an adult education course in the District administrative capital took the ideas of self-help, village industry, co-operation etc. back to his own village twenty miles away. His neighbours were suspicious and only vaguely interested:

..Where did you get this news? How do we know you are not making it up? Bring us the person who told you these things..

The man then invited the government team who had given the original lecture to come and talk to a small group in the village, telling it again exactly what the villager himself had said. Given that the 'news' was non-specific it is impossible to measure its immediate effect, but it is clear that as soon as the officials, the 'white' men had spoken and had sat about awhile and answered questions, 'something had been said' which was not said before; the villagers had now 'heard' the news and could act on it if they wished.

(ii) The second case concerns perhaps the most progressive village in Lesotho. By their own effort the people have laid in a water supply, improved footpaths and roads, built a school and a community centre. In each of these projects both the initiative and the continuing drive have come from a triumvirate of the chief, the evangelist and the teacher who insist that they have been effective only through a number of village committees 'which the people were persuaded to organise with us'. But if, as they say, 'normal' Basuto inertia once prevailed—and often still prevails—in that village as elsewhere, why should these three have been able to arouse the energy of the villagers and to sustain their interest long enough to achieve such exceptional results?

The chief is, by definition, 'inside' the village, but both the evangelist and the teacher were born outside the District and have each spent some part of their working lives in the Republic of South Africa. The series of committees sanctioned by all three of them provides a neutral channel of communication, neither wholly inside nor wholly outside the local system. The source of new ideas or information apparently then ceases to be relevant and the possibility of change can be contemplated Any innovation can be hooked on to what is traditionally known—in this case the chief—and is given the kudos of modernity by the white-trained professionals:

..If the chief, the evangelist and the teacher together endorse it, it must be acceptable to all of us—even if we never get around to doing what they say..

(iii) The Farmech Scheme was designed to introduce mechanised farming into a part of Mafeteng District.[10] After several seasons the Scheme was widely regarded as a failure, but it was given a last chance with the appointment of a third manager.[11] While his technical abilities certainly enhanced his reputation and gave him an edge over his predecessors, it is here relevant that, unlike both previous managers, the third is described in Mafeteng

[10] This project is described at length in Wallman 1969a: ch. 5; 1969b.
[11] This man and his two predecessors appear also in my 'Notes on Three Innovators' (Wallman 1970).

as 'a white man who is a Mosuto'. In the context of Lesotho, this implies that he has the prestige and authority that are associated with whites as a category, but he is at the same time friendly and sympathetic. Having been born and brought up in Lesotho as the son of a rural trader, his command of the language is faultless and his knowledge of Basuto life such that he is entirely at ease among village people. They say, with some surprise, that he loves the country as much as they do; in fact he regards the scheme as an opportunity to indulge a lifelong ambition to contribute to its development.

If these qualities were grounds for the manager's acceptance by the Basuto, they did not endear him to the majority of the white community. A white man working for, employed and paid by, a dubious African council must be a Communist or at least a *kaffir boetie*.[12] There is in any case a tendency to regard anyone not working in the ubiquitous civil service as working against it. In the beginning, the manager and his young volunteer assistant were openly snubbed in some quarters. In time, however, other aspects of the manager's background became more generally known. The most significant of these appear to have been his inoffensive political stand on South Africa, his place in one of Lesotho's oldest white families, and his reputation as probably the best polo-player in eastern South Africa. These things would have made even an unlikeable man welcome in colonial Basutoland circles.

The manager's acceptability at either end of the social scale made it possible for him to tackle the reorganisation of the Scheme unimpeded by any disqualifications of personal status.

Conclusions

People invited to change their habits of life may be put off by any number of factors. Not least of these are the characteristics of the innovator himself. In the area of planned change, any project—even one which meets locally recognised needs and is faultlessly administered throughout—has small chance of success if it comes, or appears to come, from the wrong source.

For practical purposes, the definition of the 'wrong' source is less problematic than it might appear. Status characteristics are

---

[12] Afrikaans. 'little brother of the kaffir', a pejorative, equivalent to 'nigger-lover' in America.

manifest wherever they are relevant, and their effect is readily observable in context. As long as every practitioner's bag contains maverick examples of innovations rejected, analyses of the characteristics of particular innovators will pay off,—if only to the extent that statuses and status combinations which negate the innovator role cannot be controlled or avoided unless they are first identified.

From the theoretical point of view, it seems to me significant that, in the three successful cases cited, the innovator (or innovator team) occupied both inside and outside statuses: each combined the prestige of rank outside-ness—in this context, of the white world—with the familiar involvement of a brother. The innovations they brought were therefore 'safe' and 'new' at once.

These examples argue well for hybridisation: role hybrids make the best innovators (cf. Ben-David 1960). They also demonstrate that the innovator role cannot be fitted into Banton's typology (Banton 1968:39). It is clearly not 'basic'—like sex roles, nor 'independent'—like leisure roles. Nor does the intermediate category 'general' explain much if occupational roles are prototype (as ibid.:33). Innovation is less an occupation than it is a peculiar combination of status and situation which cannot be differentiated in terms of relative independence. In Banton's terms, the role of innovator is neither basic to nor independent of incumbency in other roles.

There are three possible explanations of this: (i) the innovator role is somehow exceptional; (ii) Lesotho, the setting of this case, is peculiar; or (iii) roles cannot in practice be differentiated according to Banton's model.

(i) Relative to other roles there is no evidence to suggest that the innovator role is extraordinary. Incumbent innovators may be marginal, intercalary and/or deviant, but the role itself carries as good a set of norms and expectations as any: it is conceptually ordinary.

(ii) Lesotho is neither urban-industrial nor isolated-rural, but it is like countless other settings in this respect. Its peri-urban quality is none the less significant to status and role analysis. Banton writes: 'this role of schoolteacher maybe more independent in town than in nearby villages' (ibid.: 35). Bailey's recent definition of community as a setting within which members have a reputation is illuminating (Bailey 1971). Whether the reputation is good or bad is not the point. It is significant that the strands of reputation become more multiplex (and contentious?) as the scale of interaction decreases (ibid.: 7). The innovator in Lesotho cannot therefore escape the implications of his other statuses: the setting is neither so isolated-rural that everyone knows *everything* about everyone else, nor so urban-anonymous that no one is interested in the whole man anyway.

(iii) Interpretation of the innovator seems, in fact, inextricably dependent on situation. A different definition of situation entails a different interpretation of behaviour and, indeed, different behaviour. The innovator role cannot be placed on the basic-to-independent continuum because the norms and expectations of innovators vary with social and sociological context and can only be realistically differentiated if these factors are taken into account. Since the innovator role is not extraordinary (as (i) above), then the usefulness of Banton's model is minimal.

The interplay between role and situation is, of course, widely recognised.[13] The analyses of Goffman (1959) and Nadel (1957) are most impressive,—Goffman's because his (not very systematic) psycho-dramatic framework allows some marvellous practical insights in the sense that he has made explicit what all of us already knew; Nadel's because he demonstrates the extent to which the situation *is* the structure, and provides sociological means of dealing with many versions of the same role.

The problem of assessing, measuring and predicting the kind and extent of the interplay remains. We tend to construct models which we never test, sometimes because they are not testable (all sciences need better models), more often because the union of theory with application is, in anthropology, considered somewhat illicit.

Even if the union *is* improper, there is no doubt that it is sometimes fruitful and the hybrid often peculiarly vigorous. In the context of a volume dedicated to applied anthropology I can argue that we should capitalise our hybrid status more blatantly, encouraged by the possibility that relevant innovations in the discipline may depend on it.

[13] Banton also deals with it, if weakly, in the volume cited here (Banton 1968: 135–7).

LIST OF WORKS CITED

ADAMS, T. W., 1971. *AKEL: The Communist Party of Cyprus*, California.
AIJMER, GÖRAN, 1967. 'Expansion and extension in Hakka society', *Journal of the Hong Kong Branch of the Royal Asiatic Society*, **7**, pp. 42–79.
ALABASTER, ERNEST, 1899. *Notes and Commentaries on Chinese Criminal Law and Cognate Topics*, London.
ALASTOS, D., 1955. *Cyprus in History*, London.
ALLOTT, A., 1971. 'Theoretical and practical limitations to registration of title in tropical Africa', Seminar on problems of land tenure in African Development (mimeo), Leiden.
AMIN, S., 1966. *L'Economie du Maghreb*, 2 vols., Paris.
——, 1970. *The Maghreb in the Modern World*, London.
APTHORPE, R., 1968. *Land Law and Land Reform Policy in Eastern Africa*, Milton Obote Foundation Land Law Reform Seminar (mimeo), Uganda.
ARGYLE, W. J., 1969. 'European nationalism and African tribalism', in *Tradition and Transition in East Africa* (P. H. Gulliver, ed.), London.
ASHFORD, D. E., 1961. *Political Change in Morocco*, Princeton.
——, 1967. *National Development and Local Reform: political participation in Morocco, Tunisia and Pakistan*, Oxford.
BAILEY, F. G., 1969. *Stratagems and Spoils; A Social Anthropology of Politics*, Oxford.
——, 1971. *Gifts and Poison: The Politics of Reputation*, Oxford.
BAKER, HUGH D. R., 1966. 'The five great clans of the New Territories', *Journal of the Hong Kong Branch of the Royal Asiatic Society*, **6**, pp. 25–47.
——, 1968. *A Chinese lineage village: Sheung Shui*, London.
——, 'Some aspects of kinship in the traditional Chinese City' (in press).
BALANDIER, G., 1970. *Political Anthropology*, London.
BALLER, F. W., 1892. *The Sacred Edict, with a translation of the colloquial rendering. Notes and vocabulary*, Shanghai.
BANTON, M., 1968. *Roles*, London.
BARNETT, H. G., 1953. *Innovation*, New York.
BARTH, FREDRIK, 1959a. *Political Leadership among Swat Pathans*, London School of Economics Monographs on Social Anthropology, no. 19, London.
——, 1959b. 'Segmentary opposition and the theory of games. A study of Pathan organization', *Journal of the Royal Anthropological Institute*, **89**, pp. 5–21.
——, 1963. *The Role of the Entrepreneur in Social Change in Northern Norway*, Bergen.
——, 1966. *Models of Social Organization*. Occasional papers of the Royal Anthropological Institute, no. 23, London.
——, 1967. 'On the Study of Social Change', *American Anthropologist*, **69**, pp. 661–9.

BATTEN, T. R., 1957. *Communities and their Development*, London.
BEATTIE, J., 1971. *The Nyoro State*, Oxford.
BELAL, A. A., 1968. *L'Investissement au Maroc (1912–1964)*, Paris.
BEN BACHIR, S., 1969. *L'Administration Locale au Maroc*, Casablanca.
BEN BARKA, M., 1966. *Option révolutionnaire au Maroc*, Paris.
BENCHEIKH, T., 1968. 'Modèles de planification agricole au Maroc', *Bulletin Economique et Social du Maroc*, **30**, **109**, pp. 35–48.
BEN-DAVID, J. 1960. 'Roles and Innovations in Medicine', *American Journal of Sociology*, **65**, pp. 557–68.
BIEBUYCK, D. (ed.), 1963. *African Agrarian Systems*, London.
BODDE, DERK and MORRIS, CLARENCE, 1967. *Law in imperial China, exemplified by 190 Ch'ing dynasty cases (translated from the Hsing-an hui-lan) with historical, social, and juridical commentaries*, Cambridge, Mass.
BOEKE, J. H., 1953. *Economics and Economic Policy of Dual Societies*, New York.
BOHANNAN, P., 1954. 'Migration and expansion of the Tiv,' *Africa*, XXIV, pp. 2–16.
——, 1963. ' "Land", "Tenure" and "Land Tenure" ', in *African Agrarian Systems* (D. Biebuyck, ed.), London.
BOISSEVAIN, JEREMY, 1964. 'Factions, Parties and Politics in a Maltese Village', *American Anthropologist*, **66**, pp. 1275–87.
——, 1965. *Saints and Fireworks: Religion and Politics in Rural Malta*, London School of Economics Monographs on Social Anthropology, no. 30, London.
——, 1969. *Hal-Farrug: A Village in Malta*, New York.
BRIGNON, J. et al., 1967. *Histoire du Maroc*, Casablanca.
BROCK, B., 1969. 'Customary Land Tenure, "Individualisation" and agricultural development in Uganda', *East African Journal of Rural Development*, **2**, pp. 1–27.
BURKE, F. G., 1964. *Local Government and Politics in Uganda*, Syracuse.
CAPLOW, THEODORE, 1968. *Two Against One: Coalitions in Triads*, Englewood Cliffs, N.J.
CARTIER, MICHEL, 1970. 'Une tradition urbaine: les villes dans la Chine antique et médiévale', *Annales: économies, sociétés, civilisations*, **25**, no. 4, pp. 831–41.
CHAMBERGEAT, P., 1963. 'Les élections locales au Maroc', *Annuaire de l'Afrique du Nord*, **2**, pp. 102–3.
CHAN, WING-TSIT (trans. and ed.), 1967. *Reflections on things at hand, the neo-Confucian anthology compiled by Chu Hsi and Lü Tsu-ch'ien*, New York and London.
CHERKAOUI, A., 1968. *Le contrôle de l'Etat sur la Commune*, Rabat.
CHRISTODOULOU, D., 1959. *The evolution of the rural land use pattern in Cyprus*, World Land Use Survey, Monograph, no. 2, London.
COHEN, ABNER, 1969a. *Custom and politics in urban Africa*, London.
——, 1969b. 'Political Anthropology: the analysis of the symbolism of power relations', *Man* n.s., **4**, no. 2, pp. 215–35.
COHEN, JEROME ALAN, 1966. 'Chinese mediation on the eve of modernization', *California law review*, **54**, no. 2, pp. 1201–26.
——, 1958. *The Dream of the Red Chamber* (trans. Florence and Isabel McHugh, from the German version by Fritz Kuhn), London.

LIST OF WORKS CITED

COHEN, MYRON L., 1969. 'Agnatic kinship in south Taiwan', *Ethnology*, **8**, no. 2, pp. 167–82.
——, 1973 (in press). 'The politics of religious organization in rural China: A case study from South Taiwan'.
COHEN, R., 1969. 'Anthropology and political science: courtship or marriage?', in *Politics and the Social Sciences* (S. M. Lipset, ed.), London.
COLSON, E., 1966. 'Land, law and landholdings among the Valley Tonga of Zambia', *South-Western Journal of Anthropology*, **22**, no. 1, pp. 1–8.
——, 1971. 'The impact of the colonial period on the definition of land rights' *Colonialism in Africa 1870–1960* (V. W. Turner, ed.), **3**, pp. 193–215.
COSER, LEWIS, 1956. *The Functions of Social Conflict*, London.
CROCE, B., 1965. *Storia del regno di Napoli*, 6th edn., Bari.
DAHRENDORF, RALF, 1959. *Class and Class Conflict in Industrial Society*, London.
DAVIES, R. T., 1965. *Spain in decline*, London.
Dream of the red chamber, The, 1958. (English translation by F. McHugh and I. McHugh from the German version by Kuhn, F.), London.
DUNNING, R. W., 1959. 'Ethnic Relations and the Marginal Man in Canada', *Human Organisation*, **18**, pp. 117–22.
DU SAUTOY, P., 1958. *Community Development in Ghana*, London.
EAST AFRICAN ROYAL COMMISSION, 1953–5. *Report*, Cmnd. 9475 London (H.M.S.O.), Cambridge.
ELIAS, NORBERT, 1959. *Über den Prozess der Zivilisation: Soziogenetische und Psychogenetische Untersuchungen*, 2nd edn., Bern and München.
ELVIN, MARK, 1970. 'The last thousand years of Chinese history: Changing patterns in land tenure', *Modern Asian Studies*, **4**, no. 2, pp. 97–114.
EMMET, DOROTHY, 1958. *Function, Purpose and Powers: Some concepts in the study of individuals and societies*, London.
FAVRET, J., 1968. 'Relations de dépendance et de violence dans la Kabylie précoloniale', *L'Homme*, **8**, no. 4, pp. 18–44.
FEI HSIAO-TUNG, 1953. *China's Gentry, essays in rural-urban relations* (revised and ed. Margaret Park Redfield), Chicago.
FEI, J. C. H. and RANIS, G., 1964. *Development of the Labour Surplus Economy: theory and policy*, New Haven.
FELDMAN, R., 1970. *Custom and Capitalism: A study of Land Tenure in Ismani, Tanzania*, (mimeo), Dar-es-Salaam. (Revised version forthcoming in *J. Development Studies*).
FINCHER, JOHN, 1968. 'Political provincialism and the national revolution', in *China in revolution, the first phase, 1900–1913* (Mary C. Wright ed.), New Haven and London.
FOLEY, C., 1964. *Legacy of Strife: Cyprus from rebellion to civil war*, Harmondsworth, Middlesex.
FORTES, M., 1948. 'Time and Social Structure: an Ashanti case study', in *Social Structure: Essays presented to A. R. Radcliffe-Brown* (M. Fortes, ed.), Oxford.
——, 1958. 'Introduction', in *The Developmental cycle in domestic groups* (J. Goody, ed.), Cambridge.
FOSTER, G., 1961. 'The Dyadic Contract: a model for the social structure of a Mexican Peasant Village', *American Anthropologist*, **63**, pp. 1173–92.

FRANK, A. G., 1966. 'Urban Poverty in Latin America', *Studies in Comparative International Development*, 2, no. 5.
——, 1969a. *Capitalism and Underdevelopment in Latin America*, New York.
——, 1969b. *Latin America: Underdevelopment or Revolution*, New York.
FREEDMAN, MAURICE, 1956. Review of Chang Chung-li, *The Chinese Gentry*, *Pacific Affairs*, 29, no. 1, pp. 78–80.
——, 1958. *Lineage Organization in Southeastern China*, London School of Economics Monographs on Social Anthropology, no. 18, London.
——, 1963. *A report on social research in the New Territories* (mimeo), Hong Kong.
——, 1966. *Chinese Lineage and Society: Fukien and Kwangtung*, London School of Economics Monographs on Social Anthropology, no. 33, London.
——, 1967. 'Ancestor worship: two facets of the Chinese case', in *Social Organization: Essays presented to Raymond Firth* (Maurice Freedman, ed.), London.
——, 1970. 'Why China?' in *Proceedings of the Royal Anthropological Institute of Great Britain and Ireland 1969*, pp. 5–13, London.
FRIED, MORTON H., 1957. 'The classification of corporate unilineal descent groups', *Journal of the Royal Anthropological Institute*, 87, pt. 1, pp. 1–29.
——, 1966. 'Some political aspects of clanship in a modern Chinese city', in *Political Anthropology* (Marc J. Swartz et al. eds.), Chicago.
——, 1970. 'Clans and lineages: how to tell them apart and why—with special reference to Chinese society', *The Bulletin of the Institute of Ethnology*, (Academia Sinica, Taipei, Taiwan) no. 29, pp. 11–36, Taiwan.
FRIEDLANDER, R. A., 1964. 'Holy Crusade or Unholy Alliance. Franco's "National Revolution" and the Moors', *South Western Social Science Quarterly*, 44, no. 4, pp. 346–56.
FROELICH, J.-C., 1968. 'Sorciers et magiciens: question de mots', *L'Afrique et l'Asie*, 83-4, pp. 74–9.
FUNG, YU-LAN, 1949. 'The philosophy at the basis of traditional Chinese society', in *Ideological differences and world order* (F. S. C. Northrop, ed.), New Haven.
GELLNER, E., 1964. *Thought and Change*, London.
——, (n.d.) 'Scale and Nation', (unpublished paper prepared in advance for participants in Burg Wartenstein Symposium no. 55, July 31–August 8).
GERAY, C., 1967. *Toplum Kalkınması Deneme Calısmaları-Bünyan Ornegi*, Ankara.
GILFILLAN, S. C., 1935. *The Sociology of Invention*, Chicago.
GILPIN, S., 1970. *Female Wage-earners in Kinshasa* (unpublished B.Litt. thesis, University of Oxford.)
GLUCKMAN, MAX, 1959. *Custom and Conflict in Africa*, Oxford.
——, 1968. 'The Utility of the Equilibrium Model in the Study of Social Change', *American Anthropologist*, 70, pp. 219–37.
GLUCKMAN, M., and DEVONS, E., 1964. 'Introduction', in *Closed Systems and Open Minds: the limits of naïvety in social anthropology* (M. Gluckman, ed.), Edinburgh and London.
GOFFMAN, E., 1968. *Stigma*, Harmondsworth, Middlesex.
——, 1959. *The Presentation of Self in everyday life*, New York.
GOUSSAULT, Y., 1962. 'Quelques aspects de la politique agraire marocaine

depuis l'indépendance', in *Réforme Agraire au Maroc* (J. Dresch, ed.), Paris.
——, n.d. 'Animation et Encadrement dans les Périmètres Irrigués du Maroc', Paris.
GREEN, R. H. and SEIDMAN, A., 1968. *Unity or Poverty*, London.
GRIFFIN, K., 1971. *Underdevelopment in Spanish America*, London.
GRIVAS, GEORGE, 1964a. *Memoirs*, London.
GRIVAS-DIGHENIS, G., 1964b. *Guerilla Warfare and EOKA's Struggle*, London.
GROVES, ROBERT, G., 1965. 'The origins of two market towns in the New Territories', in Royal Asiatic Society, Hong Kong Branch, *Aspects of social organization in the New Territories*, Hong Kong.
——, 1969. 'Militia, market and lineage: Chinese resistance to the occupation of Hong Kong's New Territories in 1899', *Journal of the Hong Kong Branch of the Royal Asiatic Society*, 9, pp. 31–64.
GULLIVER, P. H., 1969. 'Introduction', in *Tradition and Transition in East Africa* (P. H. Gulliver, ed.), London.
HAYES, JAMES W., 1962. 'The pattern of life in the New Territories in 1898', *Journal of the Hong Kong Branch of the Royal Asiatic Society*, 2, pp. 75–102.
HENRIQUES, F., 1962–8. *Prostitution and Society*, vol. I: *Primitive, Classical and Oriental* (1962); vol. II: *Prostitution in the New World* (1963); vol. III: *Modern Sexuality* (1968), London.
HILDEBRAND, P. E. and PARTENHEIMER, J., 1958. 'Socio-Economic Characteristics of Innovators', *Farm Economics*, 40, pp. 446–9.
HILL, SIR GEORGE, 1952. *A history of Cyprus*, vol. IV: *The Ottoman province—the British colony, 1571–1948*, Cambridge.
HINDERINK, J. and KIRAY, M. B., 1970. *Social Stratification as an obstacle to development*, New York.
HO, PING-TI, 1968. 'Salient aspects of China's heritage', in *China in crisis*, vol. I: *China's heritage and the Communist political system*, Book 1 (Ping-ti Ho and Tang Tsou eds.), Chicago.
HOUDAS, O. V., (ed.), 1969. *Le Maroc 1631–1812*, Amsterdam.
HOUSTON, D., 1954. 'The significance of irrigation in Morocco's economic development', *Geographical Journal*, 120, pp. 314–28.
HSIAO, KUNG-CHUAN, 1960. *Rural China, imperial control in the nineteenth century*, Seattle.
HU HSIEN-CHIN, 1948. *The Common Descent Group in China and its Functions*, New York.
ICHIKO, CHŪZŌ, 1968. 'The role of the gentry: an hypothesis', in *China in revolution, the first phase, 1900–1913* (Mary C. Wright, ed.), New Haven and London.
INGLEHART, R., and WOODWARD, W., 1967. 'Language conflicts and political community', *Comparative Studies in Society and History*, 10, pp. 27–45.
INTERNATIONAL BANK FOR RECONSTRUCTION AND DEVELOPMENT, 1961. *The Economic Development of Uganda*, Entebbe.
JENNESS, D., 1962. *The Economics of Cyprus: a survey to 1914*, Montreal.
JONES, G. I., 1949. 'Ibo Land Tenure', *Africa* XIX, pp. 309–323.
JORGENSON, D. W., 1961. 'The Development of a Dual Economy', *Economic Journal*, 71, pp. 309–34.

JORGENSON, D. W., 1967. 'Surplus Agricultural Labour and the Development of a Dual Economy, *Oxford Economic Papers.*
KAMARCK, A. M., 1967. *The Economics of African Development*, London.
KAPIL, I., and GENÇAĞA, H., 1971. *Migration and Urban Social Studies*, U.S.A.I.D., Ankara.
KEDOURIE, E., 1960. *Nationalism*, London.
——, 1970. *Nationalism in Asia and Africa*, New York.
KELSO, T. M., et al., 1967. *Morocco: Role of fertilizer in agricultural development*, Tennessee.
KERR, A. D. R., 1967. *Agriculture in Bukedi District, Uganda* (Arapai Agricultural College) (typescript), Soroti, Uganda.
KIRAY, M. M., 1970. *Squatter Housing: fast de-peasantization and slow workerization in underdeveloped countries* (mimeo), Ankara.
KUHN, PHILIP, A., 1970. *Rebellion and its Enemies in Late Imperial China: Militarization and social structure, 1796–1864*, Cambridge, Mass.
KYRIAKIDES, S. (1968) *Cyprus: constitutionalism and crisis government*, Philadelphia.
LACLAU, E. 1971. 'Feudalism and capitalism in Latin America', *New Left Review*, **67**, pp. 19–38.
LACOSTE, Y., 1968. *Géographie du Sous-Développement*, Paris.
LA FONTAINE, JEAN S., 1962. 'Gisu marriage and affinal relations', in *Marriage in Tribal Societies* (M. Fortes, ed.), Cambridge Papers in Social Anthropology No. 3, Cambridge.
——, 1970. *City Politics: a study of Leopoldville 1962–3*, Cambridge.
LEACH, E. R., 1954. *Political systems of highland Burma*, London.
——, 1955. 'Polyandry, Inheritance and the definition of marriage', *Man*, **55**, pp. 199–.
LÉVI-STRAUSS, CLAUDE, 1949. *Les structures élémentaires de la parenté*. Paris.
——, 1956. 'Les Organisations Dualistes Existent-Elles?' *Bijdragen tot de taal-, land- en volkenkunde 112*, pp. 99–128, reprinted as: 'Do Dual Organizations Exist?', in C. Levi-Strauss, 1968. *Structural Anthropology*, pp. 132–163, London.
——, 1969. *The Elementary Structures of Kinship*. (trans. J. H. Bell, J. R. von Sturmer, and R. Needham; R. Needham, ed.), London.
LEWIS, W. A., 1954. 'Economic Development with Unlimited Supplies of Labour', *Manchester School*, **22**, May, pp. 139–91.
——, 1958. 'Unlimited labour: further notes', *Manchester School*, **26**, pp. 1–32.
LITTLE, K., 1971. 'Some aspects of African urbanisation south of the Sahara', in *Anthropology* (McCaleb Module), Manila.
LO WAN, 1965. 'Communal strife in mid-nineteenth century Kwangtung: The establishment of Ch'ih-ch'i'. *Papers on China* **19**, pp. 85–119 (East Asian Research Center, Harvard University, Cambridge, Mass.)
MAQUET, J., 1961. *The Premise of Inequality in Ruanda* (International African Institute), Oxford.
MCMASTER, D. N., 1966. 'Changes in the extent of distribution of cultivation in Uganda, 1952–58', *Uganda Journal*, **30**, pp. 63–74.
MENNESSON, E., 1961. 'Importance social des exploitations minières dans la région de Nador', *Mines et Géologie*, no. 14, pp. 93–106.

LIST OF WORKS CITED 257

MESKILL, JOANNA M., 1970a. 'The Chinese genealogy as a research source', in *Family and Kinship in Chinese Society* (Maurice Freedman ed.), Stanford.
——, 1970b. 'The Lins of Wufeng: the rise of a Taiwanese gentry family', in *Taiwan, studies in Chinese local history* (L. H. D. Gordon, ed.), New York and London.
MICHAEL, FRANZ, 1964. 'Introduction: Regionalism in nineteenth-century China', in Stanley Spector, *Li Hung-chang and the Huai Army: A study in nineteenth century regionalism*, Seattle.
MIDDLETON, J., and TAIT, D., 1958. *Tribes without Rulers*, London.
MIDDLETON, J., 1966. 'The resolution of conflict among the Lugbara of Uganda', in *Political Anthropology* (M. J. Swartz, V. W. Turner and A. Tuden, eds.), Chicago.
MIEGE, J-L., 1963. *Le Maroc et l'Europe 1830-94* (4 vols.), Paris.
MONTAGNE, R., 1972. *The Berbers: their social and political organisation*, London.
MOORE, BARRINGTON JR., 1969. (first pub. 1966), *Social Origins of Dictatorship and Democracy: Lord and peasant in the making of the modern world*, Harmondsworth, Middlesex.
MOROCCO 1. 1967. *Plan Quinquennal 1968-72*, Ministère des Affaires Economique du Plan et de la formation des cadres, Rabat.
MOROCCO 2. n.d. *Situation à la veille du plan quinquennal et programme d'action*, Ministère d'Agriculture, Nador.
MOROCCO 3. 1964. *Avant Projet d'Aménagement et de Mise en Valeur de la bassé Moulouya*, Office National d'Irrigation, Rabat.
MURPHEY, RHOADS, 1972. 'City and countryside as ideological issues: India and China', *Comparative Studies in Society and History*, **14**, no. 3, pp. 250-67.
NADEL, S. F., 1957. *The Theory of Social Structure*, London.
NAVAL INTELLIGENCE DIVISION, 1942. *Morocco*, London.
OBOTH-OFUMBI, A. C. K., 1960. *Padhola*, Nairobi.
OGOT, B. A., 1967. *History of the Southern Luo*, vol. 1: *Migration and Settlement 1500-1900*, Nairobi.
ORR, C. W. J., 1918. *Cyprus under British Rule* (reissued, 1972), London.
OTHIENO, T., 1967. *An Economic Study of Peasant Farming in Two Areas of Bukedi District, Uganda* (unpublished M.Sc. thesis, Makerere University College), Uganda.
OULALOU, F., 1969. *L'Assistance étrangère face au développement économique du Maroc*, Casablanca.
PAPACHRYSOSTOMOU, CHR., 1969. *Archeion Pesonton* (in Greek), Nicosia.
PASTERNAK, BURTON, 1968a. 'Agnatic atrophy in a Formosan village', *American Anthropologist*, **70**, no. 1, pp. 93-6.
——, 1968b. 'Atrophy of patrilineal bonds in a Chinese village in historical perspective', *Ethnohistory*, **15**, no. 3, pp. 293-327.
——, 1969. 'The role of the frontier in Chinese lineage development', *The Journal of Asian Studies*, **28**, no. 3, pp. 551-61.
——, 1972. *Kinship and Community in two Chinese Villages*, Stanford.
——, 1973. 'Chinese tale-telling tombs', *Ethnology*, **12**, pp. 259-73.
PAYNE, S. G., 1967. *Politics and the Military in Modern Spain*, London.
PETERS, E. L., 1967. 'Some structural aspects of the feud among the camel-herding Bedouin of Cyrenaica', *Africa*, **37**, no. 3, pp. 261-82.

Pons, V., 1969. *Stanleyville*, Oxford.
Potter, Jack M., 1968. *Capitalism and the Chinese peasant: Social and economic change in a Hong Kong village*, Berkeley and Los Angeles.
——, 1969. 'The structure of rural Chinese society in the New Territories', in *Hong Kong: a society in transition—Contributions to the study of Hong Kong society* (I. C. Jarvie, ed.), London.
——, 1970. 'Land and lineage in traditional China', in *Family and Kinship in Chinese society* (Maurice Freedman, ed.), Stanford.
Republic of Turkey, *General Census 1965* (State Institute of Statistics), Ankara.
Rogers, E. M., 1959. 'A Note on Innovators', *Farm Economics*, **41**, pp. 132–34.
——, 1962. *Diffusion of Innovations*, Glencoe.
Romaniuk, J., 1961. *L'aspect démographique de la Stérilité des femmes Congolaises*, Louvain.
Sahlins, M., 1965. 'On the Sociology of primitive exchange', in *The Relevance of Models for Social Anthropology* (M. Banton, ed.), (Association of Social Anthropologists Monograph 1), London.
Sartori, G., 1969. From the sociology of politics to political sociology', in *Politics and the social sciences* (S. M. Lipset, ed.), London.
Seddon, J. D., 1970. 'Demography in Morocco', *Family Planning*, **18**, no. 4, pp. 99–101.
——, 1973. 'Local Politics and State Intervention: Northeast Morocco from 1870–1970', in *Arabs and Berbers: from tribe to nation in North Africa* (E. Gellner and C. Micaud, eds.), London.
——, in preparation, *The Human Geography of Nador Province, northeast Morocco*.
Sharman, A., and Anderson, L., 1967. 'Drums in Padhola', *Uganda Journal*, **31**, pp. 191–9.
Sharman, A., 1969. ' "Jokiug" in Padhola: Categorical relationships, choice and social control', *Man* n.s. **4**, pp. 104–17.
——, 'Women of Padhola' (manuscript).
——, 1970. *Social and Economic Aspects of Nutrition in Padhola, Bukedi District, Uganda* (unpublished Ph.D. thesis, University of London).
Skinner, G. William, 1964–5. 'Marketing and social structure in rural China', *Journal of Asian Studies*, **24**, nos. 1, 2 and 3, pp. 3–43, 195–228, 363–99.
——, 1971. 'Chinese peasants and the closed community: An open and shut case', *Comparative Studies in Society and History*, **13**, no. 3, pp. 270–81.
Southall, A. W., 1952. *Lineage Formation among the Luo* (International African Institute, Memorandum XXVI), London.
——, 1957. *Padhola: Comparative Social Structure* (mimeo), East African Institute of Social Research, Makerere University College, Uganda.
Stephens, R., 1966. *Cyprus: a place of arms*, London.
Stirling, P., 1965. *Turkish Village*, New York.
Tax, S., 1953. *Penny Capitalism*, Chicago.
Thoden van Velzen, H. U. E., 1972, 'Coalitions and Network Analysis', in *Network Analysis: Studies in Human Interaction* (Jeremy Boissevain and J. Clyde Mitchell, eds.), The Hague.
Timur, Serim, 1971. *Turkiyede aile yapısı*, (unpublished Ph.D. thesis,

Hacettepe University, Ankara) (Using Institute of Population Studies national survey, *Turkiyede Aile Yapısı ve Nüfus Sorunlari Arastırmasi*, 1968, Ankara.)

TROIN, J. F., 1967. 'Le nord-est du Maroc: mise au point régionale', *Revue de Géographie du Maroc*, **12**, pp. 5–41.

TWITCHETT, DENIS, 1959. 'The Fan Clan's charitable estate, 1050–1760', in *Confucianism in action* (David S. Nivison and Arthur F. Wright, eds.), Stanford.

UGANDA GOVERNMENT, 1966. *Report on the Uganda Census of Agriculture*, Vol. III. Ministry of Agriculture, Forestry and Co-operatives, Entebbe.

UGANDA PROTECTORATE, 1955. *Land Tenure proposals*, Entebbe.

——, 1960. *Report on the commission of inquiry into disturbances in the Eastern Province*, Entebbe.

VOGET, F., 1950. 'A Shoshone Innovator', *American Anthropologist*, **52**, pp. 53–63.

WAKEMAN, FREDERIC, JR., 1966. *Strangers at the Gate: social disorder in south China, 1839–1861*, Berkeley and Loss Angeles.

WALLMAN, S., 1965. 'The Communication of Measurement in Basutoland', *Human Organisation*, **24**, pp. 236–43.

——, 1968. 'Lesotho's *Pitso:* Traditional Meetings in a Modern Setting', *Canadian Journal of African Studies*, **2**, no. 2, pp. 167–73.

——, 1969a. *Take out Hunger: Two Case Studies of Rural Development in Basutoland*, London School of Economics Monographs on Social Anthropology, no. 39, London.

——, 1969b. 'The Farmech mechanization project, Basutoland (Lesotho)', in *The Anthropology of Development in Sub-Saharan Africa* (The Society for Applied Anthropology Monograph no. 10) (David Brokensha and Marion Pearsall, eds.), pp. 14–21, Lexington, Kentucky.

——, 1970. 'Notes on Three Innovators', *Journal of Modern African Studies*, **8**, pp. 477–82.

——, 1972. 'Conditions of Non-Development', *Journal of Development Studies*, **8**, pp. 251–61.

WATERBURY, J., 1970a. *The Commander of the Faithful: the Moroccan Political Elite—a study of segmented politics*, London.

——, 1970b. 'Morocco' in *African Handbook* (Colin Legum, ed.), London.

WATT, JOHN, 1970. 'Leadership criteria in late imperial China', *Ch'ing-shih wen-t'i*, **2**, no. 3, Ch'ing pp. 17–39 (Society for Ch'ing Studies, New Haven, Conn., and St Louis, Mo.).

WEINGROD, A., 1967. 'Political sociology, social anthropology and the study of new nations', *British Journal of Sociology*, **18**, pp. 121–34.

WILSON, GODFREY and MONICA, 1945. *The Analysis of Social Change*, Cambridge.

WOOLMAN, D. S., 1969. *Rebels in the Rif: Abdelkrim and the Rif rebellion*, London.